THE SMART APPROACH
HOME
DECORATING

THE SMART APPROACH TO
HOME DECORATING

CREATIVE HOMEOWNER®, Upper Saddle River, New Jersey

COPYRIGHT © 1999

CREATIVE
HOMEOWNER®

A Division of Federal Marketing Corp.
Upper Saddle River, NJ

Editorial Director: Timothy O. Bakke
Art Director: W. David Houser

Decorating Books Editor: Kathie Robitz
Associate Editor & Photo Researcher: Lynn Elliott
Contributing Writers: Megan Accardi, Laura M. Alovosus, Jane Cornell, Lynn Elliott, Alison Murray Morris, Kathie Robitz, and Joanne M. Still.
Copy Editor: Megan Accardi
Proofreader: Paul Rieder

Graphic Designer: Jan H. Greco
Illustrators: Vincent Alessi, Clarke Barre

Front Cover Concept: Annie Jeon
Front Cover Photography: Kari Haavisto

Back Cover Design: Jan H. Greco
Back Cover Photography (clockwise): Andrew McKinney; Bob Greenspan (Susan Andrews, stylist); Kari Haavisto.

Manufactured in the United States of America

Current Printing (last digit)
10

The Smart Approach to Home Decorating, First Edition
Library of Congress Catalog Card Number: 98-84952
ISBN: 1-58011-050-9

CREATIVE HOMEOWNER®
A Division of Federal Marketing Corp.
24 Park Way
Upper Saddle River, NJ 07458
Web site: **www.creativehomeowner.com**

ACKNOWLEDGMENTS

For the wealth of information and guidance they have provided, thank you to the American Society of Interior Designers (ASID), the International Society of Interior Designers (ISID), the International Furnishings and Design Association (IFDA), the National Kitchen & Bath Association (NKBA), the National Association of the Remodeling Industry (NARI), and the Color Association of the United States.

CONTENTS

Reader's Digest
Illustrated Guide to Gardening

VICTORIAN ENTERTAINING   Freeman

TIFFANY TASTE   JOHN LORING

The complete FLOWER ARRANGER'S companion

INTRODUCTION

I nterior design sense is a lot like money—some people are born with it; others acquire it. And just like the wise investor, a good designer takes advantage of the methods that can enhance his or her skills. This may be said of the professional and nonprofessional alike, for anyone who has ever selected a color or arranged furniture is essentially a designer. What distinguishes one person's level of skill over another's is a proficiency for working with all of the basic elements that fill up and shape space: architecture, color, pattern, texture, natural and artificial light, furniture, and accessories. In *The Smart Approach to Home Decorating*, you'll learn all about them, plus how to apply the principles that every designer relies on: scale, proportion, line, balance, rhythm, and harmony.

Because so much of what you do (or hesitate to do) to your home is a matter of confidence, *The Smart Approach to Home Decorating* explains everything you need to know to make educated decisions about decorating projects. It starts with an easy explanation of space—how to analyze it and work with what you have. Simple instructions for creating your own floor plan and furniture templates at the back of the book let you try out different layouts. A chapter on color, pattern, and texture gives you the inside information you need to design flawless schemes with paint and fabric. And you'll learn how to select the perfect wall, window, and floor treatments to pull together one cohesive look. If you're debating about whether to buy new furniture or reuse existing pieces,

Left: *The informality of today's lifestyle invites home decorators to create their own rules about style and comfort, which may include mixing tradition with casual taste.*

you'll find the answer in the chapter on furniture. Besides describing furniture styles, it offers important advice for judging quality in a piece and when it pays to refinish versus buying new items.

The Smart Approach to Home Decorating also addresses the special concerns of kitchen and bath design. So that you can make them efficient *and* handsome, you'll find space-planning guidelines from the National Kitchen & Bath Association, as well as a rundown on the latest in cabinetry, fixtures, fittings, and finishing materials. You may also have questions about decorating as it pertains to specific rooms of the house. The chapter on decorating room

Clockwise (from above): *An informal dining room is enhanced by its adjacency to outdoor living space. A daybed in the corner of a room creates an intimate place to read. The privacy of this home's location permits bathing in the fresh air. An eclectic collection of china and ceramic pieces make an attractive tablescape. A curtained deck is an inviting spot for alfresco meals. This kitchen's layout keeps messy work stations hidden from the dining/family room areas.*

by room comes with tips from professional interior designers who offer their advice about foyers, living rooms, family rooms, dining rooms, bedrooms, kitchens, and baths—and how to make each one special. And because today's living extends beyond the front and back doors, *The Smart Approach to Home Decorating* takes you outside with ideas for giving outdoor living spaces such as patios, decks, and porches the same consideration as indoor rooms. To help you with the overall process, Smart Steps in every chapter take you through each phase of the decorating process in an organized way to make each project creative and fun.

As the renowned celebrity decorator Billy Baldwin once said, "The first rule of decorating is that you can break almost all the rules." *The Smart Approach to Home Decorating* shows you how to make up your own rules with style and flair.

UNDERSTANDING & ARRANGING YOUR SPACE

Good design always begins by analyzing the space. Ask any interior designer, and he or she will tell you to make a careful examination of the space—including its size, shape, architecture, and intended use—before considering the colors, fabrics, carpeting or any other furnishings that may become part of the decorating plan. This chapter will help you understand the conceptual nature of space and explain how to examine your own so that you'll be able to play up its pleasing physical attributes and tone down its less attractive features.

You'll also learn how to manipulate space to make it more functional—small rooms will feel larger, and grand spaces will seem more intimate and cozy when you learn a few easy tricks that can alter your perception of the size and shape of a given space. Selecting and arranging furnishings will be less frustrating, too, because you won't have to do it by trial and error. Your understanding of scale and proportion, two fundamental concepts relating to space, will take the guesswork out of buying something that might otherwise be too big or too small for a particular room. Your eye for creating pleasing arrangements on walls, shelves, and tabletops will become more sophisticated as well, as you discover how to apply your new knowledge to the technique of putting together flawless groupings of art or other interesting objects. (Also see Chapter Six, "Adding Character," on page 100, for more guidance.)

Left: *The mixture of casual furnishings and formal architecture strikes a harmonious balance in this traditional-style space.*

Later in this chapter you'll learn how to take accurate measurements as well as how to sketch your ideas on paper just as professional interior designers do. Furniture templates, which you can find in the Appendix, will help you try out different ways to arrange your floor plan. But your first challenge as your own designer will be to become familiar with the basics.

THE FRAMEWORK OF SPACE

Most of the time homeowners decorate by intuition, and practice makes perfect—sometimes. There are no strict rules to follow; however, every serious student of design begins by learning several fundamental principals relating to space that are always useful when applied practically. These principles include scale, proportion, line, balance, harmony, and rhythm.

SCALE AND PROPORTION

Scale and proportion work hand in hand. In decorating, *scale* simply refers to the size of something as it relates to the size of everything else, including people and the space itself. *Proportion* refers to the relationship of parts or objects to one another based on size—the size of the window is in proportion to the size of the room, for example. Good scale is achieved when all of the parts are proportionately correct relative to each other, as well as to the whole.

Although it is easy to see that something is too large or too small for its place, it takes a deliberate effort to achieve good proportion. Usually, it requires patience and experimentation with various objects and arrangements until something finally looks right, so just keep at it.

LINE

Next to consider is *line*. Simply put, line defines space. Two-dimensional space consists of flat surfaces, such as walls, floors, and ceilings, which are formed by intersecting lines. Adding depth, or volume, to a flat surface creates three-dimensional space such as a room. However, lines do more than define physical space; they also suggest various qualities. For example:

- *Vertical lines* imply strength, dignity, and formality. A good example is a classical column, which always appears stately and strong.
- *Horizontal lines*, on the other hand, convey relaxation and security, such as a restful bed or a sturdy platform.
- *Diagonal lines*, such as a balustrade or a gable, express motion, transition, and change.
- *Curved lines*, like those of a winding path, denote freedom, softness, and sensuality.

As you start to select the furnishings to include in your room's design, look for ways to incorporate a variety of lines into the plan. Most modern rooms are rectilinear. To relieve the repetition of the squares and rectangles inherent in the architecture and make them more interesting, introduce a few curves or diagonals with furniture and accessories.

BALANCE

Balance is another important concept related to space. It refers to the equilibrium among forms in a room. All of the furnishings, large and small, should be distributed evenly throughout the space, not just to one side of the room, for example. With balance, relationships between objects seem

Clockwise (from far left): *The mirror over the mantel helps to counterbalance the grand scale of the windows in this living room so that the other furnishings do not seem out of proportion to the tall space. The designer deliberately emphasized the dramatic height of these windows by adding another strong vertical line with the placement of the prints. Everything about the diagonal lines of this staircase and the ascending order of the pictures suggests movement. To avoid the formality of a symmetrical arrangement in this casual space, each chair is positioned slightly differently in relationship to the chest.*

natural and comfortable to the eye. For instance, two framed pictures of relatively equal size and weight look appropriate hanging side by side on a wall, whereas the pairing of two pictures of unequal size and weight seems awkward and out of balance. Balanced relationships between objects can be either *symmetrical* or *asymmetrical*.

Symmetry. This refers to the same arrangement of parts, objects, or forms on both sides of an imagined or real center line. A good example of symmetry is the placement of a chair and sconce on each side of a fireplace. For the arrangement to be pleasing, however, the chairs must be of equal size, as must the sconces, and placement must be identical. Anything that is even slightly off will be distract-

ing. Because symmetrical arrangements appear formal, they look appropriate in a traditional setting.

Asymmetry. This refers to the balance between objects of different sizes as the result of placement. For example, picture a grouping of tall, slender candlesticks on one side of a mantelpiece and a short, wide vase on the other. As long as the scale is correct, asymmetry can be every bit as pleasing as symmetry. Because asymmetrical arrangements appear informal, they look at home in a contemporary setting.

HARMONY AND RHYTHM

Two other concepts, *harmony* and *rhythm*, concern creating patterns in space. Harmony is achieved in design when all of the elements relate to one another. In other words, everything coordinates within one scheme or motif. Matching styles, colors, and patterns are good examples. Rhythm refers to repeated patterns. You'll read more about these two concepts in Chapter Two, "Color, Pattern, and Texture," on page 20. For now, keep in mind that harmony pulls a room together, while rhythm moves you around the room. The key to creating good harmony and rhythm is balance; always add at least one contrasting element for interest.

ANALYZING YOUR SPACE

Chances are good there are some things you like about the existing space, as well as things you don't like. On the plus side, the windows may overlook a beautiful view, or the sunlight may stream into the room at the perfect hour of the day. However, there may be too many doorways and not enough solid walls for placing furniture, or the fireplace or some other large built-in feature, such as a bookcase, may be awkwardly situated. Maybe the room is too small for comfortable entertaining or too large to feel homey. Sometimes the space is oddly shaped; it may be long and narrow, for instance, or the ceilings may seem

Left: *An asymmetrical arrangement of jars, fruit, and a candlestick looks appropriately informal atop a rustic cupboard.*

Right: *An octagonal table with curved legs and the rounded upholstered pieces soften the strong straight lines in a converted living space with exposed beams and rafters.*

Left: *By all means, play up a fabulous view, but pay attention to the orientation of the windows at various times of the day. If you use the space mostly during the day, is there too much or too little natural light for your comfort?*

Begin by listing what you think are the best and worst features of the space. Call attention to important aspects, such as the orientation of the windows at various times of the day. Depending on when you typically use the space, you'll need to know whether it gets sunny in the morning (east-facing windows), at midday (south-facing windows), or in the late afternoon (west-facing windows.) Alternatively, the space may get very little natural light (north-facing windows). If you routinely take a nap in the family room before dinner, think twice about positioning the sofa across from windows with a western exposure, for example. Also, take note of the view. Big, beautiful windows lose much of their allure when there isn't something pleasant outdoors to admire.

Next, look at the layout in terms of permanent features, such as doors and doorways, windows, stairs, and closets. Are there too few? Too many? Does the location of any them interfere with the layout? Are any shapes awkward? Consider adjacent spaces, too. Do they present problems concerning noise or privacy?

Jot down all of the different activities you expect the space to accommodate, along with any additional storage you may require.

Even if your budget is limited, make a list of all the possible solutions to your space problems. These might include enlarging the layout by building on or incorporating adja-

too high or too low. Unless structural changes are an option, you'll have to work with the space you have rather than against it. In many cases, the negatives are not so much the structural aspects of the space but the scale of the objects chosen to fill it and how they have been arranged. Follow these Smart Steps to design functional as well as aesthetically pleasing space.

ONE: *Create a notebook.* Use a loose-leaf binder to keep notes and any other information relating to your project, including your analysis of the existing space and your ideas and goals for it. Later on you can use it to hold paint chips, fabric and wallpaper samples, and pictures from magazines of rooms and furniture styles to which you may want to refer during this or a future decorating project.

cent existing space, or adding, eliminating, or moving a wall, doorway, or window. Of course, structural changes such as these can be costly and complicated and will require consultation with an architect or qualified remodeler. But the time for considering the possibility of making any one of them is during the early planning phases of your project, not after you've ordered new furniture based on the old layout.

TWO: *Walk the space.* Go into the room, walk around it, spend time in it. It's a good idea to carry a clipboard and paper so that you can record information to add to your notebook later. Is there an easy flow from one area to another, or are the aisles tight or cluttered? Observe the traffic pattern from all entrances into the room. Notice the direction in which the doors swing. Is the furniture arrangement comfortable and attractive? Is there a focal point—one substantial element, such as a fireplace or a large piece of furniture—that anchors the space? If the space is large, there should be more than one focal point. Are activity areas clearly defined, or do they spill into one another? What's your overall impression? Does the room feel cozy or cramped? Airy or cavernous? Are the furnishings the right size? Remember, with space, everything is relative. The living room may not be too small; the sofa may be too big for the living room, for example. Sometimes it's the arrangement of furnishings that creates a problem. Pushing seating up against the walls isn't always the best placement. It's better to create small conversational groupings at opposite sides of a room if the space is large, or place one grouping in the center of a small space. Make sure you can move around these areas; traffic should never interrupt them. In

Right: *Sometimes the only solution to a space problem is to make structural changes. To open up a small kitchen to an adjacent dining room, the owners removed a wall but left structural supports intact.*

later chapters, you'll learn how color, pattern, and light also affect your perception of space.

THREE: *Measure up.* Invest in a good steel measuring tape, and take careful, accurate dimensions of the space. If you can, ask another family member or a friend to help; he or she can hold the end of the tape in one corner while you measure the entire length of a wall in a single step. This eliminates the possibility of the cumulative error that often occurs when measuring a wall in increments. If a window or doorway breaks up the space, measure from one corner of the wall to the outer edge of the opening, and then proceed from the outer edge to the next corner.

After obtaining the overall dimensions of the room, measure all the openings (doors and windows) and any other

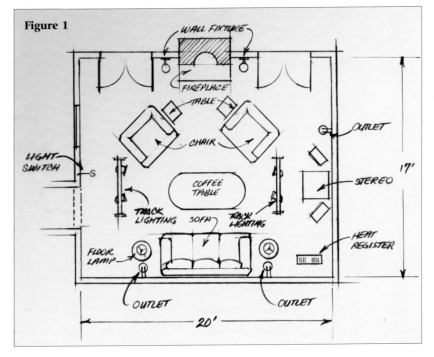

Figure 1

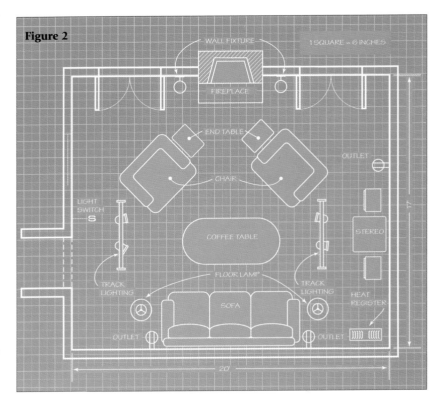

Figure 2

Left: *Figure 1 illustrates the type of informal sketch you should make of the space. Your rendering doesn't have to be perfect, and your measurements can be just good estimates.*

Below: *Figure 2 illustrates a formal plan that can be drawn on $1/4$-inch graph paper. At this stage, all measurements must be accurate.*

cable input, phone jacks, radiators, heat registers, air ducts, and light fixtures, as well. Indicate adjoining rooms or areas on the sketch, too. You don't want to block access to any of them.

FIVE: *Draw plans.* Once you evaluate the existing space thoroughly, get ready to draw the layout to scale on $1/4$-inch graph paper. Each square will represent one foot. For example, if a wall measures 15 feet, the line you draw to indicate that wall will use 15 squares. To make straight lines and accurate corners, use a T-square; for the arch that symbolizes an open door, use a compass. If you don't have these tools on hand, be as careful as possible, and use any

fixed features, such as a fireplace, staircase, closets, built-in bookcases, and cabinetry.

While you're at it, measure the existing furniture, too—even those pieces you may be thinking of replacing. With a few adjustments to the layout, you may decide to retain some of them. Later you can refer to these measurements when you're ready to add furniture to your plan.

Another reason to measure all of the furniture pieces at this point is so that you can compare their heights with those of the fixed features in the room. Keep in mind that when you draw your sketch and floor plan later, they will reflect only the widths of these objects. For visual interest, you'll want a pleasing balance of tall and short elements in the final design.

FOUR: *Make an informal sketch.* As you walk through the space, make a free-hand drawing. Note all dimensions on the plan or in the margin, including the height of the ceiling. (See Figure 1, above.) Pencil in electrical switches and outlets,

straight-edged instrument to draw your lines. You might invest in a handy ruler or yardstick.

On your drawing, record the measurements the same way a design professional does: For 3 feet and 2 inches write 3'-2" and for 14 feet and 3$\frac{1}{4}$ inches write 14'-3$\frac{1}{4}$". Figure 3, on this page, shows the symbols to use for the room's major features. When your drawing is complete, you'll have a good idea about how much and what size furniture will fit into the space.

SIX: *Create furniture templates.* Next, make cutout templates of the furniture, using the same $\frac{1}{4}$-inch scale. Although you can refer to so-called standard sizes for furniture, be aware that there are variations. One manufacturer

Above: *Always obtain accurate dimensions of furniture before buying. When planning this dining room, the designer had to factor in the space required to get in and out of the chairs before making a final decision about the sizes of the table and hutch.*

Left: *Figure 3 illustrates the standard architectural symbols used for various permanent features that should be indicated on your floor plan. Refer to the Appendix for additional symbols.*

may make a 96-inch sofa, while another makes one that is 96$\frac{1}{2}$ inches. It's okay to estimate for your rough sketch, but you should be precise on your final drawing. Although a $\frac{1}{2}$ inch here or there won't make any significant difference to your layout, it's best to use accurate measurements. For new furniture, refer to the manufacturer's spec sheet, which will include dimensions. Don't ever buy a piece of furniture you think looks like the right size. After paying for it and waiting weeks for its delivery, you don't want to find out your guess was wrong. If it's a custom order, you're stuck with it. Even with furniture you already own, don't assume standard size; measure it.

Use the standard furniture symbols in the Appendix to draw your templates. We've drawn each one to scale based on average dimensions, but you'll have to adjust the scale to your furniture's true size.

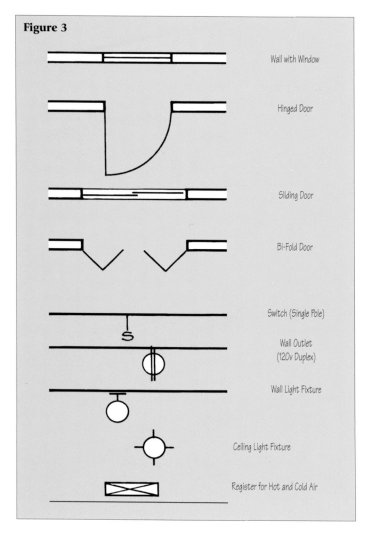

Figure 3

	Wall with Window
	Hinged Door
	Sliding Door
	Bi-Fold Door
	Switch (Single Pole)
	Wall Outlet (120v Duplex)
	Wall Light Fixture
	Ceiling Light Fixture
	Register for Hot and Cold Air

Cutouts to include in your template kit could be sofa beds, tables, chairs, free-standing bookcases, cupboards, or armoires, chests of drawers, and so on. If you are designing for the kitchen or bath, refer to those chapters and to the templates on pages 236–243 in the Appendix. Just remember that the appliances and fixtures in these two rooms cannot be moved as easily as pieces of furniture. There are technical considerations with regard to plumbing, electricity, and zoning regulations that affect placement. You may want to put your ideas on paper, but consult a kitchen or bath specialist or a licensed contractor before making actual changes.

RESHAPING EXISTING SPACE

With scaled templates in hand, you can move things around your scaled layout to see how to group pieces into different arrangements. Always note the traffic pattern in your floor plan when arranging furniture, however, and start by placing the largest, most important pieces first. For major aisles that will be used to move in and through the space, allow at least 3 feet if at all possible. Sometimes you can use furniture as a sort of boundary that prevents traffic through a work or conversation area—seating that is arranged around two or three sides of an area, for example. However, never place furniture in the middle of a major traffic lane.

If the shape of the space bothers you—it's too long, too narrow, too wide, too low, too tall—there are several sim-

Clockwise (from top): *To trick the eye into perceiving this narrow living room to be wider than it actually is, the designer situated the major seating pieces on the diagonal; the addition of a square coffee table reinforces the effect. A Gothic-style cornice and accent lighting draws attention to the garden-bay window over the sink, which serves as a focal point in this kitchen. Gathered fabric swoops down gracefully from rosettes that have been installed above the windows to lend a sense of height to a low ceiling.*

Smart Tip about Clearing the Canvas

If you are having trouble creating a pleasing arrangement of furniture in a room, it can help to remove all of the contents and start from scratch. This is a good idea if you have trouble picturing things on paper or if you aren't going to buy a lot of new furniture and just need a fresh start. If at all possible, strip the room down completely, removing all the furnishings, including window treatments, rugs, wall art, and accessories. This way you can observe the true architectural nature of the space without distractions that influence your perceptions. For example, minus the trappings of curtains, you can see that two windows may be slightly different sizes or installed too close to a corner. Other things you may notice might be odd corners, uneven walls, radiators or heating registers that are conspicuously located, or any other quirky features that are unique to your home.

Don't be in a rush to start filling up the room again. Live with it empty for a few days so that you can really get a sense of the space. Then slowly begin to bring things back inside, starting with the largest objects. You'll know immediately when you've crossed the line with something that doesn't belong. But you have to be willing to pull back and pare down.

ple tricks you can play on the eye to camouflage the problem visually. For example, if the room is

❧ *Long,* divide the space by creating two separate, major groupings of furniture. Use area rugs to anchor each group in the divided space. You can also use square shapes, such as a square area rug, to "widen" the space.

❧ *Narrow,* arrange furniture on the diagonal. In the bedroom, for example, place the bed catty-cornered. In the living room, angle the sofa between two walls. Again, introduce more squares, such as a square coffee table.

❧ *Low,* add height with tall furnishings, such as bookcases, which will make the space feel grand. You might also consider tall lamps, such as torchieres, or window treatments that extend above the window frame and hang from the area just below the ceiling to the floor. Use as many vertical lines in the room as possible, even on wall and fabric treatments. Vertical-stripe wallpaper or curtains are good examples. (See Chapter Two, "Color, Fabric, and Texture," on page 28.)

❧ *Tall,* lower the scale of the space by incorporating more horizontal lines in the room. Install molding half or three quarters of the way up the walls to visually shorten them. Hang pictures lower on the wall. (See "Adding Character," in Chapter Six, on page 100.)

FOCAL POINTS

There has to be one dramatic element in a room that draws your immediate attention. This is the focal point. If you're lucky, it may be a distinctive architectural element, such as a fireplace, a built-in cabinet, a handsome staircase or entry door in a foyer, or a spectacular window. If the room doesn't have one, create a focal point with furnishings. This could be a beautifully dressed bed; a large central seating group; dramatic window treatments

One excellent example is a drop-leaf dining table that can be stored unobtrusively against a wall in the living room, then opened up when necessary. If you entertain overnight guests occasionally but not often enough to reserve a special room for the purpose, buy a convertible sofa. Keep extra linens in an antique trunk that can also act as a coffee table, or purchase a large ottoman with a

Left: *Though compact, a converted attic makes room for two separate functions in one space. At one end, a demure sofa, a few small tables, and lamps create the perfect haven for relaxing with a book, a cup of afternoon tea, or listening to music.*

Below *On the other side of this cozy space, the homeowner—a professional interior designer—meets with her clients at a built-in peninsula-style counter that serves as a desk as well as a subtle partition between the office and sitting areas.*

on an otherwise undistinguished window; a massive table, armoire, or cabinet; or wall art, particularly if it is highlighted. (See Chapter Three, "Light by Design," on page 44.) The focal point should be one of the first elements penciled onto your plan.

MULTIPURPOSE SPACE

No matter how much space we have, most of us complain about needing more. One way to get it is to use a room or an area for more than one purpose. For example, the kitchen may also serve as a home office or family room; a hallway is another spot that can double as an office; even a living room can serve more than one function, whether that of a part-time dining room, guest room, or study. Seemingly impossible spaces can be adjusted to accommodate more than one function as well. Furniture that folds up when not in use is helpful.

hinged top that opens up to roomy storage. In a dining room/office, use a folding screen to hide electronic office equipment when not in use, and house stationery and other supplies in the bottom half of the china cabinet. Another option, when the home office is shared space with another room in the house, is to purchase an armoire that features a fold-down desk, storage shelves, and accommodations for a computer, printer, and fax machine. Just close the doors when the work day is done.

You can also divide space with furniture. Remember: There is no rule that says all of it has to be arranged against a wall. Use tables or upholstered pieces to delineate separate functional areas of a room. Painting one wall a different color to visually separate one area from the other is another means of dividing space. If the front door opens directly into the living room, situate an open-shelving unit perpendicular to the door to create an entry area. If you've always wanted a quiet little getaway in your home but don't have the extra room, use a landing or the end of a corridor. A comfortable chair, a small table, and a lamp are all you need for a little peace and quiet with a good book or a CD player and headphones. Use your imagination and try out other ways to make the most out of every square inch of space in your home.

As much as you may want to enlarge the functional capabilities of space by dividing it up into separate zones, don't overdo it with a series of stuffy little warrens, either. To keep the overall appearance of the space free-flowing and balanced, you'll have to provide at least one visual link that moves the eye along. There are a few different ways to do this. One is to use the same palette throughout. You may want to vary the intensity of the color from area to area, but sticking to the same basic hue creates a cohesive back-

Above: *Some general guidelines exist regarding minimum clearances around furniture, but you'll have to use common sense as well. For example, you'll need more than the standard distance between you and the coffee table if your legs are exceptionally long.*

drop for everything. Another option is to "stretch" space by using the same floor treatment so that there is no separation as you move from one area to another.

FURNITURE PLACEMENT BY ROOM

There are recommended guidelines for clearances you should follow when arranging furniture. Just remember, they are not strict rules. You might try using them as starting points or to analyze an existing space. Then rework some things to suit your taste and lifestyle. The important thing is to make the room comfortable for the people who use it.

Living Rooms and Family Rooms. The kitchen may be the heart of a home, but the living room is where people can put their best foot forward. It's also the place, along with the family room, where many of us relax in front of the TV, listen to music, read, or just hang out. It's important, therefore, to have an attractive, comfortable arrangement of furniture in the living room, whether you use it only on occasion or everyday.

If you entertain often, rate the existing room's ability to accommodate large as well as small groups. Professionals recommend a distance of 4 to 10 feet between the sofa and chairs. Anything less is too cramped; anything more discourages easy conversation. For a comfortable amount of legroom, the coffee table should be positioned between 14 and 18 inches from the sofa.

When there's a large party, make sure there is space for guests to move around or break up into small groups. Most designers suggest one major seating area created by grouped upholstered pieces, plus several lightweight portable chairs located around the room. When company comes, these chairs can be moved around for socializing.

Do you watch TV in the room? If so, grab your measuring tape again. For optimal viewing, the distance between the TV monitor and the seating located opposite it should be three times the size of the screen. In other words, to comfortably watch TV on a 30-inch screen, you should sit 90 inches away from it.

Is there a focal point? All of the furnishings should take their cue from that important feature in terms of scale, proportion, and balance.

If you use the living room as a part-time home office, guest room, or dining area, look at how your existing arrangement is working now. Is the space organized in a way that keeps each function from interfering with another? Ideally, there should be a traffic lane that is at least 3 feet wide to move from one zone to another. If you don't have that much room, look for other ways to contain things. Your plan may have to include an armoire or chest that can keep items such as extra pillows and blankets, office supplies, or files tucked away until you need them.

Dining Rooms and Kitchen Eat-in Areas. Certainly the table is the focus of any dining space, which could be a large formal room, a niche in the kitchen, or even a spot in the corner of the living room. When analyzing your existing dining space, your first question should be, "Is seating around the table comfortable?" Good space planning calls for suitable room to get up, down, and around easily. A seated adult occupies a depth of about 20 inches, but needs 12 to 16 inches more to pull back the chair

Left: *A fireplace is a natural focal point, and an arrangement of seating in the center of the room in front of the hearth can be quite cozy. The rug defines the visual boundary that separates the sitting area from the traffic aisles denoted by the bare wood flooring.*

Left: *This rectangular dining table requires at least 32 inches of clearance between it and the walls for easy maneuvering in and out of chairs and serving.*

Below: *In this spacious bedroom, there's ample room to safely get in and out of the bed without knocking into other furnishings.*

and rise. Placing chairs at angles to the wall can save a few inches, but you'll need either a round or square table for this strategy. Rectangular tables require 24 inches per person and 32 to 36 inches of clearance between the table and the wall. On the serving side, the table-to-wall distance should be at least 44 inches.

Bedrooms. It may be your adult retreat, where you get away from the kids, or it may be your teenager's domain, where adults are off limits; nevertheless the bedroom is primarily the place one sleeps, so it's only logical to begin designing this space by placing the bed. For your comfort, as well as for safety, there are minimum clearances recommended for the space around the bed. When two people share the room, there must be an aisle that is spacious enough for either party to get in and out of bed easily and without bumping into an open door or having to climb over another person.

Begin by measuring the floor space on each side of the bed. The minimum clearance between the edge of the bed and the wall should be 24 inches. In addition, allow at least 36 inches between the edge of the bed and any door that opens into the room. If you place two beds side by side, maintain at least 18 inches between them. This will accommodate a small night table and a pathway for the average adult to swing out of bed and walk between the beds comfortably.

Now that you understand how to analyze and design comfortable, safe, attractive space, you're ready for the next chapter: how to use a designer's most powerful decorating tool—color.

COLOR, PATTERN, & TEXTURE

Blending color, pattern, and texture in decorating is similar to composing music. If you hit the right note with color, it sets the tone for the room: A formal living room may call for a traditional dove gray and cream color scheme, whereas the family room of a beach house may be better suited to lively tropical colors. Pattern creates rhythm, a measured flow between a number of elements throughout a room. A motif on a pillow, for example, may be repeated on a window treatment, on a wall stencil, or even in a painting. Texture is like a visual caesura, a pause that prevents the design from becoming predictable. Light reflected off of a stainless-steel countertop brightens a kitchen filled with oak cabinetry; a chenille bedspread adds a cozy quality to the pared-down simplicity of a modern bedroom.

The trick in decorating, as in musical composition, is to create a harmonious balance between all the elements. You don't want to end up with The Clash when you were trying for Beethoven. By investing some time in learning those theories behind the selection of color, pattern, and texture, you can begin to develop a mix that soothes your senses the way a pastoral piece of music does. The science of color is partly concerned with its precise measurement and the intricate chemistry of dyes and pigments. It also ventures into the more subjective realm of perception and psychology: exploring how colors relate to one another, how they affect the viewer, and how quantities, textures, and patterns

Left: *With the help of guidelines that are used by professionals, the process of choosing colors, patterns, and textures for a room will become easier.*

alter the effects. A bit of color theory can provide a further foundation for the art of interior design.

COLOR YOUR WORLD

Color is the most versatile tool a designer can employ. It is both the easiest way to improve space and an effective way to alter it. It is the most exciting decorating element. Yet many of us find the power of color intimidating and, fearful of stepping into new territory, stick with neutrals. The palette for walls is often white or cream—colors that work fine as a backdrop for more richly hued furnishings but are less successful in rooms with neutral-colored pieces. Aside from the strength of color itself, the enormity of color choices available in paints, wallpapers, fabrics, and flooring options can also overwhelm us, making us retreat to the safety of white for the walls and neutrals throughout. So how do you break the monotony and establish an exciting color scheme? First you'll have to overcome your fear of color, then narrow your choices. An explanation of the color wheel is a good place to begin.

HOW COLOR WORKS

Light reflected through a prism creates a rainbow, known as the color spectrum. Each band of color blends into the next, from red to violet. The longest band is red, then orange, yellow, green, blue, and violet. Modern color theory takes those bands from the spectrum and forms them into a circle, called the *color wheel*, to show the relationship of one color to another.

The color wheel includes *primary colors* (red, blue, and yellow), *secondary colors* (green, orange, violet), and *tertiary colors* (red-blue, blue-red, and so on). Secondary colors are made by mixing two primaries together, such as blue and yellow to make green. A primary color and a secondary color are mixed to make tertiary colors, such as blue and green to make turquoise.

Above: *A checkerboard wall in lime green and white adds visual excitement to a simple breakfast area. Blue-purple accents—an analogous color—enhance the scheme.*

Intensity and Value. Colors, or hues, vary in their intensity—that is, the level of the color's purity or saturation. The primaries, secondaries, and tertiaries represent colors at their full intensity. There are several ways to lessen a color's intensity. You can lighten it with white to form a *tint*, darken it with black to create a *shade,* or add gray to arrive at a *tone.* In addition to changing the intensity of a color, these methods affect what is known as the color's value. *Value* is the lightness or darkness of the color. Tinting gives a color a lighter value, and shading, of course, makes it a darker value.

PUTTING THE COLOR WHEEL TO WORK FOR YOU

Now that you've got it in front of you, use the color wheel to help you envision certain color combinations. An *analogous* scheme involves neighboring colors that share an underlying hue.

Complementary colors lie opposite each other on the color wheel and often work well together. What, you ask? A red and green living room? Well, yes, in full intensity that might be hard to stomach, but consider a rosy pink room with sage green accents. The same complements in varying intensities can make attractive, soothing combinations. A *double complementary* color scheme involves an additional set of opposites, such as green-blue and red-orange.

Alternatively, you could go with a *monochromatic* scheme, which involves using one color in a variety of intensities. That way your décor is sure to be harmonious. When developing a monochromatic scheme, lean toward several tints or several shades, but avoid too many contrasting values—that is, combinations of tints and shades. This can make your scheme to look uneven.

If you want a more complex palette of three or more colors, look at the *triads* formed by three equidistant colors, such as red/yellow/blue or green/purple/orange. A *split complement* is composed of three colors—one primary or intermediate and two colors on either

Color Wheel Combinations

The color wheel is the designer's most useful tool for pairing colors. Basically, it presents the spectrum of pigment hues as a circle. The primary colors (yellow, blue, and red) are combined in the remaining hues (orange, green, and purple). The following are the most-often used configurations for creating color schemes.

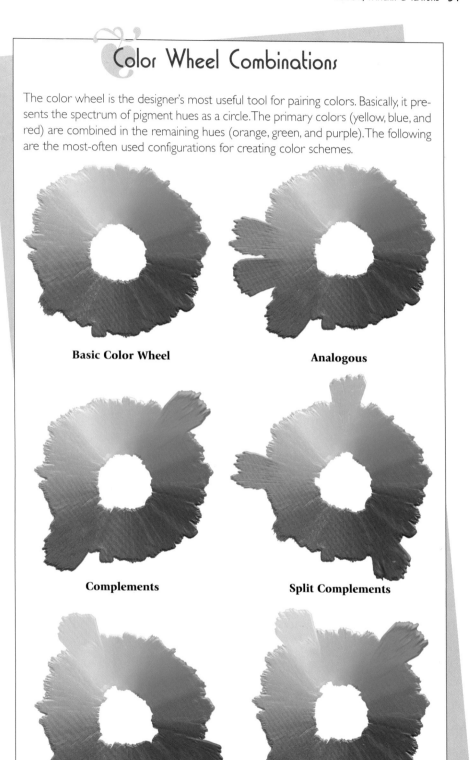

Basic Color Wheel

Analogous

Complements

Split Complements

Triad

Tetrad

side of its opposite. For example, instead of teaming purple with yellow, shift the mix to purple with orange-yellow and yellow-green. Lastly, four colors equally spaced around the wheel, such as yellow/green/purple/red, form a *tetrad*. If such combinations sound a bit like Technicolor, remember that colors intended for interiors are rarely undiluted. Thus yellow might be cream, blue-purple a dark eggplant, and orange-red a muted terra cotta or whisper-pale peach. With less jargon, the color combinations fall into these two basic camps:

❧ *harmonious*, or *analogous*, schemes, derived from nearby colors on the wheel—less than halfway around; and

❧ *contrasting*, or *complementary*, schemes, involving directly opposite slices of the pie.

THE PSYCHOLOGY OF COLOR

Few of us get past kindergarten without acquiring a favorite color. Over the years our tastes change and we allow ourselves to appreciate more than one hue, but most of us can still name a preference when pressed. Picking out a few colors you like best—colors that make you feel happy—is as good a place as any to begin establishing your color scheme because it is largely an emotional decision. In narrowing down your choices and combining them with the preferences of those who will share the space, try to include both warm and cool colors. The warm hues—reds, yellows, oranges, peaches, and creams—are generally most effectively used in rooms where there will be a lot of activity because they make us feel livelier. Kitchens, office spaces, even bedrooms if you're a morning person, are all natural places for brighter, warmer, more uplifting hues. Cool colors tend to be more soothing and restful. You may want to reserve your blues, greens, and lilacs for the rooms where you go to unwind.

However, color responses are subjective and changeable. The pervasive use of green in schools and hospitals in decades past, for example, has prompted a visceral dislike of the color's "institutional" shades for many people. Some studies have suggested that red rooms may heighten blood pressure and yellow rooms make the occupants more argumentative.

Sharp contrasts or schemes that feature bold colors can be fun in rooms used only occasionally, but they can become

Left: *Soft violet walls and crisp white tiles are an imaginative choice for a soothing bathroom. The cool color helps to visually expand this small room.*

tiresome on a daily basis. Of course, these are general guidelines. Some people never tire of a favorite color—even if it is repeated in every room of the house.

Cultural Effects. We may be less aware of how our culture and era shape our color responses. In America and much of Europe, blue is a perennial favorite color, while red ranks first in other locales, such as Spain and Japan. Western brides dress in joyful white—a mourning color in some Far Eastern societies. Even within one culture, the accustomed palette changes. In the Victorian era, early Impressionist paintings shocked viewers, who saw them as garishly bright. Yet to our jaded eyes, the same paintings seem restfully pastel. Even closer to our own times, we might chuckle or wince at colors and combinations from a decorating guide dated 1955 or 1969—colors that struck the readers of the day as perfectly keen or groovy. And a few decades hence, our own most stylish efforts may suffer a similar fate.

The pull of comfortable, traditional colors and the push for novel, fashionable choices have shaped the American palette since the nation's early days. But the home decorator can hold to one constant: Human beings seek variety in their surroundings. Light colors seem upbeat, clean, and lively but turn cold and monotonous if unrelieved. Dark colors are plush and enclosing but in excess can turn gloomy. Midtones are attractively comfortable, but a room decked completely in midtones can be dull and monotonous. Bright, saturated hues are eye-catching accents but uncomfortably demanding in quantity. In short, one could do worse than to follow the old decorating maxim, "Something dark, something light, something dull, something bright."

ALTERING SPACE WITH COLOR

As a designer, you can use warm colors and cool colors quite effectively to manipulate the way a room is per-

Above: *Since the dining room isn't used as often as, say, the kitchen or bedroom, it can accept a richer color scheme. Here, deep red walls are tempered by off-white trim and gingham.*

ceived visually, as well as emotionally. For instance, you can cozy up a large room with warm colors. Because warm colors appear to advance, walls swathed in sunny hues seem closer together and make a room feel more intimate. Conversely, cool tones and neutrals appear to recede and can be used to open up a smaller space.

These color tricks can be employed more subtly as well. For example, suppose you've got your heart set on a cheery, predominantly yellow living room. But it's a smaller room and you'd also like to expand it visually as much as is possible. Do you have to switch your palette to blues and neutrals?

Not necessarily. The less-intense version of a color will generally reduce its apparent tendency to advance or recede. Investigate the other intensities, the shades and tones of yellow, to see whether there's one that does the job.

Generally speaking, sharp contrasts have the same impact as a dark color, reducing perceived space. Monochromatic schemes enlarge space. Neutrals of similar value make walls retreat and can flow unobtrusively from room to room.

Light and Color. Lighting can change color dramatically as well. The quality of natural light changes through the course of the day, too. (See Chapter Three, "Light by Design," on page 44.) Make sure you consider this when choosing a color. Paint some test samples on the wall, and watch how the colors change depending on the position of the sun. Do they need to be adjusted? Rooms with a northern exposure will be filled with bluer, cooler light, which weakens warm colors but intensifies cool hues. Ones facing south will have a warmer, yellowish light. That light can have the opposite effect on colors. All in all, colors interact in complex ways, so these generalizations are not absolute, but they're good starting points for making initial judgements.

PATTERN

You can add pattern to a room in a variety of ways—wallpaper and fabric being the two most popular. Because pattern is largely a vehicle for color, the same rules that guide the selection of color effectively narrow the field when it comes to selecting a pattern or complement of patterns. The designer's old friend, scale, from Chapter One, is the other important consideration when picking patterns.

Large-scale patterns are like warm colors in that they appear to come toward you. They can create a lively and stimulating atmosphere and generally make a large space seem cozier. In a small space, handle a large-scale pattern with care or it can overpower the room. That doesn't mean rule it out completely, but perhaps use it sparingly. Small-scale patterns appear to recede, making small spaces seem larger. They can also be used effectively to camouflage odd angles or corners that you find in attic ceilings. Try a subtle, nondirectional pattern for this kind of application. In a large room, the effect of a small pattern can be bland. From a distance, it

Left: *Pattern adds variety to the warm neutral tones in this cozy bedroom. A miniprint wallpaper is a subtle backdrop for a mix of floral and geometric bed linens.*

may read as a single color. If you're using a small-scale pattern in a large space, pick one with vibrant colors.

How to Mix Patterns. Mixing patterns can be intimidating, in part because it's subjective to experimentation, judgement, and "eye." Responding to this fear, manufacturers provide an abundance of coordinated wallcovering and fabric collections, available through wallpaper books and in-store design services. Such collections, selected by professionals, can save you a lot of legwork and still leave scope for your own input. If you prefer to mix your own patterns, try to match the scale of the pattern to that of the area over which it is to be used. The general rule is to use large prints on large-sized furnishings, medium prints on medium pieces, and small prints on accent pieces. A sofa, for instance, looks better than a dining room chair with a large-scale pattern. A delicate stencil makes a better border for a table top than on a wall. But these rules are not hard and fast.

Another trick for mixing patterns is to provide links of scale, motif, and color. The regularity of checks, stripes, textural looks, and geometrics, particularly if small-scale and low-contrast, tends to make them easy-to-mix "neutral" patterns. A small floral can play off a thin ticking stripe, while a cabbage-rose chintz may require a bolder stripe as a same-scale foil. You may choose to use the same or similar patterns in varying sizes or develop a theme by focusing on florals, geometrics, or ethnic prints.

The most effective link is shared colors or a similar level of intensity between the prints. A solid-color companion that pulls out a hue shared by two prints provides another connection. Exact matches are the backbone of manufacturers' coordinated collections. But to arrive at your own personal mix, you can interpret the principle loosely, and experiment to see which pattern combinations work for you.

Above: *The window seat in this living room is a study in pattern scale: A large check covers the seat cushion, stars and stripes were chosen for the medium element—the throw pillows—and the pincushion pillows are in a small-scale woven fabric.*

TEXTURE

Texture doesn't have the obvious impact on a room that color and pattern wield. But how a material feels, as well as how it looks, does influence room design. Incorporating a variety of textures in a room adds to its richness in a way that's most comparable to the subtle inclusion of the line varieties discussed in Chapter One. A mix of textures plays upon the senses and adds another layer of complexity and sophistication to a design scheme. As with every aspect of decorating, mixing textures involves a balancing act. To give a room a distinctive character, you might let one texture predominate the room, but the right contrast can make the scheme more intriguing.

ADDING TEXTURE

The easiest way to incorporate texture into a design is with fabric. Brocades and damasks, *moirés* and chenilles, tweeds and chintzes—all conjure up different looks and sensations. Fabrics, however, are just the beginning. Tactile interest can emanate from any material or surface that is coarse or smooth, hard or soft, matte or shiny. Coarse and matte surfaces, such as stone, rough-hewn wood, stucco, corduroy, or terra cotta, absorb light and sound. Glossy and smooth surfaces, which range from metal and glass to silk and enamel, reflect light.

Spatial Effects. To start adding texture into your design, assess your room's needs. Does it lack warmth? Or does it feel too closed in? Texture affects a room spatially. Coarse or matte surfaces will make a room seem smaller and cozier. A living room of only glossy surfaces can seem cold and impersonal without a velvet slipcover on the sofa to add warmth and contrast. Smooth and shiny surfaces do the reverse—they make a room look larger and brighter. A study that feels too stuffy, for instance, may benefit from the addition of a mirror or a glass-topped table. Light reflected off either object will brighten the space.

Pattern and Color. Keep in mind that texture also affects pattern and color. With fabrics, texture can either soften or enhance a pattern. For instance, patterns are crisp on

Below: *Plush leopard-print and silky striped pillows are just two of the textural elements that add interest to this all-neutral living room. Notice how the marble-topped coffee table with antiqued metal legs plays against the plump upholstered furniture.*

Left: *Armchairs in a heavy, woven upholstery are combined with the smooth richness of a leather sofa and ottoman. The effect keeps the room's large size from being overwhelming.*

tures—foils, flocks, embossed papers, and real fabric, to list a few. Paint can be applied in matte or gloss finishes and special painted effects, discussed in detail in Chapter Five, can add texture. Tile and other architectural embellishments, such as cornices and moldings, can also imbue a room with more tactile richness.

Window treatments are another natural outlet for texture. Fabric choices for draperies and curtains, as well as the fabrics and other materials available for blinds and shades, are enormous and varied. Texture can be enhanced by the way fabric is hung. Pleating, for example, creates a play of light and shadow. You can combine layers of fabric or fabric and blinds to show off different textures.

On the floor, carpets can be smooth, knobby, sculpted, or flecked for visual texture. Rugs, rush, coir, sisal, wood, or cork are warming texture options.

glazed chintz but are blurred on terrycloth. A coarsely textured surface tones down the intensity of a paint color, and gives the color subtle variations. High-gloss surfaces increase the intensity of a color. Think of how the gray color of a tweed jacket looks "heathered" and muted. On a silk shirt, however, the same gray color would look shimmery and more intense—a completely different effect. Every room has an existing element of texture—a stone fireplace, brass hardware, a gleaming hardwood floor, a stuccoed wall, or an iridescent tile border—that you may want to take into consideration when planning your design.

Relatively featureless rooms may be improved by adding contrasting textures. Wallpaper comes in a variety of tex-

Quarry tiles, ceramic tiles, marble, and slate make a room cooler. Varying the materials can make the effect more interesting. An Oriental rug over a varnished wood floor is a classic example.

PULLING IT ALL TOGETHER

You've analyzed your room, you've determined how you want it to function, and you'd like to make it restful and soothing. As luck would have it, blue is your favorite color. So now what? How do you get from there to choosing the "right" shade of blue, deciding where to use it, picking a coordinating wallpaper pattern, selecting fabrics for the furniture, and ensuring plenty of tactile richness to boot? Take it slowly, in steps—Smart Steps, that is.

Design Materials

As you have likely gleaned from this discussion of color, pattern, and texture, designers rely on certain materials to carry various effects into a living space. Most design materials have specific functions and applications where they are preferable to other options in their category. In flooring materials, for example, ceramic tile may perform well in a kitchen setting but not as effectively in a living room. Within many categories, there are varying degrees of quality. Throughout this book, the appropriate applications of different materials and tips on how to judge the quality of some materials is addressed in pertinent chapters. In Chapter Four, for instance, you'll find an examination of flooring materials. Chapter Five contains in-depth coverage of paints and wallpaper options. Here, because textiles are such integral players when it comes to delivering color, pattern, and texture, is a brief overview of some common decorating fabrics and their make-up.

Brocade: Often weighty fabric woven of silk, cotton, wool, or a combination. A raised, floral design (called a jacquard) is its distinguishing feature. Typically used for upholstery and draperies.

Cambric: A plain, tightly woven linen or cotton fabric with a sheen on one side. Curtain panels, pillows, and lightweight slipcovers can be successfully made from cambric.

Canvas: A course, woven cotton material, available in heavy or lighter gauges. Canvas is strong and inexpensive. Will hold up for upholstery, slipcovers, or draperies.

Chintz: Cotton fabric, often in floral or other all-over print, coated with a resin that gives it a sheen. Dry cleaning is necessary. Used for pillows, curtains, and some upholstery.

Cotton duck: A cream-colored cotton that comes in various weights. Ideal for no-sew curtains. See *canvas*.

Crewel: Plain woven, natural cotton fabric with wool embroidery. Traditionally used for upholstery and draperies.

Damask: Another jacquard material made of cotton, silk, wool, or a combination with satin raised design. Widely used for draperies and upholstery.

Gingham: Plain-weave cotton fabric woven in block or checked prints. Its crisp look makes this fabric popular for trim, curtain panels, draperies, tablecloths, and bedspreads.

Lace: Cotton or cotton-polyester blend material featuring open-work designs. Frequently used for curtains.

Linen: An unusually strong fabric made from processed flax. Works best when used simply, such as tab-topped curtains.

Moiré: A finish on a silk or acetate fabric intended to resemble watermarking. Washing removes the finish; dry clean only. Depending on thickness, good for draperies and upholstery.

Muslin: A course, plain weave cotton in white or cream. It is often sheer, not heavy as canvas is. Used for sheeting, curtains, and light slipcovers.

Organdy: Light cotton washed in acid for a crisp finish. Used for trimming and curtains.

Satin: A silk, linen, or cotton weave with a glossy surface and dull back, sometimes with a *moiré* finish. Not particularly durable, but fine for draperies and light-use upholstery.

Silk: A soft, shiny fabric made from the fine fibers produced by silkworms. It is favored for swags and formal drapery.

Taffeta: Silk and acetate weave that appears shiny and maintains shape. Useful for trimmings and draperies.

Tapestry: A heavy, woven cloth that imitates handmade tapestries. Often used for upholstery, pillows, and wall hangings.

Toile de Jouy: An eighteenth-century cotton or linen fabric printed with pastoral scenes. First produced in the French town of Jouy. Used for curtains, upholstery, and pillows.

Velvet: Made from cotton, viscose rayon, or polyester, velvet features a smooth, iridescent-looking pile. Finer velvets are good for draperies; heavier ones for upholstery.

SMART STEPS

ONE: *Create a sample board.* One way designers organize the colors, patterns, and textures they plan to use in a room is to create a sample board. The white, foam-cored presentation board sold in art supply stores, measuring at least 8½ x 11 inches, is ideal for this purpose. Attach to the board with rubber cement (or tack to it with removable sticky material) any swatches of fabric, wallpaper patterns, or paint color chips you're considering. Keep the swatches and other items in the same proportion on the board as they would be in the room. For example, a paint sample that you're considering for the walls will be quite large, whereas an accent color will take up far less space. The fabric you plan to use on the sofa should take up more space on the board than one you're thinking about for a small window treatment or footstool. As a general rule of thumb, designate about two thirds of the board for wall and ceiling treatments, and divide the remaining third between floors and furnishings. Add and remove things as you experiment with different looks, and be certain to look at the board in the room for which it's created at different times of day, under both natural and artificial lighting conditions.

TWO: *Develop your color scheme.* Bringing to bear all you now know about color (how it affects mood and how it can seemingly expand or decrease space, what you like, what your family likes), pick one. Frequently, you can establish your color based on elements already in the room that you don't plan to replace—an upholstered furnishing, a carpet, or even a favorite painting. Once you determine the main color, look at its complement or triad on the color wheel, and pick an accent or two. If you're painting your walls, go to the paint store and get

Right: *To pull off this color-coordinated garden room, the designer created a sample board of fabric swatches for the seat cushions and the throw pillows, paint chips, and a piece of the rug.*

sample chips of each of your colors in every intensity you can find. If you're planning to wallpaper, borrow the books with the kinds of patterns you like, and pore through them until you find something that works. Often you can pull your accent colors from the wallpaper pattern you choose.

THREE: *Consider mixing fabric patterns.* Most wallpaper makers offer fabrics to coordinate with their wallpaper patterns. Consider these, but also visit fabric stores to find other coordinating prints for upholstery and window treatments. Don't forget to check out ready-made slipcovers and window treatments, too. To experiment with mixing patterns, start simply. Geometric patterns often mix well together—stripes with checks or plaids or dots. It is always easier to mix patterns that contain one or more common colors. Two different patterns can be linked by color, fabric weight, texture, and degree of formality. You can mix patterns in different scales, but don't go overboard. Use a large pattern on a large element, such as a sofa, smaller prints for windows, and something smaller still for pillows. Same-size patterns fight for attention. As a general rule, a good mix includes small-, medium-, and large-scale prints. Checks with stripes, dots with plaids, florals with geometrics are all possibilities when coordinated tastefully. Designers develop a knack for picking eye-catching combinations—and through trial and error, you will, too. Look through magazines or wallpaper books for ideas. In any room where you're mixing patterns, it is important to give your eyes a place to rest. Be sure to add solid-color furnishings to the room as well.

FOUR: *Pick one print and stick with it.* If mixing does not appeal to you and you prefer to use one bold print, make sure the scale is large enough to carry the room. Paint the walls a saturated color picked out from the fabric. Use a second color for other large upholstered pieces or window treatments. Then pick the sharpest, brightest hue from the pattern for accents. Add variety with textiles—a rug, for example. Balance the pattern throughout the room.

FIVE: *Customize your plan.* Color schemes aren't one-size-fits-all. The most successful ones are custom-tailored for a particular space. In your clear-eyed assessment of your needs, here are some aspects to consider:

Physical Space. Consider not just whether the room is large or small but how the dimensions drive the plans. In a big room, would you rather scale down for a more intimate mood or emphasize the room's lofty spaciousness? In tight quarters, will you pull out every space-enhancing trick or bring on rich, deep colors to create a cozy "jewel box"? Is the space disjointed by doorways, windows, and jogs, asking to be unified in a smooth sweep of color? Or is it a bland box that begs for detail? There may be elements you

Clockwise (from right): *Sometimes the simplest approach is best: Stripes on the wall, curtains, and armchair are contrasted with one floral and one solid-colored pillow in a cozy reading corner. Yellow and blue in equal intensity—but not equal amounts—brighten a bedroom. A plain-Jane breakfast area is transformed by warm peach walls and floral roman shades. The complementary colors of red and green can be very livable choices when toned down to softer hues.*

Right: *When you choose a color scheme, make sure to incorporate accent pieces in those colors. Here, the forest green and sunflower yellow theme is continued in the glasses, plates, flowers, and even the coffeemaker.*

Below: *The rich jewel tones of the Oriental rug are picked up by the royal blue sofa and the red tulips. The tapestry throw pillows tie the scheme together.*

want to downplay. What are the room's fine features—the ready-made focal points?

Is the room located in a suburban ranch, a town house, a clean-lined apartment, a country house, or a beach bungalow? The color scheme may reflect a distinctive architectural period or regional character. You don't have to listen to the house's suggestions—an East Coast apartment can have a Southwest flavor or a country house some big-city slickness—but playing against type takes more design ingenuity.

Also consider the prevailing climate. If you face chilly, rainy winters, consider the psychological warmth of sunshiny tints and deep textures. In hot regions, smooth surfaces and light backgrounds seem particularly fresh and cool.

Lifestyle Concerns. Will the room be a high-traffic space, requiring washable, forgiving surfaces and colors? A space reserved for company occasions might be jazzed up with glamorous, less-practical choices. What activities take place in the room—reading, crafts, watching TV, or conversation? Is it a family space? A family space may need a color scheme that won't show dirt. Do family members have any strong opinions on color that you'd like to accommodate? If so, consider incorporating a favored color by using it as an accent or even as the base color for the entire scheme.

Will you spend long hours in the room or brief periods? Rooms you pass through briefly can usually carry off more-dramatic colors and patterns than rooms where you linger.

Atmosphere. What sort of mood would you like the room to project? Elegant? Homey? The room's purpose often prompts the color choices. You might, for example, lean toward an invigorating tint for a home office. The atmosphere should also relate to the room's purpose. You may, for example, need an energetic color for a home office.

Natural Light. The room's orientation can influence the palette, depending on whether you're trying to tone down or maximize the available light. In a true sun room, dark or bright textiles, which are prone to fading, might be reserved for easily changed accents. Before tailoring a room for sunshine, make sure the artificial lighting also flatters the selection. The next chapter, "Light by Design," will take you through the process of creating a lighting plan, plus it will show you how light affects color and how it sets the tone of a room.

CHAPTER 3

LIGHT
BY
DESIGN

A major element in any well-designed home is good lighting. A careful lighting design will make moving about and performing household activities easier. In addition, effective lighting improves the general atmosphere and appearance of an interior, helping to define form and emphasize texture. A seemingly drab room may just be poorly lit.

The quality of the light we live with also affects our sense of well being. We learn quicker and work better in bright, warm light. When we want to rest, dim light relaxes us. All of these considerations point to the importance of thoughtfully planning lighting for the home. Whether you decide to devise a lighting scheme yourself or call in a lighting specialist, remember: Good interior designers also take advantage of the transformational power of light and so can you. In this chapter, you'll learn how to use light to manipulate the perception of space, casting it up to make a low ceiling seem higher, or washing the walls with it to make a small room appear spacious. You'll also learn how to use light in a painterly fashion to emphasize forms or objects. What could be more dramatic than the shadow play of leaves on a nearby wall or ceiling produced by aiming a small spotlight upwards from underneath a bold, sculptural plant?

Today, at the flick of a switch, you can illuminate your home inside—and out. You can program and store entire lighting schemes thanks to the latest tech-

Left: *A good lighting scheme will enhance the appearance of any room, but in order to complement your décor, it should be planned in advance.*

nology. On command, create bright light for work, then change the mood to cozy when you want to relax, or adjust it all over again for TV viewing. Set your lights on timers for safety and security, or activate them by remote control.

For complicated situations, you may want to consult with a lighting design professional, or you may feel comfortable devising a plan yourself with the help of an electrician. In any case, you need to understand something of the basic science of light, how it is measured, and its effect on color. To make wise choices from among the wide variety of lighting types available, compare them on a level playing field. That's what lighting measurements can help you do.

You'll also need to learn about the types of lighting, the different kinds of bulbs and fixtures, in addition to the terminology. This will help you with planning, and will make you more effective when discussing ideas with experts and sales staff. For instance, many of us use the words "fixture" and "lamp" interchangeably, but when lighting professionals speak of "lamps" they are talking about "bulbs." Learn to speak the language.

Once you have prepared yourself, you can begin sketching out a plan that can cover areas within one room and to create a flow from one space to another.

NATURAL LIGHT

Any discussion about lighting your home has to begin with natural light. To the human eye, the desirable norm is sunlight. Part of its appeal is its variety. Consider the clear illumination on a cloudless mountaintop. Compare that to the diffused light on a misty morning or the intense brightness on a tropical beach. Then there's the changeability of sunlight between a cool rainy day, a clear winter afternoon, and a full summer blaze, or the contrast between the color of sunlight at noon and the way it appears as afternoon wears into evening.

The amount and quality of natural light a room receives depends on the size of its windows and its orientation with regard to the sun. South-facing windows get the lion's share

Left: *When planning a light scheme, start by charting the natural light, on both sunny and overcast days.*

Right: *The soft, diffused glow from this art glass wall sconce—an ambient source of lighting—provides plenty of general illumination for the hallway.*

of direct sunlight for most of the day. East-facing rooms benefit from early mornings, while rooms that face west are sunny in the afternoon. Because its back is to the sun, a north-facing room receives only indirect natural light and tends to be cool and dim.

When you are renovating or redecorating a room, always look at the existing space and take the seasons, time of day, and orientation of the windows into consideration. Sometimes making a window bigger, or adding another one, doesn't make a room brighter. If the window's siting is toward the north, the room will just get colder. You can make a breakfast nook cheerier with a window that faces east, but don't try to take a late afternoon nap in a room with west-facing windows, unless you can control the light with shades, blinds, or lined curtains.

The natural light in the room will affect any tasks you perform as well. Never arrange furniture, such as a desk or worktable, so that you are facing directly into bright sunlight. But be careful about having your back to a window. This can create shadows on your work surface. Ideally, follow the old axiom that recommends "light coming from over the left shoulder." By charting the light, and arranging your room and selecting window treatments accordingly, you can avoid problems.

ARTIFICIAL LIGHT

Artificial light picks up where natural light leaves off. It is the illumination you provide and, unlike natural light, can also be fine tuned. In the daytime, artificial light augments natural light; after dark, it compensates for daylight completely. The key to devising a versatile plan that can change with each activity, as well as with the time of day or

the weather, begins with knowing about the different types of artificial light. Here's a review:

AMBIENT LIGHT

Ambient, or general, light is illumination that fills an entire room. Its source is normally an overhead fixture, but the light itself does not appear to come from any one specific direction. Ambient light surrounds a room generally. An obvious example of ambient light is ceiling-hung fluorescent strips in the average office environment. A covering over the strips hides the source and diffuses the light throughout the room.

A wall sconce is another good example of ambient light. The fixture washes light up the wall for an overall glow. The wall reflects the light, which diminishes the appearance of a single source. While you can tell the light is coming from the sconce, the overall glow is diffused.

The key to good ambient lighting is making it inconspicuous. Ambient light is merely the backdrop for the rest of the room, not the main feature. It changes with the surrounding environment—always providing light, but never becoming obvious. For example, ambient lighting used during the day should blend in with the amount of natural light entering the room. At night, you should be able to diminish the light level so that it doesn't contrast jarringly against the darkness outside.

TASK LIGHT

As its name implies, task lighting is purely functional. It illuminates a specific area for a particular job, such as chopping food on a kitchen counter, laboring over a woodworking project, or applying makeup.

Theatrical lighting around vanity mirrors is an excellent example of task lighting. It provides cross-illumination, while avoiding the distorting shadows often seen with overhead lighting. Task lighting should always be included in any room where specific functions take place, but its use should be optional. In other words, you can turn it on when you need it, and keep it off at other times. Task lights should not be on the same switch with the fixture that provides general illumination. To use both types simultaneously creates a harsh, too-bright effect.

Clockwise (left to right): *Each room in the house has different lighting needs: Recessed and hanging fixtures combined with under-the-cabinet strip lights work for kitchens; table lamps offer lighting flexibility for living rooms, while accent lights play up elements, such as artwork; decorative lighting accentuates architectural features, such as a cove ceiling in a master bedroom; and task lighting for reading is a good choice in guest rooms.*

ACCENT LIGHT

Often overlooked, but always the most dramatic, accent lighting draws attention to a particular element in the room, such as a handsome architectural feature or a work of art. Accent lighting makes a room come alive. It creates a mood. It shapes space. Lights recessed into a soffit above a handsome kitchen countertop casts a downward glow of illumination that offsets the counter without spilling light into the rest of the room. Cove lighting over a tub shimmers above the water and delineates a bathing area dramatically.

Without accent lighting, there may be light, but no focus, no character, no show business. With it, a design becomes exciting, theatrical, and rich.

DECORATIVE LIGHT

While accent lighting draws attention to another object or surface, decorative lighting draws attention to itself. It can be kinetic, in the form of candles or flames in a fireplace, or static, such as fixed wall candelabra. It is there to grab attention. It is lighting for the pure sake of lighting.

Because it is compelling, it can be a device to indirectly attract or distract. You can use decorative lighting to draw the eye upward toward a cathedral ceiling, for example. By capturing your eye, decorative lighting forces your focus away from anything else. It doesn't highlight anything, as accent lighting does. And it doesn't provide a great deal of illumination, as ambient lighting does. It is the device that most lighting designers love to use, the final stroke in a complex multilayered plan.

Some types of decorative lighting include candles, chandeliers, neon sculptures or signs, a strip of miniature lights—any type of light that is deliberate and contrived. Include it to unify a room—to strike a balance among the various types of lighting, including natural light from the sun and moon.

CONTRAST AND DIFFUSION

Task lighting and accent lighting are examples of high-contrast lighting—they eliminate shadows and bring an object into sharp, crisp focus. Ambient lighting and decorative lighting are more diffused. They are softer, more forgiving lights that are comfortable and relaxing. Most rooms benefit from a combination of contrast lighting and diffused light, so incorporate both in your plan.

HOW MUCH LIGHT DO YOU NEED?

Design professionals have established a set of ideal lighting levels for performing the various activities and tasks that take place in any house. Your own personal preferences should lie within the minimum and maximum levels they have established. Some people favor more light; others prefer less. Good lighting begins with taking the recommended levels of light into account and tempering them with your preferences and those of people with whom you live. In common spaces, such as the family room, living room, and kitchen, it is better to err on the side of brightness. Gear lighting in private areas, such as a study, bedroom, or workshop, to individual needs. Consult the "Smart Tip about Recommended Ranges" box, on page 51, as a starting point in establishing your own levels. Once you've determined the level of light you require for each task or activity, relate this light to the surroundings. You can avoid eyestrain by including plenty of ambient light, thereby reducing its contrast to task lighting. Task lighting, the general lighting immediately nearby, and the lowest lighting in the area (as in a room's corners) should not contrast sharply. The light you use to read by, for example, should only be twice to three times as bright as the surrounding light in the room. Using a reading light in an otherwise dark room strains your eyes by forcing them to adjust frequently from

Right: *This dining room receives ample sunlight for leisurely breakfasts. In the evenings, the shaded, eight-arm chandelier creates a cozy ambiance for dining. To prevent glare, consideration was given to the hanging height of the chandelier.*

light to darkness. The greatest range of light in any room should be a four to one ratio at most.

Direct Glare. Bare-bulb glare is obvious. You can avoid it by selecting the proper size shade, adjusting the angle of a fixture, or using a low-wattage bulb or one with frosting.

Lighting professionals caution against "glare bombs," fixtures that produce unavoidable, uncomfortable light. A common offender is the bathroom globe or strip light over the vanity; another is the exposed bulb in some ceiling fixtures; a third is an inferior fluorescent fixture that blasts you with bright direct light. In the first case, you might try replacing the bulbs with heavily frosted versions. If you plan to include track lights in your scheme, install baffles over the bulbs. They are devices that are designed to reduce spill light and glare. When you visit a lighting showroom, ask specifically to see bulbs and fixtures designed to reduce glare.

Smart Tip about Recommended Ranges of Light Levels

You can avoid eyestrain by having plenty of ambient light, thereby reducing the contrast to task lighting. Start by determining the level of light needed for the activity or task, then relate it to the surroundings. (See "Assessing Your Lighting Needs," on page 55 of this chapter.) Task lighting, lighting immediately nearby, and then the lowest lighting in the area (as in a room's corners) should range no more than a ratio of four to one, preferably three to one near task lighting. You can compare watts and foot-candles cast by various light sources to determine the ratios or approximate them with your naked eye. The following chart provides the recommended ranges of light levels for seeing activities in the homes. The more intense the activity, the greater the light level should be.

ACTIVITY	EASY OR SHORT DURATION	CRITICAL OR PROLONGED
Dining	low	low
Entertaining	low to high	low to high
Grooming	moderate	high
Craftwork *	moderate	high
Kitchen/laundry chores	low to moderate	high
Reading	low to moderate	high
Studying	moderate	high
TV viewing	low to moderate	low to moderate
Computer work	moderate	high
Workbench *	moderate	high
Tabletop games	low to moderate	moderate to high
Writing	low to moderate	high

Benefits from supplementary directional light.

When you create a layout for your furniture arrangement, it's always wise to assess it for glare. For instance, if you situate the new family room sofa to face a game table, every time you flick on the suspended pendant light over the tabletop, you're creating glare for anyone seated on the sofa. Always check the field of vision from each seated, as well as each standing, position.

Indirect Glare. Any flat reflective surface can be the source of indirect glare. That includes shiny desktops, countertops, tables, mirrors and any other glass or metal surfaces, and TV and computer screens. While not as obvious as direct glare, indirect glare can cause eyestrain, too.

To determine reflected glare, simply place a mirror in front of or on top of any surface you suspect will reflect glare. The mirror will isolate reflected light glare. Place a temporary light where you plan to install a permanent source, then do the glare check before making your final installation.

THE ROLE OF BULBS IN DESIGN

Just changing the types of bulbs, or lamps as professional lighting designers call them, in your existing household fixtures can make a major difference in the way the room looks, functions, and feels. Does this mean you should go out and replace all of your fluorescent lamps with halogen fixtures and call off the rest of your remodeling plans? That might be exaggerating the power of the right light. But don't underestimate it, either.

Understanding the differences in lamps will help you select the right light sources for every area in your house. Light is like paint. You get different effects depending on the combinations you use. And color is nothing but the reflection of different types of light. When planning a lighting scheme, always consider the relationship between color and light.

STANDARD MEASUREMENTS FOR COLOR

Scales used universally in lighting assess the color temperature the lamp gives off and how light from the lamp affects the objects it is lighting. We explored the concept of natur-

al light and its effect on color in Chapter Two. Now let's look at warm and cool artificial lights and how they affect color. The term *correlated color temperature* (CCT) is used to compare the color appearance of light in terms of warmth or coolness. Lamps, which range in color from red to orange to yellow to blue to blue-white, are ranked according to the Kelvin (K) temperature scale. This rating will help you to select lamps that are closely matched, and you can vary the coolness or warmth of lighting for specific situations. Generally, light sources below 3,000K are considered warm, while those above 4,100K are considered cool. Midrange light sources fall between 3,200K and 3,600K.

Clockwise (left to right): *When choosing bulbs for your fixtures, consider the warmth or coolness of its light. Located in a hallway, the yellow glow of two wall sconces projects an inviting ambiance. A combination of blue-white light for clarity and yellow-orange light for atmosphere creates a balanced lighting scheme in this dining room. The white light of these recessed fixtures, shown with cobalt trims in the kitchen and plain in the living room, often works well for general lighting.*

Incandescent. Like sunlight, incandescent bulbs emit *continuous-spectrum light,* or light that contains every color. Illumination from these bulbs, in fact, is even warmer than sunlight, making its effect very appealing in a room. It makes our skin tones look good, and even enhances our feeling of well-being. The drawbacks to incandescent bulbs are that they use a lot of electricity, are fragile, have a short lifespan, and produce a lot of heat.

They come in a variety of shapes, sizes, and applications. (One type features a waterproof lens cover that makes it suitable for over a tub or inside a shower.) These bulbs usually are made of glass, and can be clear, diffuse, tinted, colored, or have a reflective coating inside.

Color rendition describes how a light source affects the perception of the color of an object it illuminates. The Color Rendition Index (CRI) is a way of measuring a lamp's ability to render true color (the color of an object in sunlight). The color rendering capabilities of lamps are rated from 1 to 100 with true color at 100. If you want different lamps to light an object the same way, match and compare CCTs and CRIs. Check the CCTs first, then the CRIs.

TYPES OF BULBS

Most homes include a combination of warm and cool tones, so selecting bulbs that provide balanced lighting comfortably close to what appears normal to the eye is usually the most attractive choice. Experiment with various combinations of bulbs to create your own desired effect. Balance and layering are the two keys to success. Here is a brief description of the types of bulbs and their characteristics.

Fluorescent. These energy-efficient bulbs cast a diffuse, shadowless light that makes them great for general illumination. The old standard fluorescents are very unflattering, however, making everything and everyone appear pale and bland. There are newer incandescentlike fluorescent bulbs,

Smart Tip about Dimmer Switches

You can dim lights just slightly to extend lamp life and save energy, and there will be very little perceptible change in light level. For instance, dimming the light to 50 percent will be perceived as though the light were only dimmed to 70 percent. Therefore, there is no dramatic dilation or constriction of the eye due to light level change.

called deluxe warm white, that are warmer and more natural, rendering light that resembles sunlight. New fluorescents are also available in familiar tube versions or in folded shapes, called compact fluorescents.

Because the life cycle of fluorescents is shortened when used for periods of less than three hours, place them in situations where the light will be left on for an extended period of time. For example, a fluorescent might not make sense in a storage area where light is only occasionally needed for a few minutes. On the other hand, installing a fluorescent fixture as your overhead kitchen light makes sense because it's likely to be on for hours at a time.

Halogen. This is actually a type of incandescent lamp that produces brighter, whiter light at a lower wattage and with greater energy efficiency. The disadvantages are a higher price tag and a higher heat output that requires a special shielding for fire prevention. Halogen lamps have a slightly different shape and thicker, heavier glass bulb than the most commonly used incandescent bulb. The low-voltage version of halogen bulbs produces a brighter light than standard halogen, and is even more energy-efficient. Small in size, low-voltage halogens are typically used for creative accent lighting.

Fiber Optics. One of countless innovations gradually finding its way into the home, fiber-optic systems consist of one extremely bright lamp to transport light to one or more destinations through fiber-optic conduits. Used dramatically for accent lighting, fiber-optic lighting has the advantage of not generating

Right: *The clinical light of some fluorescent bulbs is a thing of the past. The compact fluorescent wall fixtures in this kitchen have been improved to shed a warm, natural light.*

excessive heat. This makes it ideal for highlighting artwork, which can be damaged by heat, or as a substitute for decorative neon lights, which consume lots of energy.

ASSESSING YOUR LIGHTING NEEDS

When a room isn't bright enough, most people just exchange low-watt bulbs for high-watt versions. Wattage, however, is simply a measurement of how much electricity a lamp consumes. The light output of a bulb is actually measured in lumens. If the bulbs you have been using aren't providing enough general light, substitute them with ones that have more lumens. The next time you shop for bulbs, read

the packaging, which indicates the lumens per watt (lpw) produced by a bulb. The more lumens per watt, the more efficient the lamp. When looking for intensity produced by a lamp, refer to its candlepower (Cp). The more candela (units), the brighter the source.

But when planning a suitable light design, you must take other factors into consideration. Besides the amount of natural light the room receives, consider how you will use it—to rest, work, dine, entertain, or a combination of activities. Next, assess the reflectance levels in the room, or the amount of light that is reflected from a colored surface, such as a tile floor or a painted wall. Light colors are reflective; dark colors are absorbent. Surface texture also makes a difference—mirrorlike surfaces can reflect as much as 90 percent. For example, white reflects 80 percent of the light in a room, while black reflects only 4 percent of it. In practi-

cal terms, a room with white or pale walls requires less light than one with deep, jewel-toned walls.

Next, consider the size of the room. How high are the ceilings? High ceilings require brighter lights to dispel shadows. But you'll have to tone down the level of brightness in a room with low ceilings because light tends to bounce off low ceilings and walls. How many windows and skylights are there? Do they face the sunny south, or is their exposure to the north, or somewhere in between?

Designers typically determine lighting needs by using suggested foot-candle (Fc) levels for different activities and areas. Foot-candles, which refer to the amount of light that falls on a surface, are used primarily for directional lamps. To determine the foot-candle power you will need to adequately light an area, divide the candlepower of the bulb you intend to use by the distance from the fixture to the surface squared ($Fc = Cp \div D^2$).

There are no perfect stock formulas. But by looking at how each of these factors affects the others, you can make educated choices when developing your light plan. Keeping in mind the science and technology involved in lighting will help you assess your own requirements for the room. Ideally, you'll want to incorporate a variety of options for various activities, to create ambiance, and for decoration. Use the following Smart Steps to get started.

ONE: *Examine your activities.* Above all, your lighting design should enhance the function of the room. Try preparing dinner with a new recipe or following a complicated sewing pattern

Left: *Before planning your kitchen's lighting, make a list what activities you do and where you do them. That way, the new lighting scheme will address your needs.*

Right: *Shaving and applying makeup requires task lights, such as these recessed fixtures. The star sconce, however, is a decorative feature, adding little to the general illumination.*

without the right light. Make a list of all the day and nighttime activities that may take place in room, such as TV watching, studying, cooking, and crafts.

TWO: *Sketch an informal plan.* Refer to the floor plan you drew of the room or make a new sketch. (See Chapter One, "Understanding and Arranging Space," on page 12.) Circle the activity centers—work tables, reading chairs, TV viewing spots, and so forth. Not everything you expect to do will require the same level of light.

Note each activity center with a "G" for general or ambient light, "T" for task light, "A" for accent light, and "D" for decorative light. In some places, you may want to indicate more than one type of light. An easy chair may be used at times for reading and at other times for TV viewing or even just rest, for example.

Place your general lighting first, then indicate where you'll need task lights. After you've noted every activity center for task lighting, decide where you want to install accent lighting. You might want some recessed fixtures over a countertop or art. Maybe you want to highlight beautiful crown molding or hand-painted tile. If you want to use accent lighting, but don't know where it should go, ask yourself what is the most interesting feature in the room. It may be something as simple as a wall-hung framed print, a collection of first-edition books on a shelf, or a bay window with a beautiful view.

You don't have to place decorative lighting into your plan unless it is a wired fixture, such as a neon sculpture or a track system of low-voltage halogens. But if you know you'll be using candles in the room, it is a good idea to indicate them, too. That way you can plan a place that will hold them safely.

THREE: *Check your local code.* Every municipality has its own codes regarding the placement of light and electricity around water. Before you purchase any light fixtures for the kitchen and bath, especially, check your local code with the building inspector or speak with your contractor.

FOUR: *Visit lighting showrooms.* The best way to get ideas is to visit lighting showrooms and the lighting department in home centers. This will give you a chance to take an inventory of fixture types and styles currently on the market. Also, you can take advantage of the advice of lighting specialists employed at these stores. They can help you create the right plan and choose an appropriate style of lighting. Bring along your sketch, your list of activities, as well as the design materials you have compiled containing clippings, notes, sample plans, color charts, tile, paint, and fabric samples. The lighting designer can take it from there.

As you might already expect, some in-store advice is free. Ask about it. A few suggestions may be all you need to steer you in the right direction. Otherwise, you may want to consider an in-home consultation. Inquire about fees, which may be modest. Sometimes a small investment in professional advice pays off handsomely in the final result—and in the discount professional designers can offer on fixtures.

There are also systems that computerize a variety of lighting options. A lighting specialist can design an entire program that sets the lights throughout the room on a system devised for different moods and activities. Everything is preprogammed and controlled by one central panel. However, these "smart systems" can be high-priced.

FINDING THE RIGHT FIXTURE

There's practically an endless number of fixture styles on the market to match every décor and catch everyone's imagination. The past few years have proven to be a lighting designer's dream as fixtures have become more decorative and lighting schemes more varied and eclectic. From nostalgic reproductions to architecturally inspired designs and contemporary styles, there are models to suit any look in the form of table and floor models, wall sconces, chandeliers, strip lights, recessed canister lights, track lights, ceiling fixtures, and novelty types. The copious selection of finishes in all of these styles offers lots of excitement, too. Look for everything from ceramic, glass, and colored enamels to brass, chrome, pewter, nickel, and copper; brushed,

Above: *Artwork, such as this portrait, can be accented by specialty fixtures hung directly above or below the picture.*

Left: *The pendant ceiling fixture was placed on a separate switch from the wall sconces and table lamps to allow for a greater degree of lighting control.*

matted, or antiqued, as well as dramatic designs in wrought iron and verdigris. For more interest, select fixtures with a combination of finishes, such as a verdigris with antiqued brass or copper paired with wrought iron.

For a sophisticated look, combine more than one fixture type and avoid matched pairs, such as two identical table lamps at either end of a sofa. In a bathroom, a ceiling fixture that includes a ventilating fan is especially practical. For accenting in any room, pair uplighting fixtures, such as wall sconces, with downlighting types: recessed lights or a ceiling-mounted unit, for example. Install track lighting to wash an entire wall with illumination. Do this when you want to call attention to a beautiful wallcovering, a special paint technique, or a mural.

Finally, before you purchase a light fixture, ask to see it lit up in the store. That way you can be sure it produces the type of effect you desire.

CREATING ARCHITECTURAL EFFECTS WITH LIGHTING

Lighted coves, soffits (or cornices), and valances make the most of architectural features in a room. Fixtures designed for this purpose create dramatic reflective light. Coves distribute light upward. Soffits distribute light downward. Valances distribute light both up and down. A shield, usually made of a piece of wood or plaster molding, hides the light itself. Baffles, louvers, or diffusers direct light and reduce glare. Consider incorporating one of these ideas into your design if you want to make a big splash with the lighting.

Be creative when thinking about architectural lighting. Install it along the top or bottom of cabinets or inside the cove of a raised ceiling. Integrate a lighted valance with a vaulted ceiling or a curtain sweep, vertically light a wall niche, and highlight molding. Whatever you decide, first analyze your architectural lighting needs. Ask yourself these questions:

❧ Is the reflected wall or ceiling smooth enough to be attractive?

❧ Can I alter the look of the lighting by tinting the surface upon which it reflects?

❧ Can I increase efficiency by painting the interior of the valance, cove, or soffit white? (Remember, light-colored surfaces reflect light.)

❧ Does the reflected light enhance the rest of the room's light or detract from it?

❧ Is the ceiling high enough (at least 8 feet) to keep the light from spilling onto the walls? (The top of the cove should be at least 18 inches from the ceiling.)

Talk with your contractor to see what kind of architectural effects are feasible in your design. Once your lighting plan has been established, the next step is to choose flooring.

Clockwise (left to right): *No matter what the décor of your interior, there is a fixture that suits its look—from the classic sophistication of two-arm brass sconces and table lamps with botanical china bases to the updated country style of a verdigris-finished lamp with a hand-painted shade. Retro styles also abound: This etched pendant draws its inspiration for early twentieth-century design. A beaded chandelier and a sinuously shaped floor lamp put a contemporary twist on tradition.*

CHAPTER 4

FACTS ABOUT FLOORING

Because they know the market inside-out, professional designers can present you with a wide range of options for all of your flooring needs. They can recommend the right type of flooring for how you and your family plan to use the place. They also understand that, like every other element in a room's décor, flooring makes a visual impact with regard to space, perception, and style.

If you are are acting as your own designer, one of the first things you should do is learn about the various types of flooring—from wood to stone to vinyl—on today's market. The choices are myriad and innovations in technology have widened the range of finishes.

Like a professional, be sure to consider the principles of color, texture, and pattern, relating them to your selection and to the rest of the elements in the room. (See Chapter Two, "Color, Pattern, and Texture," on page 28.) If the wallpaper features a big, bold design, for instance, you'll want to tone things down with a solid color floor or one with a small pattern. If the room is large, you can make it cozy with a number of area rugs that define intimate furniture groupings. A country-style living room might benefit from a textured tile that has rustic appeal or from braided rugs. A formal entry hall will make a stately impression with an intricate parquet border or checkerboard marble floor.

Left: *The herringbone wood floor suits the formality of this spacious entry hall and adds an element of pattern that is a counterpoint to the cream walls.*

You'll also have to consider the function of the space you are decorating before making a final decision. A natural wood floor is unrivaled for adding richness and warmth, but if you install it in a high-traffic area, be prepared to deal with scuffs, scratches, and dedicated maintenance if you want it to retain its handsome appearance.

Taking a comprehensive look at the types of flooring available and their most appropriate applications will make choosing your new floor a piece of cake. As you review these flooring options, remember that some can be mixed and matched for an interesting and creative variation that also allows flexibility of design within almost any budget. Wood planks, for example, might be bordered by ceramic tile strips, or top-quality stone

edging might provide an unusual border for a relatively inexpensive expanse of carpeting.

WOOD

In bygone eras, a wood floor was simply one that was created by laying wide wood planks side by side. Later, as the manufacturing of lumber improved, homeowners were able to choose narrower planks that look more refined than rustic. Parquet floors were created by woodcrafters with a flair for the dramatic and an appreciation of the artistic richness of wood grains set in nonlinear patterns.

Below: *A rich brown stain was chosen for the floor of this contemporary bedroom, in which dark woodwork and white details, such as the bed linens, artwork, and trim, are juxtaposed.*

Left: *As a less-expensive alternative to parquet, create floor patterns, such as this check design, with stain.*

dining rooms, where chairs or other furniture will be moved around. The hardwoods—maple, birch, oak, ash—are far less likely to mar with normal use. A hardwood floor is not indestructible; however, it will stand up to use.

Both hardwoods and softwoods are graded according to their color, grain, and imperfections. The top of the line is known as clear, followed by select, No. 1 common, and No. 2 common. In addition to budget considerations, the decision whether to pay top dollar for clear wood or to economize with a lesser grade depends on use factors and on the design objectives. For example, if you plan to install a wood floor in a small room and then cover most of it with an area rug, the No. 2 common grade may be a good choice; lesser grades are also fine for informal rooms where a few scratches just enhance a lived-in look. If your design calls for larger areas of rich wood grain that will be exposed, with scatter rugs used for color accents, a clear or select grade will make an attractive choice. Another factor to use in determining what grade to select is the stain; imperfections are less noticeable with darker stains.

FINISHING OPTIONS

Color stains—reds, blues, and greens—may work in settings where a casual or rustic feeling is desired. This, however, is a departure from the traditional use of wood. Wood is not typically used to deliver color impact; instead it blends with and subtly enhances its surroundings. Natural wood stains range from light ash tones to deep, coffee-like colors. Generally, lighter stains make a room feel less formal, and darker, richer stains suggest a stately atmosphere— the traditional library with deep-toned paneling illuminated by soft, incandescent lamps, for example. Lighter stains—as with lighter colors—create a feeling of openness and make a small room look larger; darker stains foster a more intimate feeling and can reduce the visual vastness of a large space.

Today's manufacturers have made it possible to have it all. The wood floor, factory- or custom-stained to suit a particular style or mood in a room, is still a traditional favorite. It's available in strips of 2 to 3 inches wide, or in country-style planks of 10 inches wide or more. The formal, sophisticated look of a parquet floor is unparalleled for elegance and richness of visual texture. Prefinished hardwood tile blocks are now manufactured in a variety of patterns, making parquet possible at a reasonable price.

TYPES OF WOOD FLOORING

Wood varieties available as a surface material are vast, and cost varies widely, depending on the type and grade of wood and on the choice of design (strips or parquet).

Softwoods, like pine and fir, are often used to make simple tongue-and-groove floorboards. These floors are less expensive than hardwoods but also less durable. Softwoods are not suitable for high-traffic areas, for rooms with heavy furniture (which can "dig" into the wood), or for kitchens or

Left: *A hallway floor can be complete after installation if the wood strips come prefinished and sealed.*

strips or planks already finished and sealed so that once the last nail is tapped into the flooring the project is complete. Most parquet tiles come finished and sealed as well.

MAINTENANCE

If a wood floor is appropriately installed and properly sealed with polyurethane, maintenance consists of vacuum cleaning or dust-mopping as needed. It's important to promptly vacuum up any gritty material that may be tracked in from outdoors, because sand and gravel can scratch or even gouge the surface of a wood floor. Waxing isn't necessary, although some who live with wood floors like the patina that results from periodic applications of wax.

LAMINATE PRODUCTS

Laminate flooring is the great pretender among flooring materials. When your creative side tells you to install wood but your practical side knows it just won't hold up in the traffic-heavy location you're considering it for, a wood floor lookalike might be just the thing. Faux wood and faux stone laminate floors provide you with the look you want tempered with physical wear and care properties you and your family can live with. Laminate is particularly suited to rooms where floors are likely to see heavy duty—kitchens, family rooms, hallways, and children's bedrooms and playrooms—anywhere stain and scratch resistance and easy clean-up count. Because prolonged exposure to moisture will damage the product, laminate is not recommended for bathroom use. Manufacturers of laminate offer warranties against staining, scratching, cracking, and peeling for up to 15 years.

Laminate is made from paper impregnated with melamine, an organic resin, and bonded to a core of particleboard, fiberboard, or other wood byproducts. It can be laid over virtually any subflooring surface, including wood and

Creative patterning of a wood floor can enrich a design. For example, to create an Old World look, you might lay strips in a herringbone pattern. Decorative inlay with strips or parquet patterns can enhance richness and visual interest and can be used to "frame out" activity areas in large spaces that have multiple uses, such as living and dining areas.

INSTALLATION

Unless you're particularly adept at measuring and cutting wood and have the time and skill necessary to finish the flooring surface, the installation, staining, and finishing of strip or plank floors can be a formidable project. Therefore, if the design plan calls for the laying of unfinished wood strips, factor the cost of hiring a skilled professional into your budget. Many manufacturers offer products with installation kits that make wood flooring a do-it-yourself option for those whose skills are good but don't necessarily approach a professional carpenter's level. Some make

concrete. It can also be applied on top of an existing ceramic or vinyl tile, as well as vinyl or other sheet flooring. You can even install it over certain types of carpeting, but check the manufacturer's guidelines before doing so.

INSTALLATION AND CARE

The installation of laminate flooring is a reasonably quick and relatively easy do-it-yourself project. It requires sheets of a special foam underlayment followed by careful placement, cutting, and gluing of the laminate.

Laminate is available in sheets that are ideal when your design calls for a uniform look, such as monotone stone, or a linear design that mimics strip or plank wood flooring. Laminate planks, squares, and blocks offer added design flexibility: With them, you can design your own tile patterns, lay strips of wood-look planks with alternating "stain" finishes, or border your floor with a contrasting color.

Proper care for this type of material includes routine vacuuming and an occasional damp-mopping. Add a cup of vinegar or ammonia to a gallon of water for an inexpensive but effective cleaning solution.

VINYL AND OTHER RESILIENT FLOORING

Like laminate, resilient flooring is also available in design-friendly sheet or tile form. Resilient floors can be made from a variety of materials, including linoleum, asphalt or asphalt combined with asbestos, and rubber. However, the most commonly used material in manufacturing today's resilient floors is vinyl plastic.

Price, durability, and easy maintenance make resilient flooring an attractive and popular choice. Do-it-yourself installation, an option even for those who are not particularly skilled or experienced, can mean further savings.

SHEET VERSES TILES

Resilient flooring comes in an enormous array of colors and patterns, plus many of the flooring styles have a textured surface. With the tiles, you can combine color and pattern in limitless ways. Even the sheet form of resilient flooring can be customized with inlay strips.

Cushioned sheet vinyl offers the most resilience. It provides excellent stain resistance; it's comfortable and quiet underfoot and easy to maintain, with no-wax and never-wax finishes often available. These features make the floor especially attractive for areas with lots of kid traffic. Beware though: Only the more expensive grades show an acceptable degree of resistance to nicking and denting. In rooms where furniture is often moved around, this could be a

Below: *A lively vinyl pattern on the floor perks up a plain bathroom. It has the look of a pricier tile installation.*

problem. Although the range of colors, patterns, and surface textures is wide, sheet flooring is not as flexible as vinyl tile when it comes to customizing your look.

Regular sheet vinyl is less expensive than the cushioned types, but it carries the same disadvantages and is slightly less resilient. Except for the availability of no-wax finishes, a vinyl tile floor is as stain resistant and as easy to maintain as the sheet-vinyl products. Increased design possibilities are the trade-off.

Here, as with other flooring materials, one possible way out of the choice maze is to take the unconventional step of mixing flooring materials. For example, use a durable cushioned sheet vinyl in more trafficked areas, but frame it with a pretty vinyl tile or laminate border.

CERAMIC TILE

Ceramic tile—actually fired clay—is an excellent choice for areas subject to a lot of traffic and in rooms where resistance to moisture and stains is needed. These features, combined with easy cleanup, have made ceramic tile a centuries-old tradition for flooring, walls, and ceilings in bathrooms and kitchens. Color, texture, and pattern choices available today make ceramic tile the most versatile flooring option in terms of design possibilities.

TILE OPTIONS
Some handcrafted ceramic tiles are very costly, but today's manufacturers have created a market full of design, style, and price options. It's possible to create an elegant ceramic floor design even on a relatively tight budget. You

Top: *Ceramic-backed glass tiles, dotted with colored glass accents, make a dazzling hallway floor, plus they are durable enough for foot traffic.*

Left: *Glazed hexagonal tiles resist stains and are easy to clean —a smart choice for breakfast nooks. White grout was used here, but tinting the grout was also an option.*

can control costs further with do-it-yourself installation. Tiling tools are not very expensive, and many tile retailers will rent them—some will even make the trickier cuts for you. The adhesives, mortars, and grouts available today are easier to use than ever before.

Tiles come in a variety of sizes, beginning with 1-inch-square mosaic tiles to large 16 x 16-inch squares. Other shapes, such as triangles, diamonds, and rectangles, are also available. Tile textures range from shiny to matte-finished and from glass-smooth to ripple-surfaced. Tiles are available either *glazed* or *unglazed*. Glazed tiles have a hard, often colored, surface that is applied during the firing process; the resulting finish can range from glossy to matte. Unglazed tiles, such as terra cotta or quarry tiles, have a matte finish, are porous, and need to be sealed to prevent staining.

In creating a flooring design, consider whether the other elements in the room allow for an intricate pattern or work better with one light color as the dominant feature. Once you make that basic determination, create the design directly on a copy of your floor plan.

Consider using accent borders to create unique designs, such as a faux area rug, that visually separate sections of a room "or separate, one room from another. When added in a random pattern, embossed accent tiles add interest, variety, and elegance to an expanse of single-colored tiles.

Alas, no surfacing material is perfect. To assess whether ceramic tile is the right surface for your floor, take into consideration both the positive and negative points. Ceramic tile offers long-lasting beauty, design versatility, and simplicity of maintenance, but it also has some hard-to-live-with features. Tile is cold underfoot, noisy

when someone walks across it in hard-soled shoes, and not at all resilient—always expect the worst when something breakable falls on a tile floor. If you have infants and toddlers around, it may be best to wait a few years for your tiled floor.

STONE AND MARBLE

Like ceramic tile, stone and marble are classified as "non-resilients." Like tile, these materials offer richness of color, durability, moisture and stain resistance, and ease of maintenance. They also share with tile the drawbacks of being cold

Below: *The rugged surface of this slate floor adds a textural element to a country-style dining room. The half-basket-weave pattern requires the installation skills of a professional.*

to the touch, noisy to walk on, and unforgivingly hard. Stone and marble floors are clearly, unmistakably natural. As remarkably good as some faux surfaces look, no product manufactured today actually matches the rustic irregularity and random color variation of natural stone or the richness and depth of color in veined marble.

DECISION-MAKING FACTORS

With that kind of beauty and singularity inevitably comes a high price tag. Whether it's polished marble, random-cut fieldstone, slate, brick, terrazzo, or limestone, the materials are expensive and the installation requires professional-level skills. Also, you may have to go through an interior designer for the flooring because some suppliers of stone and marble won't take small residential projects. Stone may pose a safety hazard on the floor, too, because it gets slick when wet. A

Below: *Quality influences carpet durability. Check the type of fiber used, the height of the pile, and the thickness of the yarn.*

fall on a stone floor can cause serious injury. Older persons and children are at particular risk. If you choose one of these materials, use slip-resistant rugs over it.

CARPETING AND RUGS

The terms carpet and rug are often used interchangeably, but they're not the same, in terms of manufacture or design application. Carpeting is manufactured in rolls ranging from just over 2 feet wide to broadlooms that measure as much as 18 feet wide. Carpeting is usually laid wall-to-wall and can be installed over raw subflooring. Rugs are soft floor coverings that don't extend wall-to-wall and are used over another finished flooring surface. A mat is a small rug.

Differences in fiber composition, construction, color, texture, and cost make choosing a carpet or rug a complex job. Carpeting can be made of natural wool, synthetic fibers, or blends of wool and synthetics. Other natural fibers commonly used in area rugs, scatter rugs, and mats are cotton or plant materials known as cellulosics—hemp, jute, sisal, or grasses. Synthetic fibers are acrylics, nylon, olefin, and polyester.

HOW IT'S MADE

Carpet construction refers to the manner in which the yarn fiber meets the carpet backing, and carpeting may be manufactured by several construction techniques. *Weaving*, once the industry standard, is done on a loom. Weaving has given way to today's most commonly used technique, *tufting*, in which yarn is pushed through the backing from the underside, forming loops on the surface. Some tufted carpeting has a latex backing to prevent the tufts from pulling loose. Carpeting may also be *needlepunched* or needlebonded, techniques that involve the insertion of yarn into backing with hooked needles. A knitted carpet is created when needles are used to knit pile and backing together; a latex backing is usually added in this type of construction. Finally, carpeting may be flocked. *Flocking* employs static electricity to stand short fibers on end and uses an adhesive to bond the fibers to backing.

In general, woven carpet is the most durable; flocking, the least. The durability of the other carpet types fall somewhere in between. Type of fiber used, the density and height of the pile, and the thickness and quality of the yarn all contribute to a carpet's durability.

The texture of a carpet or rug is determined by a number of factors, including the height and type of pile. The term "pile" refers to the carpeting surface, created when the yarn is connected to the backing. When carpet construction creates yarn loops on the surface, the loops may be left intact *(loop pile)* or may be cut *(cut pile)*; in some cases, a carpet may be a combination of cut and uncut loops *(tip-sheared)*. To further complicate the picture, loops, cut pile, or both may be of uniform height or may be of varied heights. The resulting possibilities range from the informal, uniformly short-loop-pile carpeting, such as Berber, to the soft velvet of a uniformly cut, deep-pile carpet. The relatively informal look of a sculptured surface is created with multilevel loops.

ADVANTAGES

Wall-to-wall carpeting adds softness and warmth to a room, both visually and physically. Carpeting also muffles room noise and, when installed on upper floors, reduces the amount of sound that is transmitted to rooms on lower floors of the house or adjacent ones.

With most types of carpeting, a padding underlayment enhances softness underfoot and increases the life of the carpet. Several types of padding—from rubber to a variety of natural fibers—exist, and some are coated with adhesive. The padding choice will depend on the type of carpet you buy; follow manufacturers' recommendations on what

type to use. Cushion-backed carpet, made with the padding, is another option.

MAKING YOUR SELECTION

Carpeting offers a huge variety of material, style, color, pattern, texture, and cost options. The simplest way to narrow

Above: *A carpet or area rug made of synthetic fibers will have more color options and offer a greater variety of patterns. This loop-pile rug features an oversized floral design on a black field.*

down your choices is to decide on a cost and examine the options within your price range. That is not to endorse making a purchase strictly on price. Quality does matter when it comes to carpeting. The most durable carpeting (in terms of construction and fiber) is usually the most expensive. The converse is also true—the less expensive the carpet, the shorter its useful life. Ask yourself this question: "Do I really intend to stick with this carpet for the next 30 years?" Sure you need a durable carpet, but just how long is long enough? Think about it before you

buy. Wool carpeting is the most durable and the most expensive; it also has the advantage of being naturally fire resistant. Carpeting made from synthetic fibers offers the greatest variety in terms of color, pattern, and texture, and in the short run is certainly more affordable. A good compromise choice would be a wool-synthetic blend, offering a reasonably wide variety of design options plus some enhanced durability without a pure-wool price tag.

Area rugs are an excellent device for creating small areas within a larger space, such as marking off an intimate conversation area in a living room. They are also a relatively inexpensive way to add accent colors and to help tie room designs together.

Some area rugs are inexpensive, manufactured floor coverings that come in a variety of sizes, colors, and patterns. Others are specialty items, such as the handmade *dhurrie* rugs from India, *rya* rugs from Scandinavia, and hooked,

Above: *Natural-fiber carpets and rugs, such as sisal or jute, are favored as unobtrusive, textural backdrops in informal interiors.*

Right: *Area rugs are often used to define conversational areas. By leaving space on all sides, you accentuate the rug, as well as show off the flooring—usually wood—underneath.*

braided, and rag rugs made in a number of places throughout the world. Perhaps the most versatile in terms of decorating are the Orientals, which can blend extremely well with a variety of styles, from traditional to modern. Authentic, handmade Oriental rugs from the Near and Far East can be extremely expensive—essentially you're purchasing a work of art for your floor. A number of manufacturers make excellent reproductions, printing traditional Oriental rug patterns on factory-made rugs. Area rugs can also be made from smaller-than-room-sized pieces of carpeting; the section of carpeting must be bound at the edges to prevent unraveling and to create a finished look.

SPACE CONSIDERATIONS

In decorating with area rugs, the general rule is to allow at least a foot of floor space on all four sides, creating a three-dimensional art piece consisting of the rug, furniture, and accessories, all set within that foot-wide frame. This rule, however, need not apply if your goal is to create special-use sections within a larger space. For example, a round hooked rug can be the perfect device for pulling together two comfortable wing chairs and a small coffee table, creating a conversation area within a large living room. In a large kitchen, an area rug slightly larger than your table and chairs can offset this eating space, separating it from the work space. A round or oval rug in a small rectangular or square space can allow you to "float" furniture away from the walls, visually enlarging an otherwise crowded-looking room.

Finally, carpet tiles, manufactured in squares of one or two feet, are an option if your decorating plans call for a softer tile pattern. Some types of carpet tiles must be glued to the subflooring, but loose-laid styles are also now available.

CARE

Carpeting and area rugs are easy to maintain—vacuum cleaning is all that is required for regular maintenance. Many small area rugs are machine-washable; others can be dry-cleaned. For both area rugs and carpeting, a wide range of spot-cleaning products are available for taking care of the occasional soiling problem. A periodic cleaning with a professional steam or shampoo machine will keep most good-quality carpets looking and smelling fresh through years of use.

Left: *If you are changing the flooring in a room, incorporate the new floor in your design. Here, the twists and turns of a parquet border highlight a staircase.*

Imagine yourself in the room on a weekday morning through the entire day and determine who is likely to come through the room at those various times. Then do the same thing with a typical weekend. On a piece of paper, make columns headed "Who" and "Activities," and then list who in the family uses the room and what activities occur there. Do the kids play with toys on the floor? Do they do arts and crafts projects with paint, glue, and glitter? Does the family gather on Saturday afternoons and snack while watching a football game on television? Is it a formal living room where you entertain your friends and business clients? Is it a busy kitchen? Does the hallway extend from your front entrance or from a busier back door where the kids drop off their hockey skates?

The answers to these questions will help you to determine how durable and resilient a flooring surface needs to be, whether warmth and softness are requirements, and how much maintenance will be necessary to keep the surface clean.

CHOOSING A FLOORING MATERIAL

Now that you've got the facts about each floor surface option, picking the right one for your design will be much less confusing. The following Smart Steps can make it downright simple.

SMART STEPS

ONE: *Make a "use/abuse" analysis.* Begin by asking yourself the most important question: How is this room used? Your answer should tell you just what kind of traffic the future floor surface will endure. With a relatively expensive investment like a floor, it's best not to guess. Instead, use this system to arrive at an accurate use/abuse analysis:

TWO: *Determine your design objectives.* Are you replacing just the flooring in the room? If so, your choices are limited by the style already established by other elements in the room. Your color choices can enhance the existing palette. If your project is a complete room makeover—including walls, furniture, and accessories—you have more flexibility, although your job is a bit more complex.

Once you've determined your design objectives, compare your use/abuse analysis to the types of flooring that meet both your style and use needs. From the list of options that are left, you can narrow down your choices even more in terms of your budget.

THREE: *Draw and use a floor plan.* After the use/abuse analysis and the list of design objectives have been completed, draw up a floor plan—a separate one for experimenting with your flooring ideas. Follow these guidelines: Measure the length and width of the room, and plot it on graph paper, using a scale of 1 inch to 1 foot. If your room is larger than 8 x 10 feet, you can tape two pieces of 8½ x 11-inch graph paper together. Measure and mark the locations of entryways and any permanent features in the room, such as cabinets, fixtures, or appliances.

Make several photocopies of your floor plan. Reserve one copy as a template. Use the other copies for previewing pat-

Below: *Because this bathroom had a lot of square footage, the homeowners prudently determined their budget before choosing the small hexagonal tiles and border.*

tern ideas for flooring that comes in tiles (ceramic, vinyl, or carpeting tiles). Buy multicolored pencils and fill in your grid. You'll be able to determine not only how the pattern will look but also how many tiles of various colors you'll need to buy to complete the project.

FOUR: *Convert your overall budget to cost per square foot.* Chances are you have a budget in mind already, with an upper limit established. After you've completed the use/abuse analysis, determined your design objectives, and created a floor plan, the next step is figuring out how much of what kind of flooring material you can afford.

Most flooring is priced in terms of square feet. To determine how many square feet are in your room, round the measurements off to the next foot. Then simply mulitply the length by the width. For example, for a room measuring 10 feet 4 inches x 12 feet 6 inches, round the figures to 11 x 13 feet. Multiply 11 x 13 feet (that's 143 square feet). You will end up with extra flooring, but it is better to have more than less.

Some flooring—like carpeting—is priced in terms of square yards. To determine the number of square yards in your room, divide the number of square feet by nine. In our example, there are just under 16 square yards in 143 square feet.

Let's say you have a budget of $850 to purchase tile for your 10-foot 4-inch x 12-foot 6-inch room. For the sake of the illustration, let's assume your subflooring is adequate, you have the tools, and the cost of adhesive and grout for your room is about $75. That leaves you with $775. To determine how much you can spend per tile, divide the remainder by the number of square feet in the room. In our example, $775 divided by 143 square feet equals about $5.40 per square foot of tile. Now that your flooring has been decided, it's time to consider treatments for walls and windows.

WALLS & WINDOWS

In a well-designed room, wall and window treatments complement each other as well as the style of a room and its furnishings. They also provide relatively inexpensive and easy ways to update an interior. Window treatments in particular can alter the function of a room, thanks to their ability to control natural light and provide insulation against drafts or heat from the outside. Wall treatments can pull together a look or set a mood in a room by introducing color, pattern, and texture.

When designing, it's important to consider these two architectural elements together. For a cohesive look, think of a window as part of a wall, and a wall as an extension of a window, then apply the basic principles of scale, proportion, line, balance, harmony, and rhythm to your plans.

Today's choices for decorating walls and windows are probably more varied than ever before. For windows, they run the gamut from neoclassical looks in swags and draperies to contemporary coverings such as pleated shades and Venetian blinds. For walls, there are infinite options, including painted effects as well as wallcoverings in simple stripes and plaids or detailed florals and textures. Your ultimate decision will affect not only the finished appearance of the room in terms of its style but also the way it is perceived with regard to size and shape. (Refer to the first two chapters, "Understanding & Arranging

Left: *In a peaceful bedroom, pinstriped wallpaper and reversible curtains in a check and floral pattern complete the charming country setting.*

Space," on page 12 and "Color, Pattern & Texture," on page 28, for more information.)

In this chapter, you'll learn how to narrow down all of the available options and make the right choices for your project. Plus, you'll find some easy instructions for applying popular painted techniques to walls as well, as designer tips to give your window treatments expert flair. If you don't want to do the work yourself, there are professionals who can turn your plans into reality, whether it's a faux-painted wall or custom window dressings.

WALLS

The very size of the wall makes it an important element in your décor. A wall can stand as a dramatic statement on its own or serve unobtrusively as a backdrop, letting the furnishings take center stage. Paint and wallcovering are your two basic choices for finishing them, but the myriad options and versatility within these two categories are bountiful.

Generally, walls in contemporary interiors should be kept simple. Fussy wallpaper patterns won't work. Wallpaper designs that represent natural materials (especially texturous ones) look best, as do walls painted in neutral hues or in faux renditions of stone.

However, feel free to dress up the walls of traditional and country-style interiors with lots of color, pattern, and pattern-on-pattern designs executed in wallcoverings or with paint. Florals, stripes, or heraldic patterns work well with traditional interiors; plaids, checks, and mini-prints look particularly appropriate in country-style settings. Sten-

Right: *Although the widely spaced painted stripes emphasize the high ceiling in this small living room, the effect is offset by a simple swag on a thick drapery rod.*

ciled borders and other unpretentious painted effects look equally at home. (See page 80.) Use these Smart Steps to help make your decision.

SMART STEPS

ONE: *Assess the condition of the walls and the existing treatment.* Before deciding whether to paint or use wallcovering, examine the condition of the surface. No matter which one you choose, make sure the walls are smooth for the best result. What's the point of investing

Right: *A trompe l'oeil* vine, *painted over a glazed yellow wall, sinuously curves around an oak cupboard, creating a focal point for the room.*

time and money in an attractive new wall treatment if there are bumps or dents that will mar the new surface? Small holes can be fixed with joint compound and a light sanding. Large holes in wallboard or cracks in plaster will need more attention, perhaps from a professional. Minor imperfections can be ignored. Wallpaper will hide them, and some painted effects, such as faux stone or aged plaster, may actually look more authentic thanks to them.

If the existing treatment is wallpaper, remove it before painting or applying new wallpaper. Paneling presents other problems. If you take it down, you risk damaging the wallboard underneath it. However, you can paint over paneling as long as you lightly sand the surface first. You can also hang wallpaper over paneling, but you will have to install a special liner paper over the paneling to give it a smooth surface for the new application.

TWO: *Narrow down your choices.* Sometimes it's easy to know what you want immediately. But at other times, the freedom and variety of a multitude of options can quickly become a case of too much of a good thing. How often have you decided to just paint the walls white or beige until you're ready to decide what to do with them? How often have you left them that way? There's nothing wrong with painting walls white or beige, as long as it isn't done as a cop-out. So for the sake of cohesiveness, choose a wall treatment at the same time that you're making decisions about the rest of the room's furnishings. For inspiration, look at the pictures in this book, visit decorator showhouses, and read home-decorating magazines. If you're putting together a period-style room, go to the library and do some research about the colors and patterns that were popular during that era. Numerous well-known paint companies and wallpaper manufacturers offer products that have been inspired by or authentically reproduce historical colors or patterns. Ask your retailer about them. If he or she doesn't have samples, ask about the company's 800 number or Web site address so you can order a brochure.

To narrow down the field even further, try out different options on your sample board. (Review Step One, "Create a Sample Board," on page 39.) Get paint chips or swatches of wallpaper, and compare them with the fabrics and carpet you've selected for the room. Live with them for a few days before making a final choice.

CHOOSING PAINTED EFFECTS

Solid-color painted walls will never go out of fashion, but these days the decision to paint can extend far beyond simply picking a hue. In addition to providing color, painted effects, such as sponging, stenciling, and *trompe l'oeil*, can add texture and dimension to an interior. These and other time-honored techniques are enjoying a renaissance of popularity because they offer an easy and inexpensive way to add uniqueness and personality to a room, whether contemporary or traditional. Some of them are simple to

do even if you're not particularly artistic. Others require an experienced hand. To give you an idea of what you can expect and whether you'll need to call in a professional, here is an overview of the most popular painted effects.

SPONGING, RAGGING, AND COMBING

Sponging, which involves using a sponge to apply or remove wet paint, is probably the easiest and most versatile of all the decorative paint techniques. It produces a highly textured surface that has great visual depth, which helps to disguise imperfections in walls and hide fingerprints and soil in heavily trafficked areas such as hallways and children's rooms. First, select your paint colors or shades of the same hue—one for the wall background and one or more for sponging. The background color, often a light neutral shade, can be applied to the wall straight from the can, whether it's a latex or oil-based product, but the paint that you choose for the sponging has to be thinned first. Latex paints can be thinned with water to create a wash. Use

Left: *Sage green paint, muted by sponging, pairs perfectly with vintage quilts and afghans. Stamped stars on the ceiling are an unexpected but welcomed detail.*

Technique: *You can work with more than one color when sponging a wall. Here, three colors are applied in successive layers over a blue-gray base.*

Above: *Dark purple was ragged over a lavender base coat for this sunny sitting room.*

Techniques (from top): *Ragging creates a more noticeable pattern than sponging. To avoid pattern repetition, change the direction of the rag as you press down. This plastic comb leaves a hard-edged pattern when combing, which is also known as* strié; *use a brush for a softer effect.*

paint thinner with an oil-based paint to make it a glaze. (The latex wash is often referred to as a glaze, too.) Commercial glazes are available and can be tinted to create the desired color. Sponges for sponge painting are available from paint stores and home-decorating centers. Wear rubber gloves when working the paint on or off the wall.

Sponging-on entails dipping a moistened sponge into the wash or glaze, wringing it out, then dabbing it against the wall repeatedly until it runs out of color. This process is carried out over the entire surface. To sponge-off, apply paint to a section of the wall (not too much, because the paint

must remain wet to sponge off), and blot it with a sponge. Rinse the sponge in an appropriate solvent (water or paint thinner) when it becomes saturated with paint.

Ragging-on and *ragging-off* are similar processes to sponging-on and sponging-off, except the sponge is replaced with a clean, lint-free cloth. For this effect, it's a good idea to have a lot of extra cloth on hand because the fabric is easily saturated and more difficult to rinse than a sponge.

With *combing* or *dragging*, the background color is revealed as a comb, brush, or other tool is dragged over a freshly applied

layer of wash or glaze. (Appropriate tools are available at home-decorating centers.) For this technique, as with sponging-off and ragging-off, it is important to maintain a brisk work pace because the paint must be wet for the combed texture to take successfully.

STENCILING AND STAMPING

Stenciling is simple, stylized, and charming. It has an honorable history going back as far as Pom-peiian villas and Early American homes in this country, and it is enjoying a widespread revival today. Stencils are frequently used as wall borders and accents in country-style interiors, as well as friezes in traditional decorating schemes such as Victorian. Craft and home-decorating stores have pre-cut stencils in nearly every imagin-able motif, plus brushes and appropriate paints. Pre-cut stencils come with instructions for use. If commercial designs don't suit you, there are materials available for cutting your own.

The success of a stenciled design depends large-ly on your ability to keep the stencil straight. Pre-cut stencils should have registration marks, but you will have to make them on any hand-cut stencils. Keeping the stencil flat against the

Above left: *Grape vines were stenciled over a trompe l'oeil trellis, and then hand-painted details were added to the leaves to make them appear more realistic.*

Techniques (left to right): *Although pre-cut stencils are readily available, you may want to make your own out of Mylar. If you are working with stamps on a surface, remember to measure and mark off the pattern.*

surface is also key. You will need a separate brush for each color you're using. Also be careful not to overload the brush with paint. After blotting the brush on a paper towel, work the stencil in a light dabbing motion.

Another quick and easy technique is *stamping*, which uses raised patterns for block-print painting. Random stamping is easy; just dip the stamp into a small amount of paint, and then press it onto the surface. Formal designs require plotting your motif on the surface beforehand.

GLAZING AND WASHING

A *glaze* is a paint or colorant mixed with a transparent glazing medium and diluted with thinner. A glaze produces a luminous translucent finish. A *wash* is a thinned-out latex or acrylic paint. It creates a flat, gauzy film of color. Both add a sense of added dimension to walls. Remember, with thinned paint, the color or shade of the wall beneath the glaze or wash will show through. Choose colors for the wall and wash or glaze with this effect in mind. It is a good idea, with quicker-drying latex especially, to do an entire wall at a time so that paint dries evenly. To apply, use a paint roller, finishing the corners and edges with a brush.

MARBLING

Applied with a steady, practiced hand, an oil glaze or latex wash can also yield a beautiful faux marble effect. *Marbling* is fabulous for adding classical details to a room, but it can also work well in contemporary kitchens and baths where natural materials abound. The technique for marbling is more advanced than the others discussed so far, however. The background and the effect are applied at the same time, and paint must be worked while the surface is still wet but not

Technique: *Marbling is an advanced technique that you can master with practice. Study a piece of real marble; then try to imitate its veined surface on a sample board.*

Left: *Dress up or change the look of architectural elements, such as this fireplace mantel and surround, with marbling. This faux finish also looks good on baseboards and columns.*

the paint to look like wood grain. After the paint dries completely, it is sealed with a transparent surface coat that gives the "wood" its luster. Recreating the grain of a specific wood species is much more complicated and generally requires professional know-how. However, as with marbling, practice helps.

TROMPE L'OEIL

Increasingly popular with designers and home-owners alike is *trompe l'oeil* painting, used to make living spaces sophisticated or fun. *Trompe l'oeil,* or effects that "fool the eye," can be full-wall murals or simply small details. They can give the illusion of depth in a small space, for example, or create scenes such as a landscape or a sky that are so realistic that they appear to be what they depict. Unless you're a skilled artist, hire a professional for this job. The box below explains how to find one.

too wet. After adding the colors, blot them off gingerly with a clean rag. You can do the veining freehand using a feather and artist's oils or acrylics, depending on whether you're applying a glaze or a wash. You'll have to blot the veins, too. Make sure they are subtly blended before brushing a final glaze on top of the design. A bit of advice: If you don't have the patience to practice this technique until you've mastered it, hire a professional artist for the job.

GRAINING

Wood graining, a technique suitable for wall panels, doors, and moldings, simulates a specific grain, such as mahogany or oak. It involves dragging with special graining brushes and detailing with rubber combs to make grains, knots, and whorls. The basic way to create the look of wood is to drag a dark brown wash or glaze over a yellow-painted background. Once the dragging is complete and before the paint dries, another tool called an overgrainer (available at home decorating and craft stores) can be used to further manipulate

Smart Tip about Finding a Special-Effects Artist

To find an artist who can give their clients a one-of-a-kind look that completes a decorating scheme, designers simply turn to their directories and pick up the phone. You may have to look a little harder, but not much. You can get a referral from a designer yourself, or check the source list at the back of any decorating magazine that features someone's work you may have admired. Designers who work at home centers or the staff at your favorite paint and wallpaper store may also have leads to recommend. And certainly, if you have admired a painted effect in someone else's house, ask how to contact the artist. Be sure to look at as many examples as possible of an artist's work before hiring him and her for your job. Any professional will be happy to show you a portfolio and supply references.

PAINT PRODUCTS—INSTANT EFFECTS

Homeowners who don't have artistic aspirations but do have the desire to add something special to painted surfaces can do so with paint products that yield special effects and easily applied textured surfaces. With all of these products come specific instructions that must be followed carefully. Some require spray applicators; others can be sprayed or rolled on directly from the can. If you're investing in one of these premium finishes, spend the extra money for high-quality tools, which can make a big difference in the final result. Because these paints cost more than standard products, you may want to use them sparingly or limit them to trimwork. Wherever you're applying an instant-effect paint, it's always a good idea to test the application on poster board before painting it on your walls. Help is available wherever these paints are sold. Instructional videos can

Below right: *Antique cupboards often have a weathered, crackled finish that developed naturally over time. But you don't have to wait 100 years or more for the same result, thanks to special paint products that can produce this aged look.*

Techniques: *Apply the crackle medium over a base coat with a foam brush. (Don't paint the same area twice.) A thick layer will produce wide crackle lines; a thin coat will create thinner ones. After the medium dries, apply a top coat of paint.*

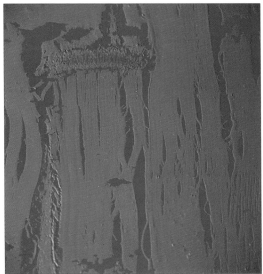

make it easier to follow directions. A few of the looks you can create with a direct application product include stone, metal, pearl, suede, denim, and a crazed or crackled finish.

Faux stone, finishes that simulate the shadowy, brushable nap of suede, and satiny pearl effects should be applied with a high volume, low-pressure sprayer. A professional painter might be able to get the desired look from this kind of paint by using a good, short-nap roller, but it is not the application method recommended by the manufacturer, especially for an inexperienced do-it-yourselfer. Another faux stone product comes as a two-process spray kit. First you apply the base coat, and after allowing it to dry, you finish it with a topcoat.

The aged effect called crackle, which resembles the dried, crazed quality of paint in old houses, can also be applied using a two-part method of paint and crackle medium. When working with paint, always keep the room well ventilated.

KID PLEASERS

Formulated and marketed for children's rooms, glow-in-the-dark paints and glittery topcoats are easy to apply. The glow paint is designed for highlighting designs such as stars, for example, that have been painted, stamped, or stenciled onto sections rather than for an entire wall application. To produce a really dramatic effect, you'll have to apply multiple coats of the paint. The glitter goes on over the base coat or the painted design with a roller. Even-handed rolling is important when using a glitter product. If you have to redo some spots with a second coat, the glitter will clump, and those areas will look uneven. As with any textured treatment, you'll have to lightly sand glitter-treated walls if you want a smooth surface when you repaint them later. Think about this before going ahead with this project.

Below *The cream color of the walls in this elegant living room was picked up from the sofa. The paint has a hint of yellow, which warms the space without being visually obtrusive.*

Right: *Pale blue is contrasted against the dark furnishings of this formal dining room. Blue in its softer shades is space-enhancing, which makes it a good choice for a long and narrow room.*

PLAIN PAINTED WALLS & TRIM

Even if you prefer to give your walls just a standard coat of paint (always a dependable decorating strategy), you've got a wide range of colors from which to choose; even neutral hues come in a variety of shades and tones. Professional designers typically bring samples of the fabric and carpet to the paint store to have a custom color mixed to match. These paints are more expensive but are worth it. Even two shades of white can clash. (See Chapter Two, "Color, Pat-

Smart Tip about Paint Basics

Most interior paints are either alkyd-resin (oil-based) products or latex (water-based) varieties. Oil and water don't mix, and generally neither do the paints based on them. For multilayered effects, stick to one type or the other.

Alkyd paints are somewhat lustrous, translucent, and hard-wearing. But alkyds, and the solvents needed for cleaning up, are toxic and combustible, requiring good work-site ventilation and special disposal methods. Professional decorative painters often prefer slower-drying alkyds, which allow more time to achieve complex special effects. Alkyd paints are better suited to techniques such as combing and ragging, where glaze is brushed on in sections and then manipulated.

Latex paints, which now approach alkyd's durability and textural range, are nontoxic and quick-drying, and they clean up easily with soap and water. Most nonprofessionals find latex paint easier to deal with and capable of creating many popular decorative finishes. In general, latex paints are best suited to effects that are dabbed on over the base coat, as in sponging or stenciling. The short drying time can be an advantage, because mistakes can be painted over and redone.

Latex paint is usually the best choice for covering an entire wall, too, because the job can be completed from start to finish in just a few hours.

tern & Texture," on page 28, for more advice.) You can also bring home sample color chips. Look at them with your furnishings in all types of light and at various times of the day. To pull your interior together, select a color that you can pick up from the upholstery or drapery fabric, in either a matching or contrasting tone.

Generally, flat paints are best for walls and ceilings. They tend to mar easily, so you may not want to use flat paints for a surface that is prone to abuse or hand marks, such as a wall next to a staircase. For trim, a semigloss finish is the typical choice, although you may prefer a high-gloss enamel. Usually glossy paints are reserved for the kitchen and bathroom because they can stand up to the moisture and grime that accumulates in these rooms.

In addition to a variety of colors and shades from which to choose, top-of-the-line paints usually go on easier and require fewer coats. They also clean easier and will remain looking fresh longer. The money you spend on a better-quality paint saves the expense of more frequent repainting.

THE WIDE WORLD OF WALLCOVERINGS

Wallpaper, fabric, tile, paneling, and mirrors are your choices in decorative wallcovering. *Mirrored glass* installed from floor to ceiling is a nifty device for creating the illusion of space in small quarters, but it is one that should be used sparingly. Solid *wood paneling* can look rich or rustic depending on the finish and trimwork. It also has insulating and sound-deadening properties. *Ceramic tile* is typically used in kitchens and bathrooms, but the vast number of decorative designs on today's market offer creative pos-

sibilities for wall décor, including murals, in any room in the house. *Fabric* such as silk, linen, brocade, wool, and suede are delicate, elegant, and expensive. *Wallpaper*, on the other hand, can be affordable, stylish, and durable depending on what it's made of—paper, vinyl, or other natural or synthetic materials—and its finish. Myriad motifs, textures, and patterns add to its appeal.

DECORATING WITH WALLPAPER

There's no getting around it: wallpaper is versatile, with an almost infinite number of styles, colors, patterns, and textures to choose from. It's also a great mimic of fabric,

Left to right: *Wallcoverings in kitchens need to be durable and should be easy to clean; vinyl is a good choice. A basic striped wallpaper is topped by a border with a nursery rhyme theme; as the children grow up, the "Cow Jumps Over the Moon" border can simply be covered by a more age-appropriate one.*

natural materials such as stone, wood, grass, or bamboo, and even painted effects. These lookalikes are cheaper to install than the real thing and are more durable and easier to care for. But what we call "wallpaper" may not be made of paper at all. (In fact, it rarely is, with the exception of some custom-made specialty designs.) Here's a rundown of more common types.

Vinyl Coverings. Vinyl is the most popular wallcovering because it can take a beating. Finger marks, grease, moisture, and water pose no threat to its long-lasting good looks and wear. There are three types for your consideration.

🐭 **Fabric-backed vinyl** has a vinyl top layer over fiberglass or cloth. It's tough, so you can scrub it when necessary. The material is heavy, and it usually doesn't come prepasted. Because it's porous, manufacturers recommend using a vinyl adhesive that contains a mildewcide, especially if you plan to use it in a room where there's a lot of moisture—a bathroom or kitchen, for example.

🐭 **Paper-backed vinyl** is lighter and typically prepasted, peelable, and washable. There are thousands of colors and patterns in its repertoire. Raised or expanded vinyls come with increased surface texture. These wallpaper products can simulate other materials such as grass cloth, granite, textured painted effects, and decorative plaster work; their texture does a good job of concealing problems with irregular and cracked walls.

🐭 **Vinyl-coated paper** is inexpensive, but it doesn't have the durability of fabric- or paper-backed vinyl. Its thin protective coating tears easily and doesn't hold up to dirt and stains. Even natural oils from your hands can permanently mar it.

Foil Coverings. Like mirrors, foil wallpapers can make a room seem larger. But for these delicate coverings, the surface of the wall must be as smooth as glass because foil will magnify any of its imperfections. Installing liner paper before applying the foil can help. A painted effect over a plain foil can look dramatic. You might consider this as one idea for creating a focal point in a bland room. Avoid using foils in sunny rooms—their reflective surfaces can result in too much glare—but do consider them to bring cheer to a room that's dark. Foils are available with or without a prepasted backing. Because they are delicate and difficult to handle, professional installation is recommended.

Flocked Coverings. Popularized in the eighteenth century, flocked coverings feature a raised, fuzzy pattern that resembles expensive cut velvet. They look at home with traditional or period interiors, but use them sparingly; they can be too ornate at times for contemporary tastes. Some flocked wallpapers are prepasted, and most are strippable. Their washability depends on the design. Certain patterns may camouflage slight wall imperfections.

Natural Coverings. Grass cloth, hemp, and other natural weaves bring texture to a room. They are particularly suited to contemporary interiors. Some are very delicate and require application over liner paper. They can also fray and are not washable. These coverings should be professionally installed.

Embossed Coverings. Lincrusta, which is made of oils, resins, and wood pulp over canvas, is a heavy linoleum-like covering. Its embossed surface features stylized designs that simulate raised moldings made of wood, plaster, tile, or leather. *Anaglypta,* which is cheaper and lighter, is made of cotton-fiber pulp. Both types were first manufactured in the late nineteenth century and are once again popular. These rich-looking, durable coverings can be painted and repainted several times over the years.

They also camouflage imperfect walls. You can use them for an entire wall application or halfway up the wall, chair-rail style. Anaglypta also comes as a border for friezes. You can find these papers in home centers today, but follow the installation directions carefully. Because of its weight, leave Lincrusta to a professional installer.

Fiberglass Weaves. Although these are mainly commercial-grade products, they do offer another option. Made of thickly woven strands of the material used for insulation, they are quite heavy. You can even apply them over concrete-block walls. What's even better, they won't rot, burn, or support mold or mildew, so they are excellent for use in areas exposed to moisture. The look of fiberglass weaves is varied and ranges from gauze-like patterns

to designs that resemble vinyl wallcoverings. If you don't see them in your retail store, inquire about contacting a manufacturer directly.

Now that you've got the lowdown on the types of wall-coverings that are on today's market, here's what you need to do to select the right one for your project.

SMART STEPS

ONE: *Apply the principles of good design.* When you're shopping for wallpaper, consider the scale and proportion of the pattern in terms of the room you're decorating. Although a particular design in a sample book may attract your eye, think of how it will affect the perception of the size and shape of the room. There is no rule that says you can't use a large print in a small space; however, oversize designs can overpower tiny rooms. Of course, they can dramatize them as well. If your project is a formal dining room or an entry hall, go for boldness. But if it's the family room, you might want to be more conservative in your choice because you spend more time in this space and a large print may tire you. In terms of line, choose a pattern that can add the allusion of height in a room with a low ceiling. Vertical stripes would be excellent in this case. Install wallpaper halfway up the wall with a border paper at chair-rail height to visually lower tall ceilings. Think about balance. If all of the other features in the room tend to be oversize, a mini-print might look out of place. And don't forget harmony. Coordinate all patterns and colors to the other hues and fabrics in the room, as well as those in adjoining areas.

TWO: *Try it out for size.* Don't ever guess about wallpaper. Just like paint, you may think it matches everything else, but once you get it home and hold it

Clockwise (from far left): *A subtle hint of metallic gold gives this wallpaper the space-enhancing quality of foil. Because of their durability, Lincrusta and Anaglypta work well in high-traffic areas, such as hallways. Wallpaper with a dark background makes large rooms, such as this dining room, seem cozier.*

up to the sofa or the curtains, you may realize you've made a mistake. Bring home wallpaper samples and try them out on your sample board. Sometimes a retailer will let you take home the book for a few days. When you think you've found the right pattern, buy just one roll at first. Cut a few wall-length strips that you can tape to the wall and live with for a week. This will allow you to get a more realistic feeling for the effect the wallpaper will make on the overall room and at different times of the day in varying levels of light. It's worth the small investment in a single roll of wallpaper to make sure it's right for your project. If you don't like it, you really haven't lost anything.

WINDOW TREATMENTS

You can accomplish a number of things with a window treatment: control the amount of natural light permitted into the room; limit summer heat gain and winter heat loss; enhance a good view or conceal a bad one; provide privacy where necessary; camouflage architectural blunders, such as ill-proportioned or oddly placed windows, or (conversely) dress the window without obscuring its handsome features; or create a focal point for a room or underscore its decorating scheme. Typically interior designers will make recommendations about window décor during the planning stages of a project. For the sake of cohesiveness, it's not a good idea to wait until everything else is done. That isn't to say that you can't change a window treatment unless you make major alterations in the room. Of course you can; in fact, it's a good way to give a tired scheme a face lift. But if you are doing a major makeover, don't leave the windows as an afterthought. Here's how to get started.

Top left: *Borders don't have to be used with coordinating wallpapers. Here, a classical swag border complements the rich red of the painted wall.*

Bottom left: *A traditional egg-and-dart border plus pinstripes accent the wall panels in this formal living room. A mini-print fills in the wainscot panels, and a wide border is used in place of a classical cornice.*

SMART STEPS

ONE: *Assess the window's style.* This is the first thing to look at; compare it with the window treatment you're considering. What kind of architectural details does the window have or lack that you can modify or enhance? (See Chapter Six, "Adding Character," page 103, for information on window styles and ornamental trim.) Always remember that decorating and architectural styles are linked; not necessarily in the strictest sense, but there should be a relationship between the two. Heavy velvet panels paired with formal swags will appear out of place in a country parlor. In the same way, ruffled calico curtains strike the wrong note in a room that's streamlined and contemporary.

Above right: *Because a neighboring house was built close by, the owner of this breakfast nook needed window treatments that allowed for privacy and let in some sunlight. A valance paired with café curtains (inset) solved the problem. The fruit print on the valance ties the window treatments to the room's color scheme.*

TWO: *Remember the function of the room.* A bedroom needs to feel cozy, so you'll want a window treatment that will keep out drafts at night but let in the air and light in the morning. A bathroom requires something that can stand up to moisture and is easily washed. The same can be said for a kitchen, which in addition to moisture must suffer the assaults of the cooking grease and the grime that sticks to it.

THREE: *Note the room's orientation.* Review the section on natural light in Chapter Three, "Light by Design," and consider the time of day you use the room and its orientation in terms of the sun. This will tell whether you need to control natural light at the time of day you're most likely to use the room. It will also help you decide whether or not the window treatment should play a role in insulating the space—particularly if the window faces north, which means it receives no direct sunlight.

FOUR: *Consider the size of the window.* Particularly in older homes, windows are often too small, even for modest-sized rooms. Sometimes that's just because the technologically advanced glazes we have today weren't available when the house was built, so the architect or builder kept the window small to avoid problems with heat loss. But you can create a more harmonious balance between window size and the room with the right treatment and installation. For a short window, install the rod above the trim or just below the ceiling line. Hang extra-long panels, and let them puddle on the floor just enough to make the windows appear grand. For a window that isn't wide enough for the wall, extend the window treatment beyond the frame on each side.

Some windows have the opposite problem—they're so large they overwhelm everything else. In this case, you can tone down the scale by keeping the look simple. If a window is too tall, don't use long panels. Break the length up by dressing the top of the window with a valance or swag that's different from the rest of the design. When windows in a room are different sizes, deemphasize the difference with curtains that are all the same length. Don't pile on several layers, and avoid heavily patterned fabrics.

FIVE: *Look in, look out.* What do you see through your windows—both from the inside and out? Whatever is seen through the windows becomes part of the décor. Likewise, remember that whatever you leave exposed to the world outside is on public view. In this crowded society, few people have the privilege of a great view with no neighbors. For most windows, you'll need something that you can open and close easily. A combination of heavy panels and sheers or shades, blinds, or shutters can be one solution to the problem.

Left: *The romantic décor of this attic bedroom called for equally fanciful window treatments, and the room's third floor, rear-of-the-house location meant that privacy was not an issue. A white sheer fabric was used for both the swag-and-rosette valance and the drapes (detail), which were fashioned into a "mutton sleeve" style that frames the windows but doesn't block the view.*

SIX: *Estimate your budget.* How much or how little you have to spend will determine whether you will order custom window treatments, buy ready-made versions, or make them yourself (something that requires skill and patience). The first option typically includes professional installation. Complex designs often require special skills because the window treatments are actually constructed on the window itself. This also means that the installer will have to remove them for cleaning and reinstall them. Ready-made window treatments are offered in several standard sizes to fit standard-size windows. See the box, "Smart Tip about Adding Professional Flair," below, which will help you put designer touches to any window treatment no matter how much or how little you have to spend.

SEVEN: *Think about maintenance.* It's expensive to have window treatments cleaned professionally and then reinstalled by an expert, so take these factors into account when making your plans. If you can't afford to spend a few hundred dollars on this periodically, rethink your choice.

Smart Tip about Adding Professional Flair

You can give your window treatment designs a professional look by using decorator tricks to customize readymades or dress your own home-sewn designs. These could include contrast linings, tassels, cording, ribbons, buttons, or couture trimmings such as buttons, coins, or bows applied to edges. Another trick is to sew a fine wire into the hem of curtains or valances to create a pliable edge you can shape yourself. Small weights that you can sew into the hem of drapery panels or jabots will make them hang better. For more inspiration look at fashion magazines.

Top left: *A rich silk fabric in a neutral color was the basis for this dining room's formal window treatment. Two layers—a swag valance with cascades on the side and full drapes that "puddle"—are ornamented with black fringe, tassels, and fabric rosettes.*

Left: *Drapery doesn't have to be limited to windows. Here, built-in shelves are adorned a black check curtain, which matches the double-layered window treatment.*

FULL FORMAL WINDOW TREATMENTS

A full formal treatment often involves two or three layers. One layer, called the *casement curtain*, is installed inside the window trim area. Typically it's a sheer, solid, or lace panel that lays straight or is gathered at the top. *Overdraperies*, often referred to simply as draperies, make up the second layer. Generally, they cover the window and the trim and, space permitting, extend beyond it either to the sides or above the window.

The words "draperies" and "curtains" can mean the same thing, but some people make a distinction between the two. Generally, draperies are pleated and hang from hooks that attach to tracks in a traverse rod, which allows them to be drawn (closed) with a cord. Curtains hang on rods from rings, tabs, or ties; they're drawn by hand. Formal draperies and curtains should be lined to give them body. An insulated interlining that reduces cold penetration and muffles sound is also a good idea. When installed, they should brush the floor. Draperies that can be drawn may eliminate the need for a shade or blinds because well-lined draperies reduce sun glare efficiently.

The third, and optional, layer of a full formal window treatment is a *valance*, sometimes called a *pelmet*, which runs horizontally across the top of the window and covers the drapery or curtain heading. To some eyes, the window treatment is unfinished without this last element, but this is strictly a matter of taste.

A simple or soft valance made of fabric may hang on a separate rod, or it may be attached to the drapery or curtain. It may be composed of the same fabric as the drapery or a coordinating one. There are various styles including a swag or cascade, a pinch-pleated version, a tab-top, or a free-form valance that can be created by draping scarves or fabrics over a rod. The fabric can be the same as the drapery fabric or one that coordinates with it. Ornate soft valances often feature vertical gathers that make horizontal pleats for *ruched*, *ballooned*, or *festooned* effects. Many valances are trimmed or shaped into points or scallops at the bottom. Ruffles, fringe, tassels, and piping all add dressy details to the edges.

A hard valance, also called a *cornice* or a *lambrequin*, is usually made of wood and covered with fabric or upholstery. It is permanently fastened to the wall with screws. Box shapes and scalloped edges are most common. Because they can't be removed easily for cleaning, the fabric covering valances should lay flat against the board backing or upholstery filler for easy vacuuming.

Fabrics that lend themselves to formal window treatments include luminous silks and damasks, velvet, wool, tapestry, and brocade. (See Chapter Two, "Color, Pattern, & Texture, " for more information on fabric.)

INFORMAL WINDOW TREATMENTS

Casual window treatments may consist of one or two layers or nothing at all. If location and privacy considerations permit, a beautiful window looks

Clockwise (starting at top right): *To take advantage of the view, a V-shaped valance was created as a minimal window treatment for this breakfast nook. A beribboned, raised swag adds visual height to a kitchen window. Materials also play a role in keeping a window treatment casual: Here, crisp red gingham drapery is topped by tassels made of cotton rope. Simple curtains call for drapery hardware, such as this leaf tieback in an antique bronze finish, which commands attention.*

attractive without the dressing—especially when there's also something pleasant to see outside. Sometimes simple casement curtains installed on handsome decorative rods or just a valance looks attractive in informal rooms. If only the lower half of the window needs covering, café-style curtains offer privacy without blocking light.

Swag-and-tail arrangements can look refined yet informal. Swags are often confused with valances because, like valances, they cross the window horizontally at the top. Unlike valances, however, the tails (or *jabots*) cascade at the sides of the window. Swags may sit over draperies in lieu of a valance, or they may be used alone. Decorative details like *rosettes* (clusters of fabric that have been gathered or pleated to look like a rose) can be used to attach swags to the window frame instead of the traditional rod. This is a good way to create a no-sew swag with just a bit of fabric gathered and fastened at each corner and left to swoop across the top of the window in the center. You can do this with inexpensive fabric remnants, sheers, or even sheeting to create an informal window dress-up for pennies. Special hardware is available that makes creating rosettes easy, too.

Fabrics that lend themselves to an informal look include anything cotton, such as chintz, ticking, toile, linen, gingham, and muslin. Unlike the fabric of formal draperies and curtains, most of these are washable. Just be sure to preshrink fabric if you are making the curtains yourself.

If minimal treatments pose a problem with light control or privacy, you can easily pair them with shades, blinds, or louvered shutters that roll out of sight when not needed.

SHADES, BLINDS, AND LOUVERED SHUTTERS

Shades are generally considered soft window treatments. They're made of a single piece of fabric or vinyl attached to a roller and operated with a cord or via a spring mechanism. Ones made of fabric can be flat, pleated, or gathered. Shades are versatile, too; they can block out the light entirely or simply filter it. Use them alone on a window for a casual look, or pair them with curtains for something formal. Popular variations include:

🍎 **Roman shades.** When pulled up, they feature sleek, flat, horizontal pleats. Roman shades are well-suited to contemporary-style interiors.

🍎 **Balloon shades.** When pulled up, the gathered fabric forms billowing festoons or fans. This eighteenth-century design suits period and traditional-style rooms.

🍎 **Pleated fabric shades.** These lightweight shades stack so tightly when rolled up, they almost disappear under a curtain. They come in a variety of colors and fabrics.

🍎 **Cellular shades.** Their pleated-fabric construction resembles a honeycomb. They are available in a wide range of styles, colors, and faux finishes.

Blinds, whether made of metal or vinyl, effectively block the sun and the outdoors in general when they are closed. Today's many styles include myriad colors, textured fabric finishes, and wood, and the choice of vertical slats or horizontal slats in standard, mini, or micro widths. Contrasting tapes are available to create interesting decorative details. Verticals are strictly suited for contemporary rooms, but the others look at home anywhere. Pair blinds with another treatment or let them stand alone.

Louvered shutters are made from wood and always lend a tony appearance to any interior. Open them for air; close them for privacy. Stained wood finishes complement country or traditional-style rooms. Some types come with a fabric panel that can be coordinated with other furnishings. "Plantation" shutters, which feature wide louvers, painted white or off-white, complement contemporary settings.

Clockwise (from far left): *Valances come in a variety of styles, including gathered, tie-top versions such as this one. Specially-shaped shutters that don't obscure the shape are an option for arch-topped windows. Shutters with fabric panels give a softer look. Tab-topped shades can stand alone as window treatments. Scalloped edges are the hallmark of balloon valances.*

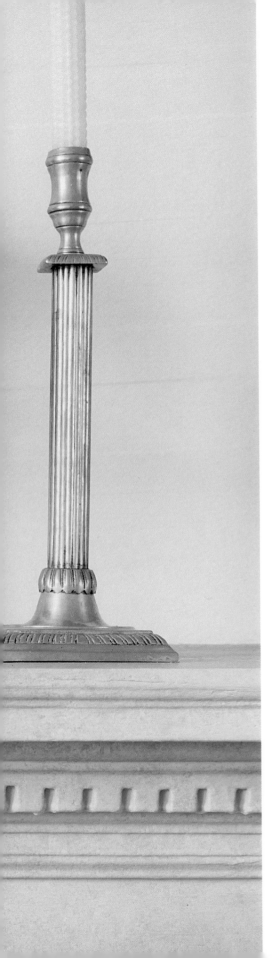

CHAPTER 6

ADDING CHARACTER

Character is what makes a house memorable. Features such as moldings, handsome door and window styles, interesting fireplace mantels and surrounds, and well-chosen accessories all help to make a home special. Luckily if your house lacks character, you can easily add it.

For interiors, character is created with the addition of architectural elements and decorative accessories. Architectural elements enhance the structural bare bones of a room. By exchanging a pair of flush, windowless doors for French doors, a dark dining room can be changed into a sunny, well-lit space; a plain ceiling can become a showpiece with the addition of an ornamental ceiling medallion and a cornice. Decorative accessories pull a design scheme together and reflect individuality. A display of majolica turns built-in shelving into a noteworthy feature; a staggered arrangement of black-and-white photography adds interest to a stairway.

In the course of planning your room design you have two perfect opportunities to give character to the space on which you're working . The first occurs early on as you assess the basic room. Does it lack moldings? Do you want a fireplace? This is the time to decide what architectural features you want to change or incorporate. The second chance arrives once you've settled on the major design elements and turn your thoughts toward your accessories. Is there

Left: *Classical motifs, such as the dentil molding and the Grecian urn ornament, embellish the mantel shelf and jamb of this painted mantel.*

a collection that you want to highlight? Is there a table-top or a niche that looks too empty? Then take stock of what items you have, and keep an eye out for accessories that appeal to you. This chapter will show you how to bring all these elements together in an attractive—and very personal—decorating scheme.

ARCHITECTURAL DETAILS

At the initial planning stage described in Chapter One, when you analyze structural features, the room under scrutiny may not have any architectural or decorative details. Unless it's been altered over time, a period house, such as a Colonial or Victorian, may be rich with orna-mentation. Today, however, many houses replicate the facades of those period buildings but eliminate the archi-tectural elements inside. If you are faced with a nonde-script room, you can introduce those features with store-bought trim or architectural salvage. The result can be an elegant foundation upon which to layer your carefully chosen design.

You can create a sense of style and history by changing door or window styles; replacing stair rails, balusters, and newel posts; or adding fire-place mantels. A window or fireplace can easily become the new focal point of a room. Other, more subtle, touches, such as molding, ceiling medallions, and hardware, give a room a well-heeled resonance.

DOORS

If an uninteresting interior door does nothing for a traditional or period room's design, you might consider replacing it with a door style that provides greater visual interest.

Most doors are made of either wood, metal, glass, or a combination of these three. The two most common types of wood doors are flush and panel. *Flush* wood doors have a smooth surface; these doors may have solid or hollow-core construction and are preferred for con-

temporary settings. *Panel* doors consist of stiles (vertical members) and rails (horizontal members) with panels inserted between them; this type is favored for traditional interiors. An older and less common type is a *plank* door. It is composed of vertical boards (usually four or more) anchored together by two horizontal members and one diagonal member, which form a "Z" on the back of the door. Plank doors are suitable for country or rustic designs. In terms of styles for wood doors, there is quite a range, including double, pocket, Dutch (divided), louvered, and folding (accordion) types.

Metal doors, constructed of hollow steel with a solid-fiber infill, are rarely used for interiors in private homes, unless there is a need for protection from fire. Aside from flush-metal doors, some styles come with glass panels or louvers that may work for contemporary rooms.

Although frameless styles exist, glass doors are usually framed in wood or metal, such as French doors or siding glass doors. The glass itself offers a variety of decorative options: It can be etched, beveled, curved (slumped), and cut, as well as composed of stained or leaded glass or art glass, such as the iridescent type.

WINDOWS

Replacing ordinary windows with decorative bows, bays, arch tops, or even casement windows is another change that pays off big in terms of style. Before you choose a replacement window, consider how it will look from

Clockwise (from top left): *Grand proportions and decorative woodwork make a Palladian-style window the main design element of this room. To accentuate the panels on this door, it was grained to look like burled wood. Gently curved French doors enhance but don't over-embellish the pared-down simplicity of this dining room; note how the divided lights (the panes) of the door echo the ones in the window. A central special-shape window, above a series of sliding glass doors, is flanked by two trapezoid windows, filling in the gable wall of this charming bedroom.*

the exterior as well as the interior of your house; the new windows should be compatible with the architecture.

Residential windows come in wood, vinyl, or aluminum. *Wood* is the old standard; it can be painted or stained to match any décor, but it requires constant upkeep because weather exposure can cause deterioration. *Aluminum-* and *vinyl-clad wood windows* are two other choices; both are rot-proof and provide good insulation. A *vinyl* window is a low-maintenance option because it does not require painting or protective coatings, it resists corrosion and denting, and it offers excellent insulation. The color selection—white, gray, beige, and brown—is limited, however. Vinyl windows are available with wood cladding on the interior. *Aluminum* windows are easy to install but offer poor insulation qualities. They can be left unfinished (a metallic color) or coated with paint, enamel, or lacquer; wood cladding is also available.

Next, consider the basic types of windows and how they function. *Fixed* windows cannot be opened and are often used in combination with *operable* windows. *Double-hung* windows are the most common of the operable types; they have two sash that move up and down, which means that only half of the window can be open at any one time. *Casement* windows are hinged vertically to swing in or out in a doorlike manner; they are operated by a crank. *Awning* windows are hinged horizontally to swing in or out. *Jalousie* windows have horizontally placed, narrow strips of glass that are opened louverlike by a crank. *Sliding* windows have top and bottom tracks on which the sash move sideways.

These practical considerations are important for your comfort, but you should also explore the various architectural styles of windows to match one with your décor. A group of three windows with an arch over the center unit is the classical makeup of a *Palladian* window. Some variations

Right: *Here, an oval window brightens a master bed that was tucked into the dark end of an attic room. Its small size also ensures privacy.*

Far right: *Filled with swag curtains, a pair of topiaries, and a bowl of lemons, this bay window creates an inviting scene, helping to soften the hard edges of kitchen countertops and cabinetry.*

have three arches (one large, two small) or one fanlight-style arch over the three windows. This window tends to visually dominate a room, so it is good as a focal point.

A *picture* window is made up of one large fixed window flanked by two casements or double-hung units. As the name describes, picture windows are for framing dramatic views.

Like Palladian and picture windows, *bay* windows are also composed of three parts. The difference is that the windows are set at an angle to each other, creating an alcove. A curved version of this window is called either a *bow window* or a *circular bay*. A large bay window adds about 4 feet of extra space to a room, where you can situate a chair or a small dining table.

Clerestory windows are made of a strip of small, horizontal panes set high on a wall, near the ceiling. These windows are a good solution in spaces where you want natural light but need privacy.

There are also a variety of special small window shapes that are almost strictly decorative. These windows can be used independently or in combination with the standard types. An *elliptical* or *arched* window is often placed above double-hung or fixed windows, but it is also used alone in situations where a larger unit won't fit, such as in a dormer or a small bathroom. An *oval* (or *cameo*) window and a *circular* window are used in much the same way; both are sometimes located on narrow staircase landings to add light. For a more modern shape, a *triangular* window or a *trapezoidal* window is often paired with a large fixed window.

STAIRS

A staircase is also a good opportunity for embellishment, particularly because it is often the focal point of a space. Decorative newels, balusters, and railings are common stock millwork items. They're available in a variety of turned profiles, as well as standard sizes. With them, a staircase that was once only functional can become an attractive part of the room.

Other specialized brackets, with carved flourishes and fretwork-like designs, can further enhance a staircase. If you view a staircase from the side, the long leg of these L-shaped pieces fits beneath the edge of a tread, with the shorter leg extending the length of the riser. The bracket is simply nailed to the carriage the same way that you attach ordinary trim.

Another way to dress up an open stair is to paint it in contrasting hues. The newel post,

Left: *The black color of the railing and balusters (the upright posts) coordinates with natural finish on the treads (the horizontal surface of the step) and the black-and-white tiles on the risers (the vertical pieces between the steps).*

railing, and treads can be painted in a dark color, while the balusters, trim, and carriage echo the color of the walls in the room. Installing ceramic tiles on the risers can also add color and pattern to stairs.

MANTELS

A fireplace is invariably the focal point of any room in which it's located. There is good reason why it's one of the most desirable features in any home, new or old. It adds warmth—visually or literally—and it's striking in looks.

You may have an existing fireplace that needs to be dressed up because of a missing mantel, or you may want to add a new fireplace to your home. Either way, learn before you go shopping for a mantel and other fireplace parts so that you get exactly what you want. Here's a quick review of the basics:

❧ A *mantel* can be just a horizontal shelf above the fireplace opening or ornamental framing around the top and sides of the opening.

❧ An *overmantel* is a decorative treatment above the mantel that often incorporates a picture, mirror, or some shelving. Many Victorian mantels had overmantels with mirrors flanked by shelves that displayed knickknacks, for example.

❧ A *lintel* is a wood or stone beam that supports the top of the fireplace.

❧ The *jambs* are vertical supports along the sides of the fireplace, holding up the mantel.

❧ A *chimneypiece* is made up of the fireplace opening, mantel, and the overmantel.

Top right: *Mantels can be as plain or as ornamented as you prefer. The sunburst medallions, fluted columns, and delicate molding details on this mantel are suitable for a traditional interior.*

Right: *In this contemporary living room, color provides the only fireplace decoration, as an unadorned gray mantel shelf is set against a purple backdrop.*

❦ A *hearth* is the floor that extends from the fireplace into the room. It is usually covered in a fire-resistant material, such as tile or brick.

❦ A *flue* is the pipe or opening through which smoke from the fireplace is released.

❦ Because the *chimney breast* contains the flue, it projects into the room. It is usually made of a fire-resistant material, such as stone, brick, or cement.

Next, consider what type of fireplace will suit your décor best. The pared-down simplicity of a contemporary interior may call for a mantel-less (flush) fireplace, such as stucco-finished wall around the opening, or an unadorned mantel. For traditional rooms, there is an unlimited choice of reproduction and salvaged mantels in period styles, including Colonial, Federal, Gothic, and Victorian. Mantels are usually made of marble, stone, wood, cast iron, or copper. A brick mantel is constructed as part of the entire fireplace; a wood mantel shelf is used for cobblestone and adobe fireplaces.

When choosing a mantel, keep certain clearances in mind. Make sure woodwork, trim, and other combustible material are at least 6 inches away from the fireplace opening. (This is the reason you'll often notice decorative tiles between the fireplace opening and a wooden mantel.) If a wooden mantel projects 1¹/₂ inches, it should be at least 12 inches from the fireplace opening.

When buying a mantel from an architectural salvage source, have your measurements ready before you go. You don't want to guess whether this expensive—not to mention heavy—item will fit. Plus, salvaged mantels are one-of-a-kind pieces; the one you want may no longer be there if you have to leave and return on another day.

If you buy a salvaged wood mantel, you may want to strip off the paint. Proceed carefully, particularly if it is ornamented. Much of the detailing on period mantels (and some current types, too) is made not from wood but from composition ornament (called "compo" for short), a pliable material that is molded into intricate designs, such as urns,

swags, and rosettes, and that is painted or stained. Paint strippers may dissolve compo, so it is a good idea to work around these ornamented areas.

MOLDING AND TRIM

Decorative trim gives a room a finished appearance. Installation is fairly easy and materials are reasonably priced. An enormous variety of stock and specialty trim exists in a wide range of materials, such as wood, plaster, and fiberglass.

From the ceiling to the floor, shaped trim called molding is used on most parts of the wall. The cornice is placed at the top, where the wall meets the ceiling. Moldings for cornices come in two main types: dramatic *crown molding* that is frequently combined with other molding styles for an opulent look or the simpler *cove molding* that elimi-

Clockwise (from top left): *Sometimes the fine detail on mantels is made from composition ornament, not carved wood. Whether you are looking for ceiling medallions, cornices, columns, or brackets, reproductions of architectural elements abound. Using those resources, the delicate features found on the ceiling, cornice, and wainscot in this classical bedroom can be added to any room.*

nates the ceiling line but doesn't stand out. The *frieze* is a wide band, sometimes ornamented with swags, that runs under the cornice but above the picture rail. As the name suggests, the *picture rail* is used to hang artwork. A *chair rail* (or dado cap) is placed on a wall, around the room, 30 to 35 inches from the floor and is often used in conjunction with a *wainscot* or *dado* (waist-high paneling) on the lower portion of the wall. *Base moldings* give the floor line a higher profile and can be as elaborate or simple as you like. Window and door trim, called *casing*, is necessary to seal the gap between the jambs and wall. But again, it can be quite plain or more decorative depending on taste.

Most of the molding profiles in use today have been around for centuries. Although the classical names for molding profiles may be off-putting, be assured their forms are as familiar to most of us as a panel door is. Some of the common profiles are *cavetto* or *cove*, a concave quarter-circle; *ovolo*, a convex quarter-round; *scotia*, a concave semicircle; *torus*, a convex semicircle; *ogee* (also called *cyma recta* and *cyma reversa*), an S-shaped form; *beaded*, a smaller, convex rounded form; and *fillet*, a flat, narrow strip separating other moldings. These profiles can be used to frame walls and openings without being intrusive on the design; they add a three-dimensional quality that most rooms need.

More ornate moldings command more attention when incorporated into a design and should suit the overall décor. Some the classic motifs that adorn moldings are: *acanthus*, a lobed leaf ornament; *anthemion*, the stylized flower and leaf of the honeysuckle; *dentil*, a series of ornamental notches; *egg-and-dart*, an oval-shaped detail that alternates with an arrow or tongue form; *guilloche*, a series of

This page (clockwise, from right): *Paneled walls can lend an air of formality and grandeur to a room. A wainscot creates a visual break on a wall that makes high-ceilinged rooms seem lower. A stylized bracket capped with a scroll adds dimension to kitchen cabinetry. The egg-and-dart molding and the Corinthian capital with an acanthus leaf motif are classical details.*

Opposite (top to bottom): *Don't overlook ceilings when adding decorative features: This Prairie-style study uses plain trim to great effect overhead. Corner blocks come in a number of motifs, with the bull's-eye being the most common.*

circular interlaced bands; and *paterae*, a cup-
shaped ornament.

ELEMENTS FOR CEILINGS

Although walls tend to get most of the
attention, rooms can benefit from an ornamented ceiling, and there are more options
than just installing an elaborate cornice.

One of the best known and most beautiful
elements for the area above our heads is the
ceiling medallion. Sometimes called a *rosette*,
ceiling medallions feature intricate nature-inspired details,
such as overlapped acanthus leafs. Originally made of plaster, the ornament was placed in the center of the ceiling;
lighting fixtures are often hung from the middle of the
medallion. Reproductions are available in plaster, wood,
metal, composition, and polymer (plastic) materials.

Ceilings are also adorned with wooden panels or pressed
tin. A *pressed-tin ceiling* is typically made of embossed metal
sheets and is meant to imitate wooden panel ceilings,
which are more expensive. Today, both pressed-tin and
wooden panels are still made for ceilings. The pressed-tin
patterns are usually stylized grids with some sort of decorative medallion or rosette in each square; wooden ceilings
are usually in coffered or sunken panel design. Pressed-tin
ceilings can be left with a metal finish but are generally
painted white or beige so that the design appears to be plaster-

work; a wooden panel ceiling is most often finished with a dark stain; it is occasionally painted.

HARDWARE AND GRILLES

Another place to look when scouting areas for embellishment is to the doors, large and small, that may provide a backdrop for decorative hardware. Door levers, knobs and cabinetry pulls can be highly ornamental and a cost-effective way to deliver style. Metalwork such as heat registers, grilles, and grates are all available in decorative designs as well.

DECORATIVE OBJECTS

Once the basic room and all its elements are in place, that's your cue to make the space truly your own. The decorative objects you choose to accent your rooms reflect your personality and can give your design an individuality as unique as your own.

Basically, decorative objects fall into two categories: art and accessories. Art can be paintings, framed prints or photos, sculpture, architectural salvage that is used as *objet d'art,* and even textiles. Accessories tend to be small objects that are introduced into a room for either a practical reason or an aesthetic one (or for a combination of these purposes). A delicately patterned soup tureen flanked by silver candlesticks makes a functional and beautiful centerpiece on a dining room table, for example.

Art and accessories shouldn't always be treated as an afterthought in the design scheme. A large piece of art can influence your room's décor, as may collections. Consider these elements as you are designing the room. Accessories may play a background role, however, and can be worked in during the last phase of the design process.

Whether you are hanging a group of prints or displaying a pottery collection, the configurations are either symmetrical or asymmetrical.

Symmetry is an arrangement that is a mirror image on either side of a central (unseen) line. Picture a sofa table with a pair of brass lamps and matching porcelain figurines flanking a flower-filled vase, for example. You can achieve *visual* symmetry with objects that don't match perfectly but are approximately the same size, height, or color. Imagining the same sofa table, if the porcelain figurines were the same size, shape, and color but different images, the arrangement would still look balanced. *Asymmetry* is the opposite of symmetry. Using visual weight as a guide, unlike elements are grouped together to achieve an informal balance. An intricate wire birdcage can be placed with a small display plate on a stand and adjacent to three topiaries in various sizes, for instance. Each element in the arrangement is a counterpoint to the other: The wide birdcage plays against the tall topiaries and the round plate. (For more guidance on symmetry and asymmetry, see Chapter One, "Understanding and Analyzing Space," on page 12.)

Clockwise (from top left): *Grouped collections have more impact: Here, cabbage-leaf pottery, displayed on built-in shelves, enlivens an all-white color scheme. Pillows in a mixture of patterns and textures are a quick way to add character. Vary the heights of accessories in an arrangement to create interest; the lamp and vase of flowers are counterbalanced by the bowl of fruit and covered jar. The elements don't need to match to be balanced, as with the birdcage, topiary, and vase on this mantel.*

ART

Historically, every inch of wall space was filled with art, creating visual chaos. Today the thinking is different. Art is shown to its greatest effect in uncluttered surroundings. A large modern painting has more impact if left alone on a wall, for instance. Small- or medium-size artworks or drawings are more impressive when placed together on a wall.

If you are displaying drawings or photography, make sure the frame is large enough to accommodate a mat. The frame should be 1 to 3 inches larger in dimension than the picture. For an up-to-date look, the trend is to make the mat at least 6 inches larger than a photograph or an illustration; this can be an effective way to draw attention to a small piece of art or photography.

When choosing matting, try picking up accent colors from your décor. If you feel your accents

Above: *Be creative when choosing your decorative accessories. Here, a row of green apples and a grouping of colorful watering cans keep this arrangement friendly and informal.*

Right: *With picture rails, you can update collections of framed photography and not create more nail holes in the walls.*

don't work with the art, look at your room's main hues. If all else fails, pick a neutral color you like from the work itself to serve as the mat's color.

Frames should coordinate with but not necessarily duplicate any other frames used in the room. Unless you're making a statement with the juxtaposition, the frame style should also reflect the overall look of the room.

When buying a frame, examine the quality of the material from which it is constructed. Does it feel flimsy? Make sure there aren't any gaps at the joints (the mitered cor-

ners of the frame). What is the condition of the metallic finish? There shouldn't be any flaking or discoloration.

It takes some trial and error to create a pleasing wall arrangement. Here's how to do it.

SMART STEPS

ONE: *Experiment with the elements.* Before you hammer a nail into the wall, place all of the art on the floor, and try out different arrangements. A vertical grouping will make a room seem higher; a horizontal one will make the room seem wider. Don't get stuck in a rut: You don't have to arrange everything in a row. A triangular shape might work for an end wall in a room with a cathedral ceiling; a rectangle or oval in an area above a mantel or sofa. Check out the other geometric placement possibilities for art on page 116.

TWO: *Find the right location on the wall.* Art should sit 6 to 9 inches above a sofa or at eye level when you are seated. Too high, and it will look like it's floating; too low, and it will interfere with headroom. When working with more than one picture, start by marking and measuring the spot for the center print. Then hang the middle row vertically, and follow with the rest.

THREE: *Check the proportions.* A framed piece that is too small will look insignificant over a large piece of furniture. The frame should be approximately two-thirds the size of the piece over which it hangs. If you still want to use the small piece, pair it with another that is approximately the same size.

FOUR: *Balance out the arrangement.* In groupings where frames vary in size, try to keep the weightier pieces on the bottom, or place two smaller elements next to it. A large piece will anchor the grouping and keep the arrangement from seeming top-heavy or from trailing off.

FIVE: *Create unity.* A mix of art that doesn't have a common theme or color can be unified by using matching frames or mats. Conversely, art with a common theme or color, such as black-and-white photography, will work well as an arrangement even if the frames don't match.

TEXTILES AS ART

Don't overlook the beauty and versatility of textiles when choosing your decorating accessories. Quilts, tapestries, appliqués, and printed cloths such as batik can stand alone on a wall, adding texture and color to the room.

Textiles can be mounted on a wall in a number of ways. Smaller cloths can be conventionally framed and sandwiched between glass. Because it is difficult to keep fabric straight and balanced within the frame, you might consider turning the job over to a professional framer.

Larger cloths or rugs can be tacked directly to a wood furring strip, or 1x2 that has been nailed into the wall studs. As an alternative, you can attach the fabric to a wooden or cast-iron dowel with decorative finials (the type used for draperies). To attach the fabric to the dowel without damaging it, create

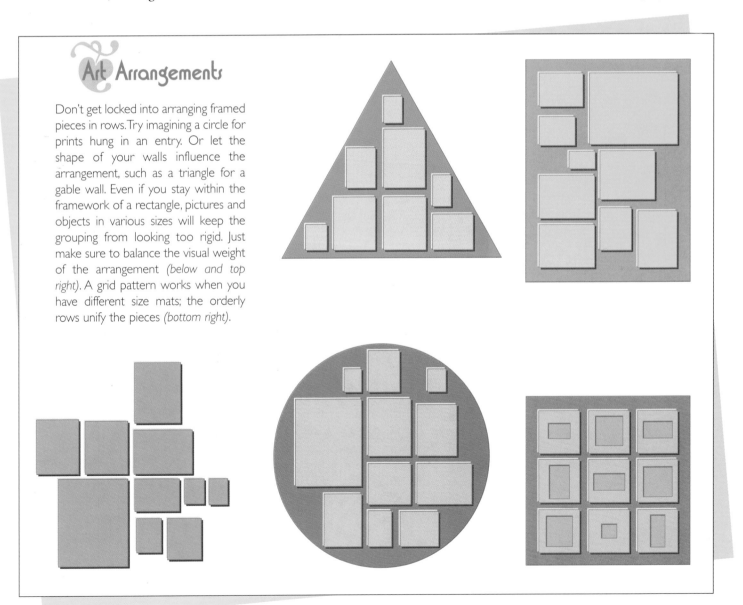

Art Arrangements

Don't get locked into arranging framed pieces in rows. Try imagining a circle for prints hung in an entry. Or let the shape of your walls influence the arrangement, such as a triangle for a gable wall. Even if you stay within the framework of a rectangle, pictures and objects in various sizes will keep the grouping from looking too rigid. Just make sure to balance the visual weight of the arrangement *(below and top right)*. A grid pattern works when you have different size mats; the orderly rows unify the pieces *(bottom right)*.

Right: *Notice how a leather-bound book is tucked under one of two matching topiaries, creating interest by varying the height.*

a pocket by looping the top piece over the dowel and stitching it together.

ACCESSORIES

With decorative accessories, there is no right or wrong in the pieces you choose. Use favorite found objects, collectibles, and tabletop items, such as candlesticks, vases, and pottery. While there are no hard and fast rules about what will and won't work, there are certain guidelines that can help you determine where and how to display the items you select. Familiarizing yourself with them will make it easy to create attractive tabletop arrangements.

SMART STEPS

ONE: *Group objects by similarities.* Choose items that share the same color, material, shape, or motif. For instance, even if the pieces aren't the same height and shape, a collection of blue-and-white delft pottery can make an impressive arrangement because the color ties the group together. Likewise, a row of Fiestaware pitchers, each in different color, will work visually because of the repeating shape.

TWO: *Vary the elevation.* Any grouping benefits from including elements of different sizes. Pairs of objects that are all the same height can be monotonous. Instead of placing two topiaries with two candlesticks, try putting the topiaries with two picture frames. Small items, such as figurines or a decorative plate, can get lost in an arrangement. Try raising them up with a small pedestal or a stand.

THREE: *Add depth.* Don't always place items in a straight line, which can look static. Instead, stagger the pieces from back to front. For example, if you are have three objects, place them in a triangle. With a larger number of objects, experiment with overlapping triangles.

FOUR: *Choose a focal point.* If the grouping is not coming together, arrange everything around one major object, such as a sculpture or a framed print.

FIVE: *Don't overdo it.* Too many items looks like clutter. Choose accessories judiciously. Store extra items away, and freshen up your arrangements periodically with these pieces.

CHAPTER 7

DECORATING WITH FURNITURE

There is no doubt that furniture plays a pivotal role in establishing ambiance and style in a home. Manufacturers offer a great selection of both contemporary and period reproduction pieces today. Although your choice is very much a matter of personal taste, there are other important points to consider before adding to or replacing anything you may already own.

As with all aspects of design, you'll want to examine the function of both the room and the furniture. Does the furniture have to be versatile and comply with a multitude of needs? How much wear and tear do you expect it to handle? Are you planning to use it in a room intended for occasional entertaining or everyday use? Should it be casual or formal, built-in or movable?

Next, you'll have to decide on a style. Taking cues from your preferences and the other elements you've chosen for your decorating scheme as well as the architectural style of your house will help you narrow down your choices.

You'll also have to think about cost. Nearly all furniture styles are available in low-end to high-priced versions. Paying top dollar doesn't necessarily mean you're buying the best—only durable materials and reliable construction can ensure that. But if an item is very cheap, something probably has been skimped on in the manufacturing or finishing process to bring down the cost.

Left: *An eclectic arrangement of different furniture styles brings personality and a cozy, casual look to this living room.*

Working with existing furniture is always an option. Although the cost of reupholstering or refinishing it may be comparable with buying something new, older pieces (those manufactured before the 1950s), may be better constructed or more valuable for sentimental reasons.

In this chapter, you'll become acquainted with all of the issues that deserve your consideration in order to make sound decisions about furniture.

THE FUNCTION OF FURNITURE

Furniture has three basic functions: for seating, sleeping, and storage. Furniture can also efficiently divide space. Within a large room, you might want to create a cozy sitting area in front of a fireplace while storing entertainment equipment at another end of the room. Or you may need to define living and dining areas within one room. A low-backed sofa can act as a room divider, as can a shelving unit or a sofa table. The key is not to block sources of natural light when dividing space with furniture.

SEATING

Furniture that functions as seating comes with a variety of options. It can roll, swivel, tilt or recline, stack, fold, or convert to another use such as a bed. Seating can also take numerous forms. Sofas, for instance, come in all shapes and sizes. There are three-seaters and two-seaters (sometimes called love seats). Other sofa terms are Chesterfield (overstuffed, tuffted upholstery with padded arms), Lawson (arms lower than the back), and tuxedo (arms the same height as the back). Backs of sofas can be termed camel back, channel back, or tufted back, all of which are firm, spring-supported styles. Pillow backs are available as either attached or loose. Multi-pillow backs, or scatter backs, have more back pillows than seat cushions. Base treatments include skirts (with various pleating designs), upholstered legs, plinth (block) bases, and bun feet.

Chairs are categorized as upholstered or occasional. Popular upholstered chairs are termed club or wing. A barrel chair has a rounded back that extends in a smooth line with the arms. A club chair is square with arms lower than its back, and a wing chair has a high back with winglike extensions at head level. Occasional chairs are usually smaller than upholstered chairs. Characterized by wooden arms and legs that are combined with seats and backs that are sometimes upholstered, occasional chairs are often traditional in design.

Left: *A two-seat sofa with a loose-pillow back is just the right size for this space. Small, thin-legged tables at each end and in front are serviceable yet help to keep the overall look of the room airy and uncluttered.*

Right: A comfortable leather club chair and tall bookcases create an idyllic reader's corner enhanced by over-the-shoulder sunlight.

Modular seating comes in any number of armless units, single-arm end modules, and corner pieces that can be arranged in various configurations to suit different spaces and needs. This type of seating is differerent from a sectional sofa, which consists of simply one corner unit and two end pieces.

SLEEPING

Furniture for sleeping ranges from futon frames to platform beds and bedsteads with head- and foot-boards. Some bedsteads also include bedside stands, lamps, and built-in storage compartments. Convertible sofa beds offer extra sleeping accommodations for small spaces. Other options are the loft bed, which is on a raised platform and frees the space beneath for other uses; bunk beds; and trundle beds, which slide under another bed when not in use.

STORAGE

Storage furniture is available to suit a wide range of needs. In the furniture industry, it is referred to as casegoods because of its boxlike structure (although tables also come under this category). It may include bookcases or any other type of open shelves, cabinets with hinged or sliding doors, cabinets that house audio or video equipment, breakfronts, chests, armoires, or desks. Casegoods come in many shapes and sizes and offer a place to display or protect collectibles and other valuables. Modular pieces can be used to create storage walls or room dividers. Storage walls are connected units that fit from floor to ceiling. They divide space while providing access to storage from both sides. Room dividers serve a similar purpose but do not extend to the ceiling or from wall to wall. They are most commonly used to divide living and dining areas.

Storage furniture for the bedroom consists of dressers, vanities, and chests. These pieces are categorized by the size of their contents. The smallest is a lingerie chest, followed by the drawer chest. The door chest is larger still, with drawers at the bottom and two doors at the top. The armoire, or wardrobe, is the largest chest available. A clothes rod inside defines it as a wardrobe.

Sometimes these pieces can serve multipurpose needs, so think about which ones you can get the most from, particularly if you are short on space. An armoire is an excellent example. It can be used in any room in the house. In the kitchen, it becomes a pantry; in the family room, it's an entertainment center; in the bedroom, it's a clothes closet; and in a spacious bath or in a hallway, it's a handy place to store linens and toiletries.

AESTHETIC CONSIDERATIONS

Once you've considered how you want to use the furniture in a room, you'll have to decide on a style that will coordinate with your décor. This is a matter of personal taste and your lifestyle. Even if you have a particular look in mind, you may want to take your time before making a final decision. Following these Smart Steps will help.

ONE: *Look around you.* What are your favorite pieces of furniture? What do you like about them? List the colors that most appeal to you. Do you have special items such as artwork or family heirlooms that you'd like to blend with new furnishings? List the things you would like to keep and what you think you may want to replace, either now or in the future. If you're on a tight budget, plan for things you might be able to save for in the meantime.

TWO: *Consider your family's lifestyle.* Do you have young children or pets? Do you spend a lot of time at home or are you always coming and going? Do you entertain frequently? How do you entertain, with a backyard barbecue or a formal sit-down dinner? Be smart: Don't buy delicate upholstered pieces for the kids to flop on with the dog. Sometimes it makes sense to put your hankering for such things on the back burner and shop for something durable. Similarly, if you're an expert chef and love to serve meals on fine china by candlelight, splurge on your formal dining room's furniture.

THREE: *Play up the architectural style of your house.* Find out when your house or apartment building was built. Research its architectural style using books on architectural history from the library if necessary. Consider a period decorating style like Victorian or Colonial if it works well with the house style. Be sure to design around architectural details such as built-in cabinets or bookcases, which add character to your home. If you have hardwood floors laid with an interesting or contrast-

Left: *A formal dining room isn't practical for everyone's lifestyle, but if you entertain often with sit-down dinners, classic, elegant furnishings enhance the mood.*

Above: *The traditional architecture of this home provides the inspiration and backdrop for the collection of fine reproduction and antique furniture.*

ing pattern around the perimeter of the room, don't obscure them completely with the furnishings you choose. Detailing around your door and window frames and at the tops and bottoms of your walls can help you decide whether a room would look best as a formal or informal setting. Think about how some types of furnishings complement these details.

FOUR: *Narrow down your choices.* If you're still at a loss, look at magazine pictures of room settings. Clip out your favorites. After you've collected a few, look at them all together. If they all have things in common, *voilà:* You may have just found your favorite style. If you've clipped examples of different styles, group the similar rooms together, and pin up each grouping in separate areas on the wall. Keep them pinned up for several days, and look at them as you

walk by. At the end of the week, can you say which group of pictures is your favorite?

CLASSIC STYLES

Three general furniture styles to consider are traditional, contemporary, and country. Within each of these categories are several different styles of furniture that work together.

Traditional. Traditional-style furniture takes its design cues from furniture made before 1900. Here you will find familiar period pieces such as a Queen Anne chair or a Chippendale table. The original designs take their names from influential people of the times as well as from architectural styles, such as Baroque, Gothic, and Victorian. Traditional sofas and chairs are often upholstered with heavy, luxurious fabrics and elaborate trim. Most furniture of this style is tailored with kick-pleat skirting and rolled arms. You'll find button-tufting and nailhead trim

homespun details. Tables and storage pieces are usually made of pine or oak, sometimes painted rather than stained.

You may choose to stay true to these design themes or create an eclectic mix of styles in your home. Think about softening the hard lines of contemporary furniture with a few country-style accents, such as handcrafted pillows or rugs. A few pieces of antique furniture can complement the architectural style of your home no matter which general décor you've chosen.

SHOPPING FOR FURNITURE

Even if you have a good idea of what types of furniture you're looking for as well as the general style that appeals to you, there is a maze of purchase options you'll have to negotiate. How do you know what you're getting for your money? What's the difference between the $800 sofa and the $1,200 one? How do you judge the quality of a table? These are important questions. To answer them, it will help to understand what's beneath the upholstery of a

as well as fringe, braid, and cord trim and other fine upholstery details on the cushions and frame.

Contemporary. Furniture styles from 1900 to the present are termed contemporary. These styles also reflect the Modern movement, including Arts & Crafts, Art Deco, and Art Nouveau. Contemporary furniture designs are streamlined and incorporate natural materials such as wood and stone with metal and glass. Upholstered sofas and chairs tend to be larger than traditional styles—you won't find buttons or skirts on these pieces.

Country. Like its European counterparts, American country-style furniture is casual and unpretentious. It often has a period flavor, but one that is rustic rather than genteel. Upholstered pieces might include ruffled skirts, pillows, and other

Above: *The chrome-frame Wassily chairs in this contemporary room are classics of the Modern style. The originals were designed by architect Marcel Breuer in 1925.*

Right: *At the other end of the style spectrum is this country interior, which features a nineteenth-century scroll-arm sofa upholstered in a lively red and white plaid check.*

sofa and how a wood chair or table is put together.

ANATOMY OF A SOFA

Quality furniture is comfortable and durable. Four elements determine the integrity of upholstered furniture: the frame, the springs, the cushions, and the upholstery fabric.

Frames. High-quality frames are made of seasoned hardwood, kiln-dried to resist warping. The frame is joined using dowels and corner blocks that are screwed and glued together. Legs

should be extensions of the frame and not attached with screws. Center legs add additional support.

Springs. The spring systems in upholstered furniture are either hand-tied coils or sagless (sinuous) constructions. Eight-way hand-tied springs are of the highest quality. These funnel-like coils are tied with twine to each of the eight adjacent coils and attached to a heavy-duty webbing underneath with steel clips. This type of construction gives even comfort and prevents "bottoming out" of the seat no matter how heavy the sitter. Four- or six-way tied springs are not nearly as supportive. Good-quality webbing is tightly woven and may be reinforced by steel straps under each row of springs.

Clockwise (from top): *What's the difference between an heirloom-quaity sofa and one that'll have to be replaced in a few years? The workmanship and the materials. One of the first things to look for is a strong frame made out of maple, preferably, or poplar, ash, or birch. Also, check for eight-way hand-tied springs that move up and down easily. Synthetic twine is the strongest, but unlike natural materials, the knots may slip out. Between the upholstery fabric and the muslin-covered springs is a protective layer of cotton. Note the webbing supporting the arm.*

Above: *The meticulous matching of the stripes in this chair's upholstery is one sign of a first-rate job, as are the sturdy seat and back cushions, which should feel substantial when lifted.*

Sagless, or sinuous, springs are S-shaped, flat wavy bands of steel that are fastened to the front rail and run front to back a few inches apart. Sagless springs have a firmer feel than coil springs and are often used in contemporary pieces that are lower to the floor.

Cushions. The frame and springs are the foundation for the cushions. A good frame is padded with cotton or poly-dacron so that the upholstery fabric never touches the wood. Quality seat cushions and loose back cushions consist of

a combination of down and other feathers wrapped around a polyurethane foam core—or loose down or feathers for back cushions. Test the quality of a cushion by lifting it. If it feels light, it may be made of poor materials. A 2x2-foot cushion should not weigh less than 2 pounds.

Back cushions are supported by springs or webbing. If back cushions are loose as opposed to attached, there are no springs. Webbing will supply the only support. This type of construction is less expensive than attached cushions and will feel less resilient than spring support. Pocketed springs are best for comfortable back cushions. You may also find some pieces with sinuous spring backs for less money.

Upholstery. You can often choose from a range of price levels, called *grades*, of fabric or coverings. These grades are assigned a letter from A to D, with A at the high end. Grading is determined by the quality of the materials, the amount of fabric needed for a good match of the pattern, and the source of the pattern design (with famous designers'

Smart Tip about Terms of the Trade

Collection: A grouping of related furniture pieces from the same manufacturer. Furniture is usually displayed in collections.

Reproductions: Copies of fine antiques made with the same materials and details as the originals.

Adaptations: Furniture designs that are loosely based on origi-nals. Tags may say "based on," "adapted from," or "in the style of."

Sectionals: Upholstered seating pieces that are made in three sections that fit together in a particular configuration.

Modulars: An unlimited number of pieces that are upholstered and may be used in many configurations.

COM: Custom-ordered material; means the furniture is made to your specifications. For instance, manufacturers may offer you a choice of COM fabrics or let you supply your own.

Apartment-size furniture: Furniture that has been scaled down.

RTA: Ready-to-assemble furniture; comes in pieces. Because you put it together, it costs less.

patterns costing more). An important factor to consider when selecting upholstery fabric is durability. In general, tightly woven fabrics wear best. Fabrics with woven-in patterns wear better than printed fabrics. Various natural and synthetic fibers offer different looks and textures as well as cleanability and wearability performance.

Natural fibers include cotton, linen, wool, and silk. Cotton is soft to the touch and durable. However, its fibers will disintegrate under prolonged exposure to direct sunlight. Cotton is also less stain resistant than synthetic fibers. Linen has a tailored, crisp feel and is one of the most durable fibers available. It is most often found in natural colors because it does not dye well. It, too, can be damaged by sunlight. Wool is extremely hardy, as well as abrasion- and stain-resistant, but should be moth-proofed before use. Silk is a beautiful but fragile fabric. Soft and luxurious, it is difficult to clean and discolors when it is exposed to strong light.

Synthetic fibers have been developed as alternatives to natural fibers and are often blended with them. Polyester is strong and easy to clean. It withstands direct sunlight and is flame- and abrasion-resistant. Rough in texture, it is often blended with natural fibers to soften its touch. Olefin is used to create heavy, textured fabrics. It is a coarse and bulky fiber that is strong and stain resistant. However, it does not wear well under direct sunlight. Nylon is the strongest and most soil-resistant fiber. Recent developments in nylon give it the look and feel of wool. It, too, is sensitive to sunlight.

As an informed shopper, you will be able to make your purchase with confidence. Never judge the quality of an upholstered piece solely by the fabric you see on it. The fabric can be easily replaced, but the frame

Smart Tip about Price Points

Keep the following in mind if you want to trim off some of the cost of your purchases:

Frame design: Curves, such as rounded arms, are more expensive to cover than straight lines.

Pattern design: Large, complex patterns are harder to match than small, overall designs.

Details: Trimmings, such as pleats, welts, braids, buttons, and fringe, all add to the final cost.

Above: *The natural woven fiber used to upholster the frames of these seating pieces requires some protection against direct sunlight. The cushions are finished in a crisp, durable linen.*

and support system cannot. Always go to a reputable furniture retailer when purchasing upholstered pieces. Because you can't see what's underneath the fabric, you'll have to ask questions about the construction. So it's important that the salesperson be knowledgeable and trustworthy. If you're still not satisfied, contact the manufacturer.

THE SIGNS OF GOOD CONSTRUCTION

Furniture can be constructed of hardwood or softwood. Hardwoods come from deciduous trees, such as cherry, maple, oak, ash, pecan, teak, walnut, mahogany, and poplar. Hardwoods are often used in high-quality furniture because they are stronger than softwoods. Softwoods come from conifer trees, such as fir, pine, redwood, cedar, and cypress. Softwoods have to be well-seasoned and kiln-dried before use, or they will split and splinter easily.

Veneers are thin sheets of hardwood that are glued to a core of less expensive wood. They were once associated with poor-quality furniture, but today's wood veneers may sometimes be stronger than solid wood: Wide boards of solid wood will warp and crack with changes in temperature and humidity, while veneer is much more stable in these conditions.

A "solid wood" label allows use of composition boards, such as plywood and particleboard, in areas of the furniture that will remain unseen. You will find these materials applied this way in medium-priced furniture. In budget-priced furniture, they may be used more extensively.

Joining Methods. Wood can be joined together with staples, nails, screws, joints, and glue. Several of these methods may be used in one piece of furniture. To evaluate quality, look for strong construction at the joints. Joints are where one part of a piece of furniture matches up with another. They are usually glued together or fastened with screws. Staples are used only on the cheapest furniture and should not be used to join any piece that bears weight. Furniture

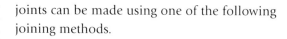

joints can be made using one of the following joining methods.

❦ *Butt joints* simply join the flat sides of two pieces where they meet. They are weak joints and should be used only in places that are not subject to stress or weight, such as where a bureau top meets the frame.

❦ *Miter joints* are often used to join pieces at right angles. The ends of the two pieces are angled to fit together perfectly. These joints may be reinforced with dowels, nails, or screws.

❦ *Tongue-and-groove joints* are used to join two boards together side-by-side, as in a tabletop. A groove is cut into one side of a board and a tongue on the other. When placed side-by-side, the tongue of one board fits into the groove of the next and so on.

❦ *Dovetail joints* are used to join drawer sides. Notches cut into the ends of each piece should fit together tightly.

❦ *Double-dowel joints* use two dowels to peg joints together. These are sturdy joints used in casegood framing and to attach legs to side rails of chairs.

❦ *Mortise-and-tenon joinery* is the strongest method of joining pieces of wood at right angles. The end of one piece of wood is shaped to fit into a hole in the other, distributing stress over a wide area.

❦ *Corner blocks* provide extra support for dowel joints. They can be held in place with either glue or wood screws.

Clockwise (from top right): *Every chair style pictured here is a classic that's available in all price ranges. It's the construction and finish that makes the difference. Tapered legs and the cotton-tape back and seat are hallmarks of Shaker design. The chair back displays features of both the Regency and Federal periods in its design. A stainless-steel and leather chair designed in 1927 by Mies van der Rohe exemplifies the Modern movement. Sinuous contours distinguish this Louis XV reproduction chair.*

Identifying Your Furniture

Poke your nose into almost anyone's basement, attic, or garage, and you'll find a hodgepodge of odd furniture. Style clues to look for include the shape of the arms, legs, and back, as well as any ornamentation and finish. Mixing similar styles is perfectly acceptable and may even add interest to a boring room. Just keep in mind that some combinations work; others don't. Here's a quick reference that can help you decide whether to take a particular piece of furniture out of storage and incorporate it into your home's décor.

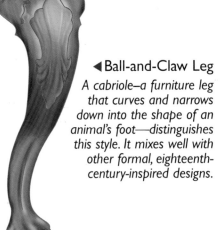

◀ Ball-and-Claw Leg

A cabriole—a furniture leg that curves and narrows down into the shape of an animal's foot—distinguishes this style. It mixes well with other formal, eighteenth-century-inspired designs.

▼ Spindle Leg

In a highly polished rich wood, spindle-legged furniture is at home with other traditional styles. Made from pine or oak and sometimes with a painted finish, it takes on a country-style personality.

▶ Chippendale Leg

The later, less ornate version of Chippendale style pairs well with any eighteenth-century look, especially formal English-inspired furniture such as Queen Anne or Windsor.

▶ Contemporary Leg

Streamlined contemporary pieces crafted in natural or man-made materials defy fads. Other styles that coordinate well with the look are simple Shaker and geometric Art Deco pieces.

◀ French Provincal Leg

The French version of country style has graceful, curvaceous legs that make it a good match with almost any furniture that has European flair.

◄ Tuxedo Sofa

A rectilinear frame and cushions look contemporary, but you can mix this plain sofa with practically any other style.

► Chesterfield Sofa

Rounded arms and tufted upholstery are its hallmarks. Pair it with any eighteenth-century-style pieces.

◄ Camelback Sofa

The undulating shape of its back inspired its name. Depending on the uphostery, it works well with country, traditional, or period pieces.

► Lawson Sofa

Both traditional and country-style furniture coordinates with this sofa, which has rounded arms that are lower than its back.

Smart Tip about Casegoods

Casegoods refers to any piece of furniture that is used for storage, such as a chest of drawers; tables are also part of this category. The furniture industry uses a variety of labels to denote the construction materials. The meanings of these labeling terms are regulated by the Federal Trade Commission.

🍎 **Solid wood** (i.e., "solid oak" or "solid pine") means that the exposed surfaces are made of solid wood without any veneer or plywood. Other woods may be used on unexposed surfaces such as drawer sides and backs.

🍎 **Genuine wood** means that all exposed parts of the furniture are constructed of a veneer of a type of wood over hardwood plywood.

🍎 **Wood** means all of the parts of the furniture are made of some type of wood.

🍎 **Man-made materials** refers to plastic laminate panels. The furniture may also include molded plastic that mimics wood panels, carving, or trim.

However, screws should not be used on everything just because they hold the joints rigidly. A good example is a chest of drawers. Glue blocks should be used to attach the top of the frame because wood panels can expand and contract, which causes the wood to split

Finishes. The final touch on a piece of wood furniture is its finish. Finishes can add color and protection through the use of stains, paints, or lacquers. A clear finish will allow the natural grain of the wood to show through. Wood stains will change the color of the wood. Finishes can make a piece of furniture look refined or rustic.

Distressing is a popular means of making new wood look old. The wood is literally battered before the finish is applied, aging it and enhancing its rustic charm. These finishes tend to hide any scratches or fingerprints the furniture may be exposed to, so they make good choices for use in active areas such as family rooms and for rustic, country-style décors.

Painted finishes are also popular for a nostalgic look. Unlike a distressed finish, however, paint tends to highlight flaws in the wood. This makes painted pieces more expensive than those with natural finishes because extra care must be taken at the factory to remove imperfections from the wood.

Finishes should always be strong enough to resist moisture. Inexpensive pieces may be simply coated with a layer of polyurethane. The finishing of high-quality furniture includes sanding, applying multiple coats of a clear finish with sanding between coats, waxing, and hand buffing. Compare the look and feel between inexpensive and expensive pieces. Always check that the surface is hard,

Below: *In a country-style setting, painted finishes, including stenciling, add charm to wood furniture. Unlike standard finishes, they may reveal imperfections in the wood.*

smooth, and even. Watch for uneven colorations, bubbles, or cracks in the surface If you're debating about whether or not to retain your existing furniture, examine the integrity of its structure and the condition of its finish. If you own genuine antiques that need repair, contact the American Institute for

Smart Tip about Quality Checks

When shopping for wood furniture, you'll find varying levels of quality and pricing. Use this checklist to judge what you're getting for your money.

Frames

- Veneers and laminates should be securely joined to the base material.
- Joints bearing weight should be reinforced with corner blocks.
- Back panels should be screwed into the frame.
- Long shelves should have center supports.

Drawers

- Drawers should fit well, glide easily, and have stops.
- Drawer bottoms should be held by grooves, not staples or nails.
- Drawer interiors should be smooth and sealed.
- Drawer corners should have dovetail joints.

Doors

- Cabinet doors should open and close smoothly.
- Hinges and other hardware should be strong and secure.

Finishes

- All finishes should feel smooth unless it is intentionally distressed or crackled.

Top Right: *A rich mahogany stain enhances this handsome desk. The raised Greek key motif, gilding, and fluted tapered legs add classical allusions to its design.*

Right: *A clear finish on this vanity permits the natural beauty of the wood's grain to provide all the ornamentation necessary to make this piece outstanding.*

Conservation of Historic and Artistic Works in Washington, D.C., to find a qualified restorer. Antiques are loosely defined as pieces more than 100 years old.

REUSING EXISTING FURNITURE

Do you have a favorite old chair, or is there a wonderful piece you found at a flea market last month that you'd love to include in your new room? If so, slipcovering, refinishing, or reupholstering may be an alternative to shopping for brand-new furniture. Although re-covering won't necessarily save you money, it will save those family heirlooms and antique shop rarities. As long as the wood frame is well-constructed and in good condition with no dry rot or worm holes, those pieces can be brought back to life with new fabric.

 SMART STEPS

ONE: *Assess the level of skill needed.* You can choose to do the work yourself or hire a professional. Depending on the shape it's in, wood furniture requires various levels of skill to restore or refinish it. Fitted slipcovers require careful measuring, good sewing skills, and many hours of labor. Reupholstering is a fine art that uses special techniques. You may be able to find classes in your area if you'd like to learn these skills.

Finding a professional upholsterer or furniture restorer is best done by word of mouth. Ask your coworkers and neighbors for references. Fabric stores that carry upholstery material might be able to refer you to someone, or look in the Yellow Pages of your local phone book under "Furniture" or "Furniture makers." Make an appointment to visit the person's shop. *Ask to see examples of their work.*

TWO: *Know what to expect.* Make sure the refinisher or upholsterer shows you what he or she plans to do with your piece beforehand and gives you an estimate for the work. First, the frame should be stripped and checked for any weaknesses. Repairs should be made to weak joints by redoweling, regluing, and rescrewing (never nailing) joints together. All hardware should be removed and the frame cleaned. If the seat platform of an upholstered piece is weak, the upholsterer should replace it and cover it with burlap. This should be hand-sewn to the springs in a diamond pattern to prevent it from slipping. A layer of horsehair gives resiliency to the seat and should be covered with cotton to prevent the horsehair from poking through. A fine

Left: *A loose slipcover that drapes over the chair and ties in the back has a slinky elegance that looks urbane in this understated interior.*

Right: *A sofa slipcovered in a mélange of vintage fabrics with a skirted bottom appears to be at home in this rustic weekend cabin.*

upholsterer will then cover the cotton padding with muslin.

The vertical surfaces of the frame should always be covered with webbing, never cardboard, and then layered with bonded Dacron. Depending on the desired plumpness of the filling, an upholsterer may use polyester wrapped in either Dacron or down. Down is the most expensive option.

THREE: *Select the fabric.* Fabric considerations for reupholstering are comparable to selecting a new piece of furniture. For a formal look, consider a brocade, damask, or velvet. If your style is casual, a linen or chintz may be more suitable. (See "Upholstery" on page 126 of this chapter and the box, "Design Materials," on page 30 of Chapter Two, "Color, Pattern, & Texture," for more information.) It's always a sensible idea to buy fabric that has been treated at the mill for stain resistance if it will get a lot of use, but it's not worth the extra money for a sprayed-on treatment that you can apply yourself.

Also, keep in mind that a talented reupholsterer can change the look of your furniture in subtle ways with fabric. For instance, a contemporary piece can be made more traditional by adding a skirt along the bottom. Neat pleats in the skirting will give the piece a tailored appearance, while ruffles will complement a country-style décor. When ordering fabric, think about extra material for coordinating window dressings and throw pillows.

FOUR: *Calculate yardage.* Some upholsterers will work with fabric you supply; others will sell it to you. Whether working with a professional or on your own, make sure you calculate the needed yardage carefully before buying the

fabric. Here are some general guidelines for how much you will need for reupholstery; slipcovers require slightly more.

❦ *Three-cushion sofa:* No skirt, 10 yards; tailored skirt, 12 yards; pleated or gathered skirt, 14 yards

❦ *Wing chair*: No skirt, 5 yards; loose seat cushion, $5\frac{1}{2}$ yards; skirted, $6\frac{1}{2}$ yards

❦ *Club chair:* No skirt, 5 yards; skirted, $6\frac{1}{2}$ yards

Lastly, avoid trendy looks. Buy classic, quality pieces that will last a lifetime. Remember, the new furniture you buy today may have heirloom value tomorrow and may possibly become a treasure for the next generation to enjoy.

DESIGNING ROOM BY ROOM

U p to this point, each element of decorating has been explored from a general perspective—one that can be applied to any space. But for every room in the house, there are unique considerations that decorators take into account when applying the various elements. You won't find that all of these issues are pertinent in your situation, but certainly some will prompt you to consider aspects of design that you may not have thought about before. This chapter discusses each room individually and explores these points in detail, with advice from interior designers.

It is important to recognize that, for many homeowners, the houses they live in are far from ideal. Sometimes you have to adjust a room's design to accommodate a lack of space elsewhere in the house. For example, much as it may inconvenience you, you may occasionally have to accommodate overnight visitors in your living room if there is no separate guest room. You should plan for this in your living room's design. The room can still look lovely and accommodate practical, multifunctional needs. Many of the circumstances addressed in this chapter pertain to multipurpose room planning; others cover the specific needs and functions of certain rooms.

The whole-house tour in this chapter begins in the foyer and proceeds through the hallway into the living room, family room, dining room, kitchen, master

Left: *Living room décor should walk the line between comfort and formality. Here, denim, check, and striped fabrics achieve a casual sophistication.*

bedroom, children's bedrooms, and bath. For many of the problematic issues presented within each section, there are possible solutions offered. Decorating tips from professional designers abound.

THE FOYER & HALLWAY

First impressions count. Your foyer should be a reflection of your style and an introduction to the rest of your house. Although many people treat the foyer as a solely utilitarian space, filling it with umbrella stands, hall trees, and the like, it can also be an ideal spot to display cherished family photographs or interesting artwork. Touches like these make your entry warmer and more inviting. They might also become the foyer's focal point.

Hallways should tie into the rooms they connect. "Do not forget to treat the walls," says Barbara Schlattman, ASID, of Barbara Schlattman Interiors in Houston, Texas. "That area 5 feet above the ground is especially important because that's what your eye sees." Faux paint finishes, art, and mirrors all add visual appeal.

FURNISHINGS

Pick up a color or pattern from an adjoining room, and use it on the walls of your foyer or hallway. If you decide to use the same wallcoverings in the foyer and living room, change the molding or floor treatment to differentiate the two spaces. Ceramic tile is a popular choice for entryways because it stands up to harsh weather conditions and dirt that's tracked in. Large foyers might have a hardwood floor with a colorful area rug in the middle. If the space is long, break it up visually with two area rugs. Always consider safety when choosing a flooring material for your foyer. The surface shouldn't be slick, and rugs must lie securely, so use a rubber pad.

If space permits, designers often add a console table and an interesting wall mirror in a foyer for both aesthetic and practical reasons. This arrangement is also fitting on stair landings where space permits. The table provides the ideal spot to drop off the mail or the keys, leave a note, or quickly write a check. A mirror helps to visually expand what is often a small or narrow space. Most designers draw the line at mirrored walls, though. The foyer is a well-trafficked spot and mirrored walls will make it look too busy.

Below: *Bookshelves and a wicker chaise create an informal focal point in a narrow hall. Off-white walls, a safe choice because they blend easily with adjacent rooms, are enlivened by a yellow door.*

Above: *Two useful elements in a hallway are a table and a mirror. The table can be a catchall for mail or packages; the mirror offers a spot for a last-minute appearance adjustment.*

Smart Tip about Foyers

Pale paint colors may brighten a narrow hallway or entry, but keep in mind that constant traffic will take its toll on the walls. Consider using warmer colors that are less likely to show marks. A gloss-finish paint will wipe clean easier than a matte-finish product, too. If you prefer wallpaper to paint, use a simple pattern that will not overwhelm the space.

LIGHTING

Hallways have to be well-lit. Use one ceiling fixture in a small hallway or wall-mounted sconces in a larger one. Halls 75 to 150 square feet in size can accommodate a single fixture, which should be at least 12 inches in diameter. A chandelier should be at least 18 inches in diameter. A small space (20 to 75 square feet) requires a fixture that is 8 inches or more in diameter. If you install a pendant lamp or chandelier, make sure it clears the top of any door that opens into the space. Recessed lamps in foyers or halls should be on dimmers. "Although having enough lighting is important, you don't want a foyer to be glaringly bright, especially when coming in from a dark night," notes Melinda Sechrist, of Sechrist Designs in Washington, D.C.

LIVING ROOMS

The living room is actually a multi-purpose space in many instances, acting as an everyday gathering spot for family, a place to entertain guests, as well as the media room where the computer, television, and stereo system all find a home. The living room might also double as the kids' play area or a guest room in a crunch. So unless your living room is off-limits except for company or it's covered in plastic (remember those slipcovers?), it must be able to withstand plenty of wear and tear.

STYLE AND COLOR

The style of the living room should complement adjacent spaces. But often it's the style and palette chosen for the living room that sets the tone for the rest of the house. Go with a look that appeals to you and complements your lifestyle. For example, if your living room functions essentially as the family room, with kids, toys, pets, and typical

Left: *Grouping furniture in one area of a large living room can make the space seem overwhelming. By creating multiple conversation areas, such as the two sections in this living room, the space becomes more intimate and manageable.*

Below: *The furnishings in a living room need to serve a dual purpose: comfort and formality. Here, a red toile fabric, used as slipcovers and curtains, fits the bill. It is inviting enough for everyday use, but it can also be dressed up for entertaining.*

When making your mind up about colors for your living room, choose hues that you wear and in which you look best. Stay away from trendy hues. Copy a trick designers like to use: repeat colors. For example, you might use a wonderful fabric on the sofa, then pick up one of the colors in its pattern for the window treatments or chair cushions. Accent solid-color sofas and love seats with vibrant throw pillows. If you're choosing white for the walls, select the paint

everyday clutter, it will be difficult to maintain the "less is more" philosophy of the minimalist contemporary style. You can try it, but it will never look the way you want. On the other hand, an informal country room will allow you to add rustic trunks and ruffled baskets that can contain the clutter and are in keeping with the homespun style.

In houses with a family room, the living room may take on a full-time formal look. Keep in mind that formal doesn't mean stuffy and uncomfortable. You might go with richer woods and colors or more delicate patterns, such as small roses or stripes, but the upholstered seating should be inviting and the other furnishings usable. You want to create an enjoyable space for conversation that makes guests and family members feel relaxed.

shade carefully. Avoid stark white in traditional settings. Warm yellow-tinted versions lend a soft tranquil feeling to rooms. Cool whites, those with blue tints, work better in contemporary settings.

Think twice about using light solid colors on the furniture in busy living rooms. An all-white sofa will look great the day it arrives, but not for long if kids, guests, and you use it everyday.

FOCAL POINT

"Every room benefits from a focal point. When you walk into a room, your eye bounces from place to place until it finds somewhere to rest—if nothing stands out, it keeps bouncing," says Dale Bruss, director of training and education for Decorating Den Interiors. "If you find that you feel a little uncomfortable in a room and you don't know why, the lack of a focal point might well be the reason. Accenting or creating one is the designer's job."

The focal point in many living rooms is the fireplace. If there is no fireplace, a large picture window can assume the role. However, a main area of focus can also be created with a dramatic piece of furniture, such as a bookcase or wall unit, a large coffee table, an eye-catching painting, or a sculpture.

FURNISHINGS

Give careful consideration to the furniture you choose for seating and storage. Always be practical. Choose pieces that can be easily moved around on special occasions when you may have to add chairs to accommodate guests or make

Above: *Rooms that are overly coordinated lack interest. A blend of new and old furniture—an antique bench with a new upholstered couch—gives this living room its eclectic appeal.*

room for the Christmas tree, for example. Seating should be comfortable and durable, especially when it takes daily use. Buy the best pieces you can afford. If you avoid trendy styles, good furniture will remain serviceable for many years. To judge the quality and construction of a piece, see Chapter Seven, "Selecting Furniture," on page 118. If you have a family room, you will probably reserve the living room for company or special occasions, so you may be able to get away with less expensive seating covered in fabric that is beautiful as well as durable.

Smart Tip about Living Rooms

You may not need new furniture for your living room—just a fresh perspective. Try rearranging the pieces. For instance, pull furniture away from the walls; create two or more conversation groups; or arrange some pieces, including sofas, on a diagonal to make a room seem wider. Also try paring down the amount of furnishings in the room. For example, two wing chairs can make a cozy setting, but three can be overkill.

Above: *Furniture placement is the tool used to define the different areas of this multipurpose living room. The home office is set perpendicular to the sofa and chair, which neatly divides the two sections both physically and visually.*

Avoid furniture suites. Just because a sofa, love seat, chair, and coffee table are grouped together in a showroom does not mean you have to buy them as a set. Furniture retailers create these groupings to sell products from the same line together, especially if you're unsure of your own design skills. But this kind of buying robs you of the fun and satisfaction of choosing furniture piece by piece. There's no reason a cherished antique or a family heirloom can't fit into your design, for example. Items like these add comfort and reflect your personality more than static sets. "Things that are too matching become very boring," says Sechrist. "Often, putting in an old piece makes the room much more interesting." You might reupholster an old chair in a floral fabric that coordinates with the new solid-color sofa or select a reproduction table in a similar style as the antiques in the room.

However, some old pieces may have to go when you're redecorating because they no longer suit the new design scheme you've created. "If it's a piece you're not crazy

about or one that clashes with your new design, even if it cost you a bundle at one time, out it goes. Try moving it to another room," suggests designer Cheryl Casey Ross, of Cross Interiors in Van Nuys, California.

When choosing furniture, keep an eye out for scale. Don't choose oversized furniture for a small living room, no matter how comfortable it is. Once you cram it into the space, in the only location it can possibly fit, you're stuck with it—in the same spot—for the duration. It's nice to rearrange a room occasionally and this will preclude that pleasure.

In living rooms that function also as family rooms, storage is a must for eliminating clutter. Select an entertainment center for the TV, VCR, and stereo. Try to find one that puts these devices behind closed doors when not in use. Add shelves to hold decorative accessories and books.

If your living room will double as a guest room, buy double-duty furnishings, such as a sofa bed or a love seat with a pullout bed. Some extra-large chairs also feature this option and are handy in smaller rooms. Another practical idea is to use an attractive trunk as a coffee or end table. That way, you can tuck sheets, blankets, and an alarm clock in the chest. Other options include storage ottomans or even a bench with a hinged top. Stay away from the large toy box you'll have to empty out every time your little one can't find the tiny figurine hidden at the bottom.

DEFINING SPACE

"Furniture should be arranged conducive to how it will be used," says Barbara Schlattman. "So if an area is going to be used for conversation, create a U-shape or box shape with the seating." This way people can face each other when they speak.

Designers also keep furniture away from the walls whenever possible. Float some pieces and create a cluster. In a large living room, create several groupings: one in a square configuration for conversation, another around the TV area, and a quiet corner for one or two people to enjoy a book. For easy passage around or through furniture clusters, leave a minimum of 28 inches clearance. For help with your furniture plan refer to Chapter One, "Analyze and Visualize," on page 12, and the furniture templates in the Appendix, on page 236.

When the living room plays more than one role, decorative screens can help divide separate areas and close off what you don't want to be seen, such as paperwork or clutter in a home office. Also, look for furniture that can house an entire office-worth of computer equipment or a media center behind doors. Use a different area rug to define separate spaces or wall-to-wall carpeting with contrasting carpet borders. Wallcoverings and wall colors can change throughout the space, but keep the change subtle to avoid creating visual chaos.

LIGHTING

Concentrate on general lighting, in addition to task and mood lighting. Ceiling fixtures or recessed canisters with dimmers are good for providing ambient light.

Right (top and bottom): *The décor of two rooms that flow into each other, such as this living room and dining room, should be coordinated. Here, a rich red color on the walls and upholstery, as well as matching curtains, unify the adjacent rooms; area rugs and furniture placement, however, are used to differentiate each space.*

The dimmers allow you to adjust light levels to create mood. If you will read, watch TV, do paperwork, or perform some other activity, you'll have to provide specific task lighting. In general, floor lamps that are 40 to 49 inches from the floor to the bottom of the shade provide generous light spread. Table lamps with shades are ideal because they direct light upward and downward with little glare. For reading, the bottom of the shade should be just below eye level. Each smaller area within the living room must have its own lighting dictated by activity. Lights might be dimmed when entertaining on a winter night as the fireplace is roaring. (See Chapter Three, "Light by Design," on page 44, for more information.)

FAMILY ROOMS

The family room is often the home's real *living* room and perhaps the busiest room in the house. This space often has to pack in a lot—from TV viewing to play. Many considerations for living rooms and family rooms are the same, so see the section on "Living Rooms," above, for more information.

STYLE AND COLOR

Because this room is going to get a workout, select patterns, colors, and materials that are durable and will still look good over time. The family room is the place to be a little more personal, so display family photos or collections. There's no need to be formal. Some designers refer to the sought-after family room look as "casual elegance."

Special consideration should be given to great rooms—family rooms and kitchens contained in one open space. Coordinate them, but create visual separation, too. This can be achieved by arranging the family-room furniture to face away from the kitchen or by alternating materials. Use ceramic tile on the kitchen floors and hardwood in the family room, or use hardwood throughout the space, and cluster family-room furniture around area rugs.

When planning the two spaces, remember that the color and style of the kitchen cabinets should be similar or identical to cabinetry in the family room. High-gloss lacquer cabinets in the kitchen will look out of place with a colonial pine entertainment center nearby. Some custom cabinetmakers will design bookshelves, computer desks, and entertainment centers to match kitchen cabinets for a fully coordinated look, and even some semi-custom or standard cabinet lines feature coordinated pieces. (See Chapter Nine, "Designing Kitchens," on page 160.)

The family room is the place to let your personality shine, though. Showcase a doll collection or a series of your favorite artist's prints. Frame some of your kids' artwork, or display your own handiwork by hanging a quilt on the wall.

Left: *Overstuffed upholstered pieces, throw pillows in quilt patterns, and painted wood cabinetry contribute to the homey, relaxed atmosphere of this spacious family room. The large coffee table provides a place within everyone's reach for drinks and snacks, craft projects, or game boards.*

Left: *Although stylish, this family room on an enclosed porch also incorporates practical features: Sisal rugs are wear-resistant floor coverings that don't show much dirt; ottomans can do double duty as tables or extra seating for guests.*

won't be uptight about having the kids use it," says Melinda Sechrist.

Select some lightweight pieces of furniture that can be easily moved—when suddenly more seating is needed around the television or you want to create mingling room when entertaining.

If the family room doubles as a playroom for kids, storage is essential. Select smaller bins that kids can handle rather than one large toy box that swallows up small items. Children are more likely to help pick up if it doesn't seem like an overwhelming task. A small bookshelf with clear bins to hold toys, baskets for stuffed animals, and shelves for games is a good idea.

FOCAL POINT

The focal point of a family room might be a fireplace, an entertainment center, or a large view of the great outdoors. With all the different activities that take place here and all the furnishings that are required, it's important to have a focal point to anchor the room.

FURNISHINGS

Your shopping list might include love seat, sofa, entertainment center, desk for computer, file cabinet, toy chest, game table, and so forth. Today's family rooms often include a snack center with a mini-refrigerator and sink. The furnishings in your family room depend on how you're going to be using the space.

Designers often advise their clients to select the best quality furnishings they can afford. Don't go for the least expensive sofa because you think, "the kids will ruin it anyway." Sturdy construction can always be reupholstered. Stay away from solid light colors that will show every bit of dirt. Use patterns which hide the wear. "If you want to have a relaxed room, you need to create a comfortable place, where you

LIGHTING

Every activity that takes place in the family room has special lighting requirements, so start by making a list of every activity that will take place in the room. A reading chair requires intense task lighting. Plan moderate task lighting over a game table. For the TV and computer, use low general lighting that doesn't create glare. Include bright supple-

Smart Tip about Family Rooms

Probably the most common activity that takes place in your family room is TV viewing. To make your "home theater" experience ideal, select window treatments that open and close easily and can block out glare-causing sunlight. Leave a distance that is three times the size of the TV screen between the screen and opposite seating for optimal viewing.

mentary lights for extra-fine detail tasks, such as crocheting or needlework. Follow the advice offered for living rooms, and consult Chapter Three, "Light by Design," on page 44.

DINING ROOMS

Although today's fast-paced lifestyles often mean quick and easy meals, the dining room should be a place where people can sit down, relax, and enjoy a leisurely meal. If you use your dining room on a daily basis, you'll have to be practical and play it safe. But if you serve meals there only a handful of times during the year, you can be a little more daring.

STYLE AND COLOR

The dining room often opens to the living room, kitchen, or foyer, so the style and colors should coordinate with those spaces. The room can take on a more formal look if the family eats primarily in the kitchen. In fact, most interior designers and homeowners like to create a show-stopping dining room for entertaining and special occasions.

Dining rooms look great with a wonderful wallpaper that includes a color found on the adjoining room's walls. Stay away from overbearing patterns. Soft florals and stripes are good choices in traditional dining rooms, while faux finishes and textured looks can perfectly complement contemporary or transitional décors. Wallpaper borders, used with an all-over wallcovering or alone, are also an option that you can use to introduce another pattern into the room.

Keep walls all the same color or wallpaper pattern for continuity. On the

Right: *Forest green is a dramatic but elegant choice for this formal dining room. The gilded mirror above the sideboard reflects light from the chandelier and candles, keeping the room from seeming too dark.*

ceiling, use a bright white paint. If you're painting the walls a light neutral hue, however, why not add color to the ceiling? Pick up the burgundy or colonial blue on the upholstered chairs as an accent and for a formal touch, for instance. Or for drama, paint the walls a deep color and accent them with trimwork.

THE FOCAL POINT

The focal point of a dining room is often the table itself or an interesting hutch, depending on the placement of the furniture and the orientation of the doorway. Add a centerpiece to the table for visual appeal. Anything from a vase of flowers to a seasonal display or dramatic sculpture will do it.

A large window, painting, or mirror can also become a focal point. If a hutch is too large for your room, replace it with a buffet topped with a colorful painting or enlarged photograph from your last vacation. This, too, becomes a focal point.

FURNISHINGS

"How many will be in the room? How will it be used? If it's small, do you really need anything in the room other than table and chairs?" asks designer Barbara Schlattman. Space can be tight in a dining room, so select as big a table as you can comfortably fit. Leave a minimum of 32 to 36 inches between the table and the wall so that you can move easily out of the chair. The floor covering is especially important in a dining room where chairs are moved in and out and the table might be expanded to accommodate more people. Choose a floor covering that will allow you and your guests to move the chairs easily. If you use an area rug, a popular choice in dining rooms, make sure it will fit under the table when it's expanded to maximum size.

Most dining-room furniture is sold in sets. A set immediately gives you a coordinated look, but it isn't your only option. "It's much more interesting to buy the pieces separately. The chairs don't have to match the table, and the hutch doesn't have to match the table, either," say Barbara Schlattman. "Styles can mix—a traditional chair with a sleek table—or work with different woods."

A china closet is practical and aesthetically appealing. But rather than displaying your crystal and dinnerware, showcase objects that reveal a little of your personality. Or select a buffet, and use the wall space to group a collection of plates.

Above (top and bottom): *If you use the dining room for more than just special occasions and dinner parties, consider creating a more informal atmosphere. A cheerful yellow-and-blue color scheme suits this country-style dining room, and the mixed collection of chairs, unified by the light blue color, emphasizes this room's casual nature. Cupboards are handy for holding china.*

Smart Tip about Dining Rooms

Change the look of your dining room by slipcovering chairs. Short-skirted slipcovers give a more informal appearance; fabrics in graphic patterns, such as checks or floral prints, complement this style of slipcover best. Long-skirted covers are elegant additions to a formal dining room, particularly in solid color or tone-on-tone fabrics. Ties, buttons, or trim can add personality.

LIGHTING

A chandelier or hanging fixture should hang above the center of the table. This may not be the center of the room, though, after arranging a hutch or other furniture. In a dining room with an 8-foot ceiling, install the fixture so that its bottom is 27 to 36 inches above the table. Raise the fixture 3 inches for every additional foot of ceiling height. A crystal chandelier looks great in a formal, elegant dining room, while a ceiling light and fan combination can add charm to a well-dressed transitional space. Display cases should have interior lighting. Wall sconces add decorative appeal and can draw attention to a buffet or painting. Make sure lighting is sufficient for instances when the dining-room table doubles as workspace. (See Chapter Three, "Light by Design," on page 44.)

KITCHENS

The kitchen represents a real design challenge. Large appliances, plenty of storage, work space, and possibly a casual eating area must come together in harmony. And in the kitchen, efficient function is crucial. "If it doesn't function, it doesn't matter how good it looks," notes Lori Jo Krengel, CKD, CBD, of Kitchens By Krengel in St. Paul, Minnesota. (See Chapter Nine, "Designing Kitchens," on page 160.)

STYLE AND COLOR

You want the kitchen to coordinate with the rest of your rooms, but since it's essentially a work space, you've got some leeway here. If the kitchen is self-contained, meaning that it's not open to another room such as the family room, then it can comfortably depart from the main style of the house. There's nothing wrong with a relatively high-tech kitchen in a traditional-style home, as long as it doesn't clash outright with the integrity of the house. You might, for example, use white cabinetry here and another type

Above: *An intricate, multicolored stenciled floor accentuates this kitchen's island, turning it into a focal point.*

Left: *Because the kitchen opens into the dining room, both areas share an earth-tone color scheme. The natural wood finish and arched backs of the island's stools echo the shape of the chairs in the dining room, providing continuity between the two spaces.*

elsewhere. But the door style might closely resemble that of the hutch in the dining room. Your accessories can also bring a taste of your main décor into the kitchen. For instance, if you are displaying a blue-and-white china collection in the family room, bring some pieces into the kitchen.

Cabinets are the dominant design element in the kitchen. If you're not sure what you want, play it safe with a traditional raised-panel door. That type of door style can take on a variety of looks, from contemporary to country, depending on the surroundings.

Light cabinet colors are best in small kitchens. If your heart is set on a dark wood stain,

Above: *Frameless cabinetry gives this kitchen a contemporary edge. The salmon and gray colors of the variegated tile floor play up the cool tones of the cabinetry and marble countertop.*

Left: *Mixing materials is a hallmark of the contemporary style. Here, rustic chairs with woven seats are paired with a stainless steel-edged pedestal table.*

brighten up the space with a light countertop and backsplash, white or almond appliances, and ample lighting—both natural and artificial.

If you want a colorful kitchen, approach it as you would any other room: Get swatches and material samples from the manufacturers. Some terrific spots to add decorative color in the kitchen are a tiled backsplash or a ceramic tile floor, a solid-surfacing countertop inlaid with a stripe or custom pattern, or even a laminate floor that features a border. Mix countertop colors and materials. For example, use butcher block or granite on the work island and solid-surfacing material elsewhere. Cabinetry can be stained in colors, such as shades of red or blue. A cast-iron sink in a vibrant blue or green always looks dramatic or, if you're more daring, there are even ranges available in bright colors, such as royal blue and red. But you may want to play it safe with neutral colors on permanent fixtures in general.

Smart Tip about Kitchens

Don't choose trendy cabinetry for the kitchen—it can quickly look dated. Instead, add bold decorative touches with those things that are easy to change—novelty hardware, for instance. Backsplashes, countertops, sinks, and wallcoverings are also good choices. Replacing these items may require a little more effort, but the job can definitely be done without tremendous fuss.

FOCAL POINT

Cabinetry is the backdrop of a kitchen, but the focal point is often the window or the area around the range. Many designers like to dress this space up with a hand-painted mural or other interesting ceramic tiles. Sleek, shiny metal range hoods also help to emphasize this area.

In a great room setup, where kitchen and family room become one, a fireplace might become the focal point. That's fine, but you'll also want to create some sort of separation between the spaces. An island or peninsula often doubles as a buffer.

FURNISHINGS

More and more kitchen designers are specifying freestanding furniture for their clients' kitchens. A hutch will provide sought-after storage space for dinnerware, glasses, or even pantry items. Glass-fronted cabinetry looks great, but the storage space inside needs to be neat and orderly.

Granite- and marble-top tables can act as a movable center island ideal for working with dough. Select a table and chairs that fit the style of the kitchen. Find interesting stools for an island that offers a casual eating area.

LIGHTING

Professional designers always try to include as much natural light in a kitchen plan as possible. Task lighting, often under wall cabinets or above the island, is a must—although it's often tempting to eliminate the added expense. There also must be a light over the sink and some type of general lighting. Some designers and homeowners prefer the look of decorative hanging fixtures to all recessed lighting. You might also want to consider lighting inside cabinetry. Because of all the different tasks performed in a kitchen, devising a light plan for this room can become complex, so consult Chapter Three, "Light by Design," on page 44, for specific guidance.

BEDROOMS

This is your getaway space, so design it to please only yourself. Invest in a luxury touch here and there—beautiful bed linens or a four-poster bed, for example. In a busy world, everyone needs a pleasant day's-end retreat.

Clockwise (from top left): *Twin beds work best for guest rooms because they can be separated or pushed together. Piles of bow-tied and trimmed pillows make a bed more inviting. A four-poster bed with patriotic bed linens is the unmistakable focal point of this attic retreat. A mix of materials—antiqued metal, upholstery, and wood—are combined in a romantic master bedroom.*

STYLE AND COLOR

The master bedroom generally conforms to the style chosen for the main rooms of the house. If possible, try not to allow the bedroom to become a multipurpose room. Don't give in to the idea that one corner could house a mini-office space perfectly—taking "work" into the bedroom is not a restful concept. If the master bedroom is shared, decide together whether or not to include a TV or stereo. To maintain a restful look in the room, choose cabinetry that conceals this equipment.

You can draw your color scheme from the palette you've chosen for one of the other spaces in the house, or you can pick favorite colors or those that look well on one or both of you. If you're a morning person and have the time to luxuriate in the bedroom until later, consider warm, invigorating colors. If you want your evening retreat to soothe away the cares of the day, pick from the cooler hues.

FOCAL POINT

The bed is usually the focal point of a bedroom, so dress it up with attractive bedding, including

Left: Chairs or benches, such as the cush-ioned one at the end of this sleigh bed, offer a handy spot to sit when dressing. A large basket is useful in bedrooms with little stor-age; it can neatly hold nighttime reading materials or extra blankets.

and getting dressed at the same time. If space permits, separate storage for each one should be included: dresser and bureau, two closets, and twin night stands. A decorative screen can provide an interesting backdrop that will also create a small dressing area. A full-length mirror, whether freestanding or mounted on closet doors, is another important element.

If there's room, also include a comfort-able chair along with a small table and a lamp. This quiet spot is great for read-ing, relaxing, or enjoying evening tea or morning coffee in the privacy of your retreat. Designers seldom purchase bed-room furniture in complete sets. Buy interesting individual pieces instead. Matched suites are passé.

Window treatments should be room-darkening to ensure you're not awakened at first light: If you install lightweight curtains, use shades or blinds underneath for controlling light. For privacy, install two-way shades or half-curtains.

comfortable throw pillows. Often the headboard or space above it catches the eye as well. An ornate headboard will serve as a focal point, as will a canopy suspended from the ceiling and arranged with coordinating fabrics. A nicely framed painting or print—or perhaps a coordinating pair or groupings—over the bed can also look attractive.

A low dresser leaves the space above it as a possible focal point. Consider an ornately framed mirror, a series of interestingly shaped mirrors, or a mirror flanked by other framed prints or a collection of items such as straw hats.

FURNISHINGS

There are some practical aspects to be addressed in a mas-ter bedroom, in which two people are often waking up

Smart Tip about Bedrooms

Whites, neutrals, or pale colors—blues, greens, or pinks—create a restful ambiance in the bedroom, making sleeping easier. Cheery colors, such as yellow, work for those who like rising with the sun (or those who need help waking up). All-over wallpaper patterns, particularly large-scale ones, can sometimes make a bedroom feel too enclosed, so use bold patterns sparingly.

LIGHTING

On each nightstand or above the bed there should be separate reading lamps for each party. For ambient lighting, an overhead light fixture is more decorative than recessed lamps. It should hang centrally. Consider an overhead ceiling fan/light combination, an asset on warm nights. Be sure to include proper task lights for applying makeup or other grooming habits. (See Chapter Three, "Light by Design," on page 44, for more guidance.)

CHILDREN'S ROOMS

A good designer will interview both the child and the parents when designing a kid's room. From the child the designer will get personal preferences, and from the parents, he or she will hope to get an idea of how the room

must function. "Too often, people focus on the look of the room, and function is an afterthought," says Michele Rohrer, Allied ASID, of Michelle's Interiors, in Grayslake, Illinois. "In a child's room, it's crucial to write down all of the functions of the room."

An older child uses it for doing homework, playing games, entertaining, and reading, in addition to sleeping. The room becomes the spot where friends come over to play. A baby's room will probably be the spot for diaper changing, lullaby singing, playing, and sleeping.

Above: *Fretwork and fish-scale shingles are the fanciful backdrops for this young girl's bedroom. Note how the swags with "mutton sleeve" panels coordinate with the bedspread and pillows.*

Left: *Because sleepovers are a part of childhood, bunk beds are a sensible choice in this boy's room. The mural and the operable toy train continue the room's Old West theme.*

STYLE AND COLOR

"When selecting a palette for a child's room, expect it to meet his or her needs for about 5 to 7 years." As children develop, aquire more interests, and make friends, they change—along with their favorite colors and decorating motifs. "A 6-year-old girl will not enjoy the same room or color scheme past the age of 12, nor can an infant room last past 6," notes Rohrer.

Themes are suitable for children of any age, although the approach may change. Select more juvenile characters and patterns for a 3-year-old's bedroom than you would a 9-year-old's—but both can still feature a jungle or train motif. As in all rooms, trendy colors and styles date it. Use them sparingly and on elements that are easy to change. "Good design is always good," says Rohrer, "If something is trendy, like daisies from the '60s, we won't do it on a large scale. We'll use daisies on a pillow maybe."

FURNISHINGS

Furnishings should be selected according to how the space will function. A full-size bed is more practical in rooms where friends use the bed for seating. Children need their own space and their things nearby, from toys to a favorite cap. These years will pass by so quickly. Most designers encourage their clients to give in to some of their kids' whims. A child's room should be fun and lively.

Trundle beds and bunk beds are often used in kids' rooms to accommodate sleepovers. Flooring should be durable and comfortable. (See Chapter Four, "Facts about Flooring," on page 62.) Area rugs are easier to remove for dry-cleaning, but they require using a nonskid mat underneath. School-

Smart Tip about Children's Rooms

Keep safety in mind when planning a child's room. Make sure there are covers on electrical outlets, guard rails on high windows, sturdy screens in front of radiators, or gates blocking any steps. Other suggestions include safety hinges for chests and nonskid backing for rugs.

Clockwise (from left): *This room can be easily updated as the baby grows: The wallpaper can be replaced, the cushions recovered, and the shades changed. Full-size game boards painted on a wood floor are a clever touch. A built-in window bench is more than just a place to read or relax—it also provides extra storage under the seat.*

age children need a desk or study area. Line a bookshelf with clear bins for easy-to-see storage. Under-bed storage keeps things out of view. Take advantage of closet space in small bedrooms by using built-in closet systems to maximize the space. "If a large closet exists, think about using it for clothing, and forego the dressers," says Rohrer. If the room is small, floor space can be used for other necessities.

LIGHTING

Combine general overhead lighting with task lighting: a reading lamp over the headboard, a desk lamp, and perhaps a night light. Avoid floor lamps, which can be easily knocked over. (See Chapter Three, "Light by Design," on page 44, for more information.)

BATHROOMS

Here, as in the kitchen, you can safely depart from the style of the rest of your house. It's a room, usually a small one, that does a big job, but there's a place for form as well as function in today's bath. (See Chapter Ten, "Designing Baths," on page 190.)

STYLE AND COLOR

The master bath and family bath are going to be used frequently, so it's especially important that you select a style and colors everyone likes. In a master bath, coordinate the colors with those used in the bedroom, or you might draw the scheme for a bath from the hall. A powder room is the place to be more daring, but keep the basics of color theory in mind. "Look at the balance. You don't want a red, green, and purple bath. You have to follow the elements and principals of design, otherwise it will look like a hodgepodge," says designer Lori Jo Krengel.

In the bath, a neutral scheme can change with your whim simply by replacing the accessories. Shower curtains, rugs, towels, and even some fixtures are relatively easy and inexpensive to change. Small items such as soap can inject color.

Clockwise (from below): *White woodwork paired with lively teal walls is a refreshing combination for this master bathroom; the wall-long vanity, with a pair of lavatories, offers plenty of storage. Tubs, such as this oval bath enclosed in beadboard and trim, are often the focal point of the bathroom. Partitioning the toilet from the tub and lavatory makes the bathroom—particularly a shared one—more efficient.*

FOCAL POINT

"There's not necessarily a focal point in a bathroom," says Krengel. "You want an overall feel." You have to decide what that will be.

You can, however, create a focal point at the vanity or the tub. A clutter-free new countertop adorned with a decorative accent piece (from a basket of bathing goodies to a vase with fresh flowers) and backed with a striking yet practical mirrored medicine cabinet can grab attention. The same is true for a tub set in a custom-designed surround. Effective lighting above the tub or on the sides of the vanity can augment drama as well.

FURNISHINGS

There are certain elements that a full bath must include: toilet, tub or shower, lavatory, and storage. Once you make your basic selections, start thinking about how you want to decorate. Permanent fixtures, except storage, should all be the same color for continuity. Add contrast with tile, paint, or patterned wallcoverings.

Storage is essential in a bathroom. If there is room, a vanity is useful and attractive. If you plan to install a pedestal sink, you'll have to find storage elsewhere. Many designers like to add freestanding pieces of furniture for extra drawer and cabinet space. This option is a practical one because it's easy to change. However, make sure wooden pieces are protected against moisture with a sealant. Take advantage of wall space behind the toilet by adding a rack or cabinet there.

Smart Tip about Bathrooms

No matter how big or small the room, details will pull the style together. Some of the best details you can include are the smallest—drawer pulls from an antique store, or shells in a glass jar or just left on the countertop. Add period flavor with crown molding, or dress up contemporary fixtures with polished stone fittings.

LIGHTING

Minimally, in a bathroom that is less than 100 square feet, one fixture is sufficient. Add another fixture for each additional 50 square feet. However, you should also plan task lighting for grooming in the sink area. You might also consider adding a light in the shower ceiling or above the tub, but make sure it is one specifically designed for a damp location and conforming to local building codes.

FINDING PROFESSIONAL HELP

If you have a design dilemma that you just can't solve yourself, consulting a professional is a good idea. These Smart Steps can help you find the right person and communicate your needs effectively.

ONE: *Narrow down your needs.* To figure out the kind of professional you need, first get a clear picture of the level of help you require. Developing a color scheme, for example, requires less specific expertise than, say, space planning for a busy kitchen. If you don't like the colors a friend suggests, you simply don't have to use them. But you may not realize until it's too late that configuring kitchen layout is too complicated a task for you. So be honest in your assessment of your skills to avoid problems.

TWO: *Locate free help.* Begin with free sources, and see whether you find answers that way. Home and decorating centers often employ designers to get potential customers through tough design decisions. If the advice you receive will mean large financial expenditures, ask the designer, casually, how much experience he or she has. In a freebie situation, it's usually not appropriate to ask for references, except in cases where the designer is not just giving advice on a single issue but designing an entire room.

Clockwise (from left): *When pulling together a decorating scheme, such as the varied elements in this sun room, you may need advice to solve a problem. If you are buying fabric from a design center, you may be able to get free advice on mixing patterns and colors. However, you may need to hire a professional when laying out a lighting scheme or changing an architectural feature, such as a fireplace mantel.*

THREE: *Search the World Wide Web.* If you have a home computer with internet access, you should know that many professional design organizations have Web sites. Some offer trouble-shooting tips or free design advice via e-mail. Web sites change over time and not all offer the same kind of resources, but there are a few worth looking into:

❧ www.interiors.org, the American Society of Interior Designers;

❧ www.nkba.org, the National Kitchen and Bath Association

❧ www.nari.org, the National Association of the Remodeling Industry

❧ www.nahb.com, the National Association of Home Builders

❧ www.aia.org, the American Institute of Architects

❧ www.aibd.org, the American Institute of Building Design

Even if you don't get free advice on-line through these Web sites you can locate design professionals in your area who may be able to help you.

FOUR: *Find a professional interior designer.* If your project really can't go forward without sound professional advice and you've figured the cost into your budget, you can easily find someone to hire. If you've admired the work of a designer in someone else's home, simply ask for the reference. Sometimes retail establishments can recommend professionals they've worked with in the past. The good old Yellow Pages are always a source. Plus, if there are designers' showhouses in your area, go visit them. A showhouse is a good way to see the work of any local talent.

FIVE: *Look at portfolios, call references, check credentials.* Make sure the person you choose to work with is registered with a professional organization, such as the ones listed in Step Three. Ask to examine the designer's portfolio to get a feeling of whether his or her style will suit you, or whether he or she has a wide enough range to meet your needs. Most importantly, don't neglect the final step of checking references. Pretty pictures of someone's dream project are easy to come by, but the whole story of a redesign or remodeling can be a nightmare. Call references, and if possible, visit sites and ask plenty of questions.

DESIGNING KITCHENS

Today's kitchen is often the gathering place for family and friends, the spot where the kids do their homework and you pay the bills, plan the family vacation, design a craft project, or have a heart-to-heart with a friend over a cup of coffee.

This one room has become so important, in fact, that prospective buyers consider it a primary factor in selecting a home. If you are thinking about remodeling the kitchen for resale purposes, you are likely to get as much back as you invest—maybe more, depending on where you live. If you are like most people, however, your motivations are much more personal.

Wouldn't it be delightful to prepare a meal in a kitchen equipped with the latest appliances and configured to let you move effortlessly from refrigerator to sink to cooktop without tripping over the kids, the cat, or your own feet? Imagine opening a cabinet without having to strain, or empty the entire contents to find one small can. Picture a countertop that isn't a catchall for the mail, dry cleaning receipts, phone books, dog treats, antacids, and all the rest of cabinet and drawer spillover. Think about breakfast in a cheery nook or eating quiet dinners in a space that isn't dark, dingy, and cramped.

The place to start, then, is with how you want the kitchen to work—for you and every other member of your household. Function is the cornerstone of

Left: *With planning and forethought, you can rework the floor plan of an existing kitchen to make it function more efficiently.*

good kitchen design. A highly functional kitchen will not make you a master chef, but it will improve the quality of the time you spend in the kitchen, which some experts say can be as much as 70 percent of your waking hours. With this in mind, remember: Even the smallest remodeling job requires careful planning and forethought. You can greatly increase the efficiency of your kitchen by paying attention to the tiniest details and the smallest of spaces.

GETTING FOCUSED

Design professionals interview their clients at length at the beginning of a project. If you will be your own designer, do the same thing. Likewise, you may even want to videotape your family (and yourself) in the kitchen during typical meal preparation or any other kitchen-based activities. If your parties often spill into the kitchen, for instance, videotape the next party, and pay attention to how difficult or easy it is to interact with guests while you're cooking or serving. Is there enough room for opening the refrigerator door when someone passes behind you? Is there space on the countertop to set up a small, informal buffet or bar?

Note the different situations that typically interrupt or assist your work flow and traffic patterns. Is the aisle you use to reach the oven the same as the one used to walk from the back door into the house? Observe how many times you have to walk across the room for something.

If you consult with a professional, don't be put off by questions. Any good design-

er has to get to know the habits, likes, and dislikes of the people who will live with the finished project. He or she wants to understand your basic requirements as well as your wildest dreams for the new kitchen.

A designer will also sketch the existing space to get an idea of what works and what doesn't. This rough drawing may include any adjacent areas that might be considered for expansion, such as a pantry or part of a hallway.

Once again, if you act as your own designer, do the same thing. Talk to everyone in the household. Ask what they think needs improvement, as well as any aspects of the space as it exists that they'd prefer to retain.

Right: *This example demonstrates that a kitchen can be highly organized and functional while retaining an inviting, personal appearance. Warm wood tones and lots of natural light are two of its key ingredients.*

For the best results, approach the project in the same calm, analytical manner as a professional, one who understands design and can be objective about what has to happen. Here's how to begin:

ONE: *Create a design notebook.* It's important to keep all your ideas and records in one place. Buy a loose-leaf binder, and use it to organize everything from magazine clippings to photos of the old kitchen (extremely important when you choose to resell the house); wish lists; notes and interviews with design professionals and family members; contracts; business cards; sample plans; shopping lists; color charts; tile, fabric, and wallpaper samples; and anything else related to the project. The file should be comprehensive yet not too clumsy to cart around to showrooms, stores, or home centers.

TWO: *Analyze the existing kitchen.* Decide what you really want to gain by remodeling. You might begin by asking the most obvious question: "What's wrong with the existing kitchen?" Maybe you and your partner enjoy cooking together, but the floor plan was designed to work for only one cook. Perhaps storage is inadequate or the appliances are old.

To be specific about your analysis, get out your notebook and record answers to questions such as, "Is the size of the family likely to grow or shrink in the near future?" If the kids are or will be in college soon, you might not need that large-capacity refrigerator. Likewise, if this is your first house and you expect to move up as your family size increases, it might be wise to refinish high-ticket items such as cabinets and hang onto older appliances that are still working, spending only a modest amount of money, time, and energy on cosmetic changes in the kitchen. Other questions to consider include:

Above: *In this kitchen, the designer situated the cooking area on an outside wall. This arrangement permits easy venting for the range hood, without requiring lengthy ductwork.*

❦ How many members of the household really cook? Note other ways each one uses the kitchen.

❦ How convenient is it to work in the kitchen? Are people always bumping into each other? When cabinet or appliance doors are open, is the traffic pattern interrupted?

❦ Is there enough storage? If you keep kitchen- or cooking-related items in other areas of the house such as the garage, or even a bedroom, it's time to analyze how to increase the storage capacity in the kitchen.

❧ What is the condition of existing materials and appliances? How old are they? Are the appliances energy-efficient? Are the walls, floors, and countertops in good condition?

THREE: *Make a wish list.* Besides the basic elements, you may want some special features in your new kitchen—a ceramic glass-top range, modular refrigeration, interchangeable cooktop components, or a warming drawer. Perhaps an elegant slate or granite countertop or a gorgeous custom range hood has caught your eye.

Create a list of all the accouterments you would like to include, whether or not you think you can afford them. When you have a close-to-perfect plan, that's the time to look for areas to trim if your budget is tight. You might choose a countertop fabricated in an affordable stone lookalike and use the dollars saved for something you can't fake, such as an energy-efficient window over the sink or a tiled backsplash.

FOUR: *Sketch the old floor plan.* Just like a professional designer, draw an existing floor plan. Do a rough sketch first, then transfer your drawing to graph paper with grids marked at ¼-inch intervals. Draw it freehand or with a straightedge, but do it to a scale of ½ inch equal to one foot. This base plan, or "base map," as it is called, should record the layout of the space as it exists. Include measurements for everything, from the width of every door to how far the refrigerator protrudes into the room.

Start by taking measurements, beginning with the length and width of the room. Then from one corner, measure the location of windows, doors, and walls. Record the swing of each door. Note each dimension in feet and inches to the nearest ¼ inch.

Next draw the cabinetry and appliances, and indicate their height. Measure the position and centerline of the sink (showing how far the center of this fixture is from the wall),

Below left: *Make a rough freehand drawing of your existing kitchen, and record accurate measurements as you take them.*

Below right: *Transfer the information from your rough sketch onto a scaled drawing on ¼-inch graph paper. Draw it to a scale of a ½ inch equal to a foot.*

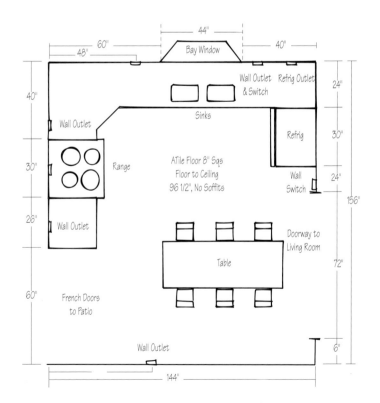

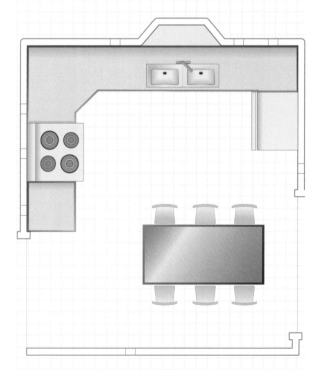

but don't forget to list its overall length and width. Also measure the height of the walls.

Include symbols for light fixtures, outlets, and heat registers on the floor plan as well. Note load-bearing walls, which cannot be moved without compromising structural integrity. If you are thinking about tearing out any wall and you don't know whether it is load-bearing, consult an architect or a structural engineer before you do anything.

It's a good idea to list your gripes about the old kitchen on the sketch. That way you can see at a glance what problem areas need to be changed.

Remember: This floor plan is only a guide. It doesn't have to be professionally drawn, only accurate in its rendition and measurements of the current space.

CREATING FUNCTIONAL SPACE

Whether you are reconfiguring existing space or adding on, the floor plan plays a large role in how well the room will function. And while a kitchen addition to an outside wall of the house offers the best possibilities for unencumbered floor space, it is the costliest option. One way to save money is to restrict your addition to a "bump-out" of 3 feet or less. This doesn't necessarily require a new foundation, and it limits the need for a new roof. Consult an architect or builder, first, to make sure the existing structure is sound and can carry the additional load. Remember to inquire about local zoning ordinances before proceeding with your plans.

However you choose to proceed, any kitchen of any size requires a thoughtful arrangement of all its elements to make it both highly functional and efficient.

THE WORK TRIANGLE

Almost everybody has heard of the kitchen's classic *work triangle*. Essentially, it is an area that puts the three major work centers—the range, refrigerator, and sink—at the three points of a triangle. The spatial relationship among these sites and how they relate to other areas in the kitchen is

Below: *This design of a work triangle demonstrates good distance limits between the three primary work centers— the range or cooktop, the refrigerator, and the sink.*

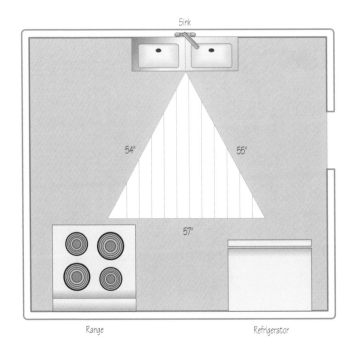

Sink

54"   55"

57"

Range   Refrigerator

what makes the room an efficient work space. The National Kitchen & Bath Association (NKBA) recommends there be at least one work triangle in a kitchen. In fact, today's busy families—and multipurpose kitchens—often call for two or more work triangles. With traditional roles at home changing, so are attitudes about cooking. Two-cook families are more common than ever, and food preparation and cooking have themselves become excuses for social events where even the guests actively participate.

In the classic work triangle, the distance between any pair of the three task centers is no longer than 9 feet and no less than 4 feet.

To conserve walking distance from point to point without sacrificing adequate counter space, the sum of all three lines of the triangle should be no greater than 27 feet and no less than 12 feet. For a large kitchen, plan two or more work triangles. Although pairs may extend inside one another, sharing one side or "leg" of the triangle for maximum performance, do not overlap the sink and range areas. Another approach is to design smaller triangles set within the larger one.

Because a goal of the work triangle is to keep normal kitchen traffic from interrupting the work flow, during your planning stage pay especially close attention to how everyone in the household comes and goes in the existing kitchen. You might even try this unusual but enlightening homespun experiment: Dust the floor with a thin coating of cornmeal; then go about your normal food preparation and cleanup. You'll be able to track your movements from cabinets to appliances to sink and the rest of the family's moves around you—or whoever does the cooking. Once you see where the kitchen becomes most crowded, you'll be able to make the necessary changes. (And don't forget to sweep up the cornmeal.) Sometimes that's as simple as relocating an appliance—particularly a small one—to a less busy area.

There is some debate today among professional kitchen designers concerning the traditional work triangle. Although most agree that it is still an important element, many see the triangular space evolving as cooking habits and lifestyles change. These designers feel that the more actual living done in the kitchen, the more expanded the basic triangle will have to become. And as kitchens grow larger—which appears to be the trend—they will embrace an increasing number of activities. This will result in the need for several autonomous triangles within the room. Whichever school of thought you believe, the bottom line still is and always will be: Design for your sake, not for the sake of design.

As you consider a new layout, check that traffic moves easily from one place to another in the kitchen and from the kitchen to other rooms in the house, as well as outdoors. It is important that through-traffic doesn't interfere with the work triangle. Otherwise, carrying a hot pot from the range to the sink could put you on a collision course with youngsters heading for the back door.

Right: *A kitchen that is configured along one wall requires the least amount of space. To maximize accessibility and allow for two people to use the kitchen at once, place the sink between the cooktop or range and refrigerator.*

Often you can correct a faulty traffic pattern simply by moving a door or removing a short section of wall. Another way to improve a kitchen's function is to experiment with basic layouts to see which suits your needs.

BASIC KITCHEN LAYOUTS

There are five basic kitchen layouts: one-wall, galley (corridor), U-shaped, L-shaped, and G-shaped. Each has its challenges and advantages.

One-Wall. This arrangement places all the equipment, sink, and cabinetry along one wall. Since you cannot create a triangle in a one-wall kitchen, maximize accessibility by placing the sink between the refrigerator and the range. Although a one-wall kitchen is more typical in a small

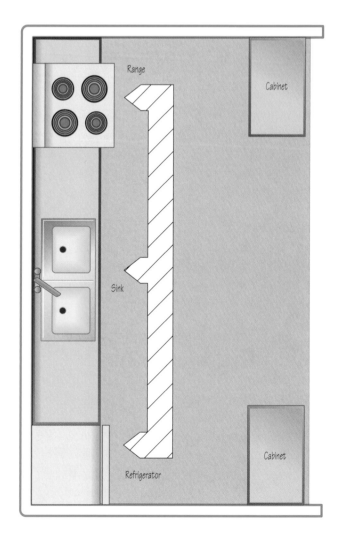

apartment, it may be found in a large, open-plan home. If you want to retain this arrangement but would like to close off the kitchen from other public areas of the house, install sliding doors or screens that can be opened or closed at will.

The Galley. Also known as the *corridor style,* this compact layout locates the appliances, sink, and cabinets on two parallel walls in order to create a small pass-through kitchen. It's easy to create an efficient work triangle in this setup, but this layout really caters to one cook. Allow a 48-inch-wide aisle after all fixtures are placed so that cabinets and appliance doors can be opened easily while someone walks through. If space is really tight, you could make the aisle 36 inches wide, but appliance doors may collide with each other if more than one is open at a time. Another tip: Avoid installing a doorway at both ends of the galley or corridor. That way, you can keep people from walking through the work triangle while the cook is busy.

To ease as many traffic problems as possible, place the refrigerator near the end of the room—away from the entrance into the kitchen. Another option is to install the primary refrigerator in the food preparation area.

The L-shape. This plan places the kitchen on two perpendicular walls. The L-shape usually consists of one long "leg" and a short one, and lends itself to an efficient work triangle without the problem of through traffic. If well designed, it is flexible enough for two cooks to work simultaneously without getting in each other's way.

Another advantage to this layout is the opportunity, if space allows, for incorporating an island into the floor plan. If you do, plan the clearances carefully. Walkways should be at least 36 inches wide. If the walkway is also a work aisle, increase

Top right: *Because it is typically narrow, a galley (or corridor-style) kitchen works best for one cook at a time. Although you should allow for a 48-inch-wide aisle, you can cut it down to 36 inches if space is really at a premium.*

Bottom right: *In an L-shaped kitchen, two intersecting walls are put to work. You can often fit a table or booth into the corner by placing it diagonally opposite the L.*

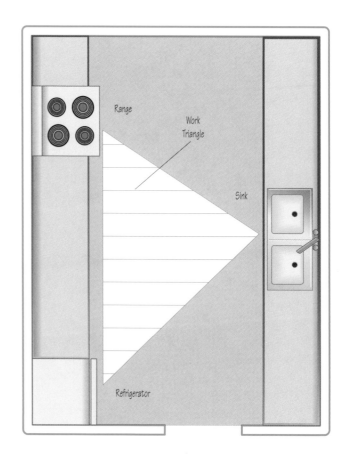

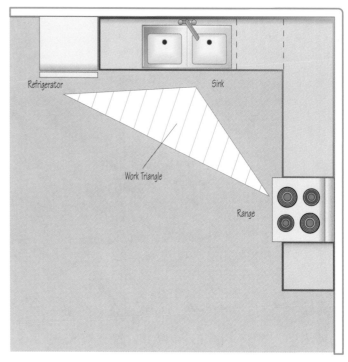

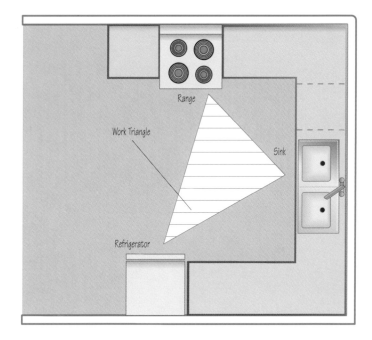

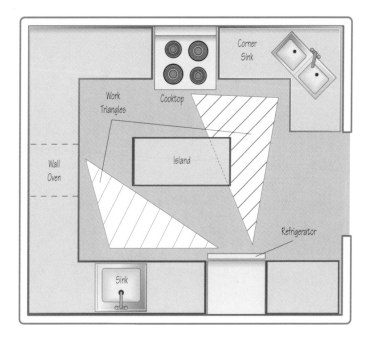

Above top: *A U-shaped design is, perhaps, the most efficient layout and provides the greatest amount of counter space between the sink and appliances.*

Above bottom: *Two cooks can easily maneuver around a G-shaped layout, which offers enough room for two work triangles. Both of them are typically anchored at the refrigerator.*

the clearance to 42 inches. A 36-inch clearance is fine for counter seating, unless traffic goes behind it. In that case, clearance should be 65 inches.

The U-shape. The U-shaped kitchen is the most efficient design. Cabinets, counters, and appliances are all arranged along three walls. The greatest benefit, perhaps, is the interrupted space for traffic flow.

A U-shaped layout incorporates a logical sequence of work centers with minimum distances between each. The sink is often located at the base of the U, with the refrigerator and range on the side walls opposite each other. The U shape takes a lot of space—at least 8 feet along the length and width of the kitchen. Corners may be a problem because they often create unusable space. However, consider angling cabinets into these otherwise "dead" areas. Upper cabinets with rolltop doors make roomy appliance garages, and bottom units fitted with carousel shelves or a Lazy Susan actually make storage more handy than standard units.

Smaller U-shaped kitchens can be dark because of the sheer mass of all that cabinetry. You can counter this with a generous-size window, skylights, or under-cabinet task lighting, or by keeping surfaces a light color.

The G-shape. This is a hybrid of the U-shape with a shorter, fourth leg added in the form of a peninsula. While the G-shaped layout is great for more than person working in the kitchen, it can feel confining.

This layout may feature a pair of sinks and a separate cooktop, as well as an oven range. One work triangle usually incorporates a sink, the cooktop, and the refrigerator, while the other houses the second sink, the oven, and, overlapping the first triangle, the refrigerator. An island is usually placed in the corner of a G-shaped layout, within easy reaching distance to both work triangles.

The G-shaped kitchen often accommodates specialty appliances, such as warming drawers, modular refrigeration, or a built-in grill, to allow as much independence between the two work areas as possible.

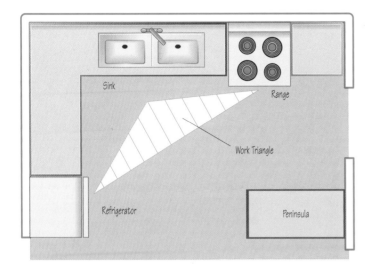

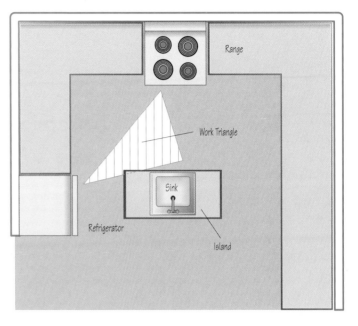

ISLANDS AND PENINSULAS

In a roomy layout, you can shorten the distance between the three key work areas by adding an island or peninsula. A peninsula base and ceiling-hung cabinets offer convenient storage for tableware and linens. In an L- or U-shaped kitchen, an island can add visual interest by breaking up the space without confining it. It also provides an extra work surface, a spot for snacks or informal meals, as well as a place to set up a buffet.

An island or peninsula can also serve as an excellent location for a cooktop or second sink, if plumbing and ventilation hookups permit. It could also prove the ideal spot for a wine rack or cooler, a wet bar, warming drawers, modular refrigerator units, or additional general storage. For maximum efficiency, be sure the design provides a clearance of 48 inches from the island or peninsula to the wall cabinets.

EATING AREAS

There are specific minimum clearances you'll need to accommodate a table and chairs, which you mustn't forget to include in your design. Plan enough floor space for all the furniture and for people to sit down, get up, and walk around it comfortably, without interfering with the work traffic.

Seating Allowances. If you feel as if you're a contortionist every time you get into or out of a chair at the table, you haven't done your space-planning homework. When

Above left: *A peninsula brings counter space and storage conveniently close without interfering with the work triangle. It works well with an L-shaped layout.*

Above right: *Depending on the location of utility lines and venting possibilities, either the sink or cooktop can be installed into a kitchen island.*

Below: *When planning your floor space, consider the minimum clearances needed for table and chairs. For a person to push back a chair and rise comfortably, plan to have 32 to 36 inches of space between the wall and the table's edge.*

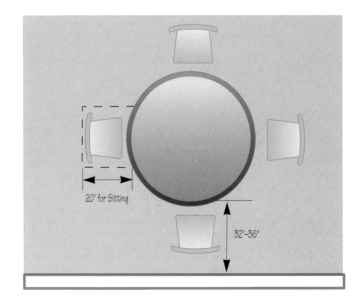

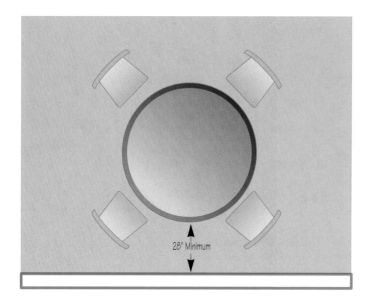

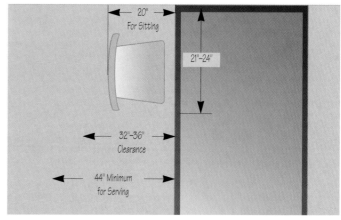

Left: *If you are working with a cramped space, you can reduce the clearance between the wall and the table to 28 inches, but you have to arrange the chairs at an angle to the wall.*

Right top: *Each person at a table will require 21 to 24 inches of table space. You should also consider serving space, which should be a minimum of 44 inches.*

Right bottom: *Booth seating is an option in kitchens that don't have enough space for a table. Plan on leaving 15 inches of knee space under the booth's table, as well as 12 inches between the table and the seat.*

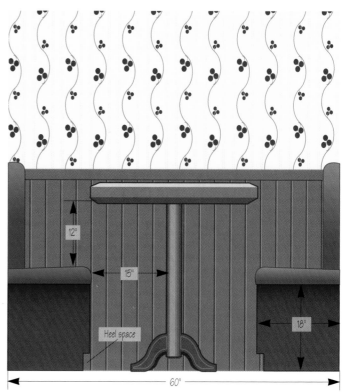

you redesign, follow the guidelines here as you plan the layout and you won't go wrong.

Even average-size people need a surprising amount of space to make a dining area accessible. Allow 12 to 15 square feet per person. That means a family of four will require at least 48 square feet in an eat-in kitchen. Assume that a 36-inch-diameter round table can seat four adults; a 48-inch-diameter one will accommodate six. Calculate 21 to 24 inches of table space per person for a square or rectangular table.

When planning space for your kitchen table, pay attention to the distance between it and the walls or cabinets. A seated adult occupies a depth of about 20 inches from the edge of the table but will need 12 to 16 additional inches of space to push back the chair and rise. This means you have to plan on 32 to 36 inches of clearance between the wall and the edge of the table. You can get away with a minimum of 28 inches if chairs are angled to the wall. However, plan on a 44-inch clearance to allow enough room on any serving side of any table, whatever its shape.

If you don't have enough room for a table, a booth (or a table with banquette) or bench seating may be the answer. A kitchen alcove or bay window offers a natural spot for either seating arrangement, or you can back it against an island, peninsula, or wall. Plan 21 inches of table space for each person with at least 15 inches of knee space underneath. This means that a family of four minimally needs a 42-inch-long table that measures 30 inches across. Because you slide in and out of a booth, the table may overhang the benches by 3 or 4 inches. Total floor space required for a four-person booth, therefore, measures only 5 feet across, compared with a minimum requirement of about 9 feet for a freestanding table with chairs.

Another popular option for in-kitchen dining is to let the island or peninsula serve double duty as an eating bar. Remember, each adult requires at least 21 inches of table space so that means a 63-inch-long counter (a typical size) will accommodate three stools at most.

Seating depends on counter height. A 28- to 32-inch-high counter requires 18-inch-high chairs with 20 inches of knee space under the bar. If you make the island or peninsula the same height as the rest of the kitchen countertops (36 inches being the standard), you'll be able to accommodate 24-inch-high stools and 14 inches of knee space. Go up to bar height (42 to 45 inches), and you'll need 30-inch-high stools with footrests, also with 14 inches of knee space.

One more aspect of kitchen design to consider is storage—an element that needs to blend function with style. Once

Below: *A kitchen peninsula can be an excellent solution to creating an informal eating area out of the way of work traffic. The seating depends on the height of the counter.*

you conclude how you want your new kitchen space to function, you're in a position to tackle the next perplexing yet all-important challenge: selecting the proper cabinetry.

CABINETRY & STORAGE

Who can't relate to this scenario: You turn the oven on to preheat it, but wait, did you take out the large roasting pan first? How about the lasagna dish, muffin tins, pizza stone, and cookie sheets that are in there, too? Now where can you put everything that was in the oven while the casserole is baking and the countertop is laden with the rest of tonight's dinner ingredients?

The oven, it seems, has become the catchall for the big, awkward stuff that you can't fit into kitchen cabinets but is just too darn ugly to leave out. Besides, the countertop is where you keep the toaster oven, food processor, coffeemaker, canisters, hand mixer, portable TV, notepad, coupon file, bills, hand lotion, car keys, and your vitamins! Wouldn't life be grand if there was a place for everything and everything was in its place? Good cabinetry outfitted with an assortment of organizing options can help you there. It can make your kitchen more efficient and a whole lot neater while establishing a style, or "look," for the room. Keep in mind, however, that cabinetry will also consume about 40 percent of your remodeling budget, according to the NKBA. So before making any expensive decisions and, hopefully, no mistakes, investigate all of the various cabinetry options that are available to you.

CABINET CONSTRUCTION

Basically, cabinets are constructed in one of two ways: *framed* or *frameless.* Framed cabinets have a traditional look, with a full frame across the face of the cabinet box that may show between closed doors. This secures adjacent cabinets and strengthens wider cabinet boxes with a center rail. Hinges on framed cabinets may or may not be visible around doors and drawers when they are closed. The door's face may be ornamented with raised or recessed panels, trimmed or framed panels, or a framed-glass panel with or without muntins (the narrow vertical and horizontal strips of wood that divide panes of glass).

Above: *In a contemporary-style kitchen, an unframed door style and minimal decoration set the tone for the rest of the décor.*

Left: *Beautiful cabinetry will consume a sizable portion of your budget. But as this kitchen demonstrates, it goes a long way toward setting the style, as well as organizing your storage needs.*

Frameless cabinets—also known as European-style cabinets, although American manufacturers also make them—are built without a face frame and sport a clean, contemporary look. There's no trim or molding with this simple design. Close-fitting doors cover the entire front of the box, no ornamentation appears on the face of the doors, and hinges are typically hidden inside the cabinet box.

Choosing one type over another is generally a matter of taste, although framed units offer slightly less interior space. But the quality of construction is a factor that always should be taken into consideration. How do you judge it? Solid wood is too expensive for most of today's budgets, but it might be used on just the doors and frames. More typical is plywood box construction, which offers good structural support, and solid wood on the doors and frames. To save money, cabinetmakers sometimes use strong plywood for support elements, such as the box and frame, and medium-density fiberboard for other parts, such as doors and drawer fronts. In yet another alternative, good quality laminate cabinets can be made with high-quality, thick particle-board underneath the laminate finish.

There are other things to look for in cabinet construction. They include dovetail or mortise-and-tenon joinery and solidly mortised hinges. Also, make sure the interior of every cabinet is well finished, with adjustable shelves that are a minimum $5/8$ inch thick to prevent bowing.

Unless you have the time and skill to build the cabinets yourself, or can hire someone else to do it, you'll have to purchase them in one of four ways: *Knockdown* cabinetry (also known as RTA, ready to assemble) are shipped flat, sometimes, and unfinished because you put the pieces together. *Stock* cabinetry comes in standard sizes but limited styles and colors; they are often available on the spot or can be delivered quickly. Like stock, *semi-custom* cabinetry comes in standard styles, but they are manufactured to fit a homeowner's specific size and finish needs. *Custom* cabinetry is not limited in terms of style or size because it is built to the designer's specifications.

CABINET ACCESSORIES AND OPTIONS

Most people would agree that no matter how much storage space they have, they need even more. The problem often isn't the amount, it's the inaccessible placement and inefficient configuration of the storage space. One of the greatest benefits today's designers and manufacturers offer is fitted and accessorized interiors that maximize even the smallest nook and cranny inside cabinets and drawers. These accommodations not only expand the use of space but increase convenience and accessibility. Among them are:

Clockwise (left to right): *A compartmentalized appliance garage makes room for a coffeemaker and carafe. Slide-outs hold a large cookbook collection and odd items such as serving baskets. A small area can hold—and hide—a lot. This cabinet's counter flips up and the door opens to reveal storage for bottled water, drawer bins for potatoes and onions, and the garbage can. There's even a rack on the inside of the door for hanging awkward-sized cooking utensils.*

Appliance Garages. Appliance garages make use of dead space in a corner, but they can be installed anywhere in the vertical space between the wall-mounted cabinet and the countertop. A tambour (rolltop) door hides small appliances like a food processor or anything else you want within reach but hidden from view. This form of mini-cabinet can be equipped with an electrical outlet and can even be divided into separate sections to store more than one item. Reserve part of the appliance garage for cookbook storage, or outfit it with small drawers for little items or spices. Customize an appliance garage any way you like.

Lazy Susans and Carousel Shelves. These rotating shelves maximize dead corner storage and put items such as dishes or pots and pans within easy reach. A Lazy Susan rotates 360 degrees, so just spin it to find what you're looking for. Carousel shelves, which attach to two right-angled doors, rotate 270 degrees; open the doors and the shelves, which are actually attached to the doors, put any item within hand reach. Pivoting shelves are a variation on the carousel design and may or may not be door-mounted. In addition, units may be built into taller cabinets, creating a pantry that can store a lot in a small amount of space.

Fold-Down Mixer Shelf. This spring-loaded shelf swings up and out of a base cabinet for use, then folds down and back into the cabinet when the mixer is no longer needed, which reduces clutter by keeping the countertop clear of appliances.

Slide-Outs and Tilt-Outs. Installed in base cabinets, slide-out trays and racks store small appliances, linens, cans, or boxed items, while slide-out bins are good for holding onions, potatoes, grains, pet food,

or potting soil—even garbage or recycling containers.
A tilt-out tray is located in the often-wasted area just
below the lip of the countertop in front of the sink and
above base cabinet doors. It looks like a drawer but tilts
open to provide a neat nook for sponges and scouring
pads that look messy when left on the counter.

Built-in Pantry Units. These fold-out or slide-out units
can be fitted into narrow areas that might otherwise
remain wasted. Store dry or canned goods here. Fold-out
units have door-mounted shelves and an in-cabinet shelf
that pivots; slide-out units fit multiple shelves in a cabinet.

Above right: *Knife storage inside a wooden countertop is handy when
chopping and slicing vegetables.*

Bottom (left to right): *Small appliance parts and canisters are kept in
outfitted drawers so that the countertop remains clear. This compact
kitchen makes the most of its U-shaped arrangement of cabinetry. Pull-out
counters at strategic areas, such as near the microwave, make convenient
landing spots for hot dishes.*

In addition to these options, check out everything a cabinet manufacturer has to offer to make the most of a cabinet's storage capacity. Other items to look for include special racks for trays and cookie sheets; drawer inserts for organizing spices and utensils, watertight recycling bins, wine racks, fold-down recipe book rests, sliding pot racks, built-in canister drawers, and plate racks.

If you decide to make do with your existing cabinets, consider refitting the interiors with cabinet organizers. These plastic, plastic-coated wire, or enameled-steel racks and hangers are widely available at department stores and home centers.

Beware of the temptation to over-specialize your kitchen storage. Sizes and needs for certain items change, so be sure to allot at least 50 percent of your kitchen's storage to standard cabinets with one or more movable shelves.

THE DECORATIVE ROLE OF CABINETS

The look you create in your kitchen will be largely influenced by the cabinetry you select. Finding a style that suits you and how you will use your new kitchen is similar to shopping for furniture. In fact, don't be surprised to see many furniture details dressing up the cabinets on view in showrooms and home centers today.

Besides architectural elements such as fluted pilasters, corbels, moldings, and bull's-eye panels, look for details such as fretwork, rope motifs, gingerbread trim, balusters, composition ornamentation (it looks like carving), even footed cabinets that mimic separate furniture pieces. If your taste runs toward less fussy design, you'll also find handsome door and drawer styles that feature minimal decoration, if any. Woods and finishes are just as varied, and range from informal looks in birch, oak, ash, and maple to rich mahogany and cherry. Laminate finishes, though less popular than they were a decade ago, haven't completely disappeared from the marketplace,

but an array of colors has replaced the once-ubiquitous almond and white finishes.

COLOR

Color is coming on strong on wood cabinetry, too. Accents in one, two, or more hues are pairing with natural wood tones. White-painted cabinets take on a warmer glow with tinted shades of this always popular neutral. Special "vintage" finishes, such as translucent color glazes, continue to grow in popularity, as do distressed finishing techniques such as wire brushing and rubbed-through color that add both another dimension and the appeal of handcraftmanship, even on mass-produced items. Contemporary kitchens, which historically favor an all-white palette, are warming up with earthier neutral shades or less sterile off-whites.

If you're shy about using color on such a high-ticket item as cabinetry, try it as an accent on molding, door trim, or on the island cabinetry. Just as matched furniture suites have become passé in other rooms of the house, the same is true for the kitchen, where mixing several looks can add sophistication and visual interest.

HARDWARE

Another way to emphasize your kitchen's decorative style is with hardware. From exquisite reproductions in brass, pewter, wrought iron, or ceramic to handsome bronze, chrome, nickel, glass, steel, plastic, rubber, wood, or stone creations, a smorgasbord of shapes and designs is available. Some pieces are highly polished; others are matte-finished, smooth, or hammered. Some are abstract or geometrical; others are simple, elegant shapes. Whimsical designs take on the forms of animals or teapots, vegetables or flowers. Even just one or two great-looking door or drawer pulls can be showstoppers in a kitchen that may otherwise be devoid of much personality. Like mixing cabinet finishes, a combination of two hardware

Clockwise (from top left): *An exuberant tile backsplash ties the look together by repeating all of the colors of the kitchen's surfaces. Whimsical hardware adds a playful accent. Fresh, vibrant hues energize this kitchen and add lots of visual interest to a large expanse of wood cabinetry.*

styles—perhaps picked up from other materials in the room—makes a big design statement. As the famed architect Mies Van der Rohe once stated, "God is in the details," and the most perfect detail in your new kitchen may be the artistic hardware you select.

Besides looks, consider the function of a pull or knob. You have to be able to grip it easily and comfortably. If your fingers or hands get stiff easily, or if you have arthritis, select C- or U-shaped pulls. If you like a knob, try it out in the showroom to make sure it isn't slippery or awkward when you grab it. Knobs and pulls can be inexpensive if you can stick to unfinished ones that you can paint in an accent color

picked up from the tile or wallpaper. If you don't plan to buy new cabinets, changing the hardware on old ones can redefine their style. The right knob or pull can suggest any one of a number of vintage looks or decorative style from Colonial to Victorian to Arts and Crafts to Postmodern.

PLANNING YOUR STORAGE

Now that you know there are cabinets and accessories to make the most disorganized person's kitchen a model of neatness and efficiency, a thoughtful approach to planning storage for the new design is in order. The time to do this is before the architectural plans are on paper or the construction work has begun. Here are a few ideas on planning storage or to get you started.

Bottom (left to right): *Slide-outs installed in otherwise wasted space in base cabinets are outfitted to house spices next to the cooktop or with racks for linen towels.*

SMART STEPS

ONE: *Analyze your needs.* Make a detailed list of your shopping and cooking habits. How do you buy food? If you buy in bulk, how much of it has to be stored in the refrigerator? A lot of canned goods and boxed grains and pasta will need cabinet space. The NKBA conducted a study several years ago that revealed that most kitchens regularly store 18 cans of vegetables, 23 spices, and six boxes of cereal. How does yours compare? If you collect wines or bottled vinegars, they may require special storage in a cooled compartment in the room.

Think about your cooking and serving utensils. Where are you most likely to use them? In the preparation area? By the cooktop? In both places? If you frequently use a wok or

or awkward to move? If so, including an appliance garage in your design makes sense, if you use these items often.

Somehow the kitchen is the catchall for many non-cooking and noneating-related items, too. If you don't think that will change once your new kitchen is completed, prepare for it. If, for example, your craft supplies, gardening tools, outdoor grilling items, and various cleaning supplies are stored on the countertop or on top of the refrigerator, reserve a space for them now—either inside a cabinet, in the pantry, or on shelves that you've held aside for such use on your formal plan for the new space.

TWO: *Install cabinet accessories.* The specialized storage options detailed earlier can be a little pricey, but they are less expensive if you purchase them with your cabinetry. Adding them later or retrofitting them in older cabinetry can boost the cost ever higher.

other typically awkward items, you might want to design special compartments or open shelves that keep them handy but hidden when not in use. The NKBA study says that most kitchens house 791 pots, pans, and dishes. (That number includes glassware and china.) Are most of your utensils presently contained in the kitchen? Or are some larger items stored in places like the basement? Would you like it to remain that way in your new design?

Are your smaller appliances, such as a mixer and food processor, hand-held or larger? Are they heavy

Above: *Some solutions to cabinet organization are simple. In this case, the homeowner used a wood plate rack that can be purchased in the housewares section of a department store or a kitchen specialty shop.*

Right: *Open-shelf storage can be quite charming in the right setting, particularly in an informal country-style kitchen. Baskets, crockery, or even a tin pail can be useful, as well as part of the display.*

There are also other accessories that can keep items neatly organized when cabinet space is at a premium. Besides the ubiquitous wire shelf and bin options, a wall- or ceiling-mounted pot rack can make use of otherwise overlooked overhead space. A knife rack that attaches to the wall or the outside of a cabinet is also handy. Wall racks that hold wine, barware, spices, mops and brooms, and ironing boards are negligible in price but invaluable space savers.

THREE: *Compartmentalize*. Make a plan now to store like things together, and tailor your shelf heights to these needs. Group utensils, pots, and pans by size. Group foods by type. Not only will this maximize the use of space, it will make finding what you need easier.

FOUR: *Plan to recycle.* Don't make recycling an afterthought. If you don't want to run outdoors to the various recycling receptacles, try to incorporate a place in the kitchen to separate them unobtrusively. Slide-out bins are an excellent solution if you can spare the cabinet space. In some kitchens, if you have a deep cabinet, a slide-out can accommodate two containers: The one in front is reserved for nonrecyclables; the second container is solely for recyclable trash.

FIVE: *Be honest about your habits.* If you're not a particularly neat person, avoid open shelving. It may look great at first because without the massiveness of closed cabinetry, the kitchen feels roomier. But if everything on the shelves looks tossed, the entire room will appear messy. The same advice applies to glass-fronted cabinets. If you really want them, plan on using them sparingly. Just one or two of these cabinets can make an attractive or colorful display for glassware or dishes.

Now that you have analyzed both your kitchen lifestyle and cooking style, you're ready to move on. The honest evaluation of your wants, needs, and preferences has prepared you to deal with the next big question—which countertop material and what fixtures should you choose?

COUNTERTOP MATERIALS

Selecting countertop material is not as simple as it once was because there are infinitely more choices in color, pattern, and texture thanks to new materials and applications. The trend is to use more than one, specifying types based on the functions at hand. For example, you might use a solid-surfacing material in one part of the kitchen, a marble insert

Above: *Outfitting a deep drawer with several compartments to separate different types of refuse makes recycling easy.*

Opposite: *A colorful collection of vintage Fiestaware looks decorative stored behind glass-door cabinets.*

at the bake center, and stainless steel next to the cooktop. Or you could pair one countertop material with the cabinetry that runs along the wall, and choose another for the island counter.

In addition to enhancing the function of your work surfaces, the countertop materials you choose can underpin your decorating theme. Wood is a natural choice a country-style kitchen, for example, whereas concrete looks handsome in a contemporary setting. The concrete can be poured or prefabricated into a mold on site. You can add color to it or create a one-of-a-kind inlaid design with stones, shards of glass, china, tile, shells, or just about anything else you can think of adding.

There are no hard-and-fast rules about any material you choose, but one important factor that should play a role in your selection is maintenance. Some materials demand greater care than others. Marble, for instance, must be sealed periodically because it can absorb liquids that will mar its looks. If you don't have time for the upkeep, can you live with the battle scars of everyday use?

Here's a rundown on choices for countertop material. After you've read about the attributes of each, you can decide which ones may be right for your application. Also, consider each type as a possibility for a matching or entirely different backsplash.

CERAMIC TILE

Ceramic tile is a perennial favorite. Impervious to water, it's perfect for installation at the sink. Tile is also durable, and doesn't scratch, burn, or stain. Aside from its practical attributes, ceramic tile offers the greatest opportunity for adding color, pattern, and texture to your kitchen. Custom designs bring personality into the room. Hand-painted, imported, and antique versions are very pricey, but you can combine inexpensive standard tiles, with raised or silk-screened patterns to create unique designs and murals nonetheless.

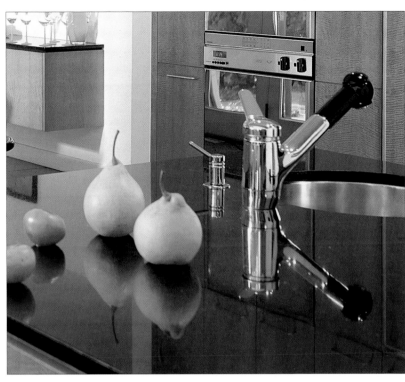

Clockwise (left to right): *Ceramic tile always makes a big design statement. The owner of this kitchen created the black-and-white check-ered pattern to suggest the look of a Viennese bakery. Coarse-grained granite and black gran-ite illustrate the different ways stone materials can be used creatively at the counter area.*

PLASTIC LAMINATE

Made of several layers of melamine, paper, and plastic resin bonded under heat and pressure, then glued to particleboard or plywood, plastic laminate is inexpensive, relatively easy to install, and available in a vast array of colors and patterns. Plastic laminate resists stains, water, and mild abrasion very well, but it can be chipped or scratched by sharp knives, and it will scorch if you put a hot pot down on it. There is no repair option available except replacement. More expensive solid-core laminates eliminate unsightly black edges at the joints because the color goes all the way through the material.

SOLID-SURFACING MATERIAL

This is an extremely durable, easily maintained synthetic made of polyester or acrylic. It's expensive, costing almost as much per linear foot as luxurious granite or marble, but it wears long and well. The material is completely impervious to water, and you can repair any dents or abrasions that may occur with a light sanding.

STONE

Marble and granite are probably the most expensive materi-als you can choose for a countertop. Though it is stone, mar-ble is actually a soft porous material that can be gouged and stained easily. Considered chic today, a granite countertop is a handsome status symbol. Like marble, it has a cool surface that pastry makers favor, but it is less absorbent. This makes it less likely to stain than marble.

Two other stone materials, limestone and concrete, are finding their way onto countertops in the hands of creative designers. Limestone is available as tiles, as is concrete, but

the latter can be poured and molded, too. Becoming even more creative, designers are adding color to concrete, and creating inlaid designs as well.

WOOD

Wood is unrivaled for its natural warmth and beauty. But it expands and contracts, depending on environmental conditions, and may warp if exposed to water. To protect a wood countertop, apply a film finish with varnish; other alternatives include applying lacquer or oil periodically. Teak is an excellent choice for a wood countertop. Another option is butcher-block, which is actually a laminated wood product. Eastern hard rock sugar maple is the most durable wood for a butcher-block application.

STAINLESS STEEL

Many of today's kitchens feature lots of metal, but they don't appear antiseptic or cold. That's largely because designers balance the look by introducing vibrant colors and other materials, such as ceramic tile or wood, into the room. Stainless steel used for a countertop, whether it is for the entire counter or just a section of it, can look quite sophisticated, especially with a wood trim. Stainless steel is vulnerable to scrapes, stains, and corrosion, so shop for a product with high chromium and nickel content.

FIXTURES

What could be more basic to the modern kitchen than a sink and faucet? Yet in today's world, there's practically nothing basic about them. Style comes in all price ranges, but high-performance technology is accompanied by an equally high price tag. There are designs and finishes to suit any contem-

Top left: *Molded concrete with a raised-pattern relief along the backsplash shows one way this material can be applied. The concrete surface was left in its natural color, but it can also be tinted.*

Bottom: *Because the island in this kitchen is used for food preparation, the owners chose a wood countertop, which can take the abuse of chopping and slicing.*

porary or traditional tastes. And far from being just necessary items in a kitchen, sinks and faucets have evolved into highly decorative elements. Here's a look at what's on the market.

SINKS

These receptacles come in all sizes, shapes, and colors, and are typically fabricated from enameled cast iron, stainless steel, a composite material (solid-surfacing, acrylic, or a mixture of natural quartz or granite with resins), or solid stone. They may be hand-painted or decorated with silk-screened designs, contoured, beveled, brushed to a matte finish, or polished to a mirror finish. The trend is to include the largest sink that you can accommodate within the confines of your space. Deep bowls make it easier to deal with awkward oversized items, such as large roasting pans and tall pots used for cooking pasta. A good example is the farm-style (or exposed-apron) sink that, at one time, would have been regarded as déclassé but is reemerging in glamorous solid colors or with decorative patterns. Shallow-basin sinks are available, when there is no other place to install the dishwasher but under the sink.

Two- and three-bowl configurations are also gaining wide popularity. This arrangement allows you to separate clean dishes from dirty ones as well as from waste materials. Some sinks come with a colander and cutting board. Typically, a waste-disposal unit is installed with one of the bowls, usually the larger one. Just peel your potatoes, then whisk the skins down the disposer. Lay the cutting board over the top of the bowl for chopping, and afterwards push the potato slices into the colander for rinsing.

Some designers recommend installing sinks in two separate areas. The primary sink often anchors the main food

Top right: *An old-fashioned exposed apron sink and mounted faucet with attached soap dish looks stylish in this refurbished kitchen. Large pots and pans can fit in its deep basins.*

Right: *An integral sink, countertop, and drainboard was fabricated from solid-surfacing material.*

preparation and cleanup areas, while a smaller secondary sink serves outside of the major work zone. A second sink is a must when two or more people cook together routinely, but it is also handy if you do crafts in the kitchen or entertain often.

Like every other kitchen product, there are numerous choices of sinks from which you will have to make a final selection, so it won't always be easy. In terms of durability, any one of the materials mentioned above will hold up well for years, if not decades, with the right care. Enameled cast-iron sinks tend to discolor but can be cleaned easily with a nonabrasive cleanser. Stainless steel and stone should be cleaned the same way. However, composite sinks are scratch resistant, with the exception of inexpensive acrylic models, so you can use an abrasive agent on them. Expect a quality sink to last as long as 30 years. In terms of installation, there are five types of sinks for the kitchen to consider. They are:

❦ **Undermounted.** If you want a smooth look, an under-mounted sink may be for you. The bowl is attached underneath the countertop.

❦ **Integral.** As the word "integral" implies, the sink and countertop are fabricated from the same material—stone, faux stone, or solid-surfacing. There are no visible seams or joints in which food can accumulate.

❦ **Self-rimming or flush-mounted.** A self-rimmed sink has a rolled edge that is mounted over the countertop.

❦ **Rimmed.** Unlike a self-rimming sink, this type requires a flat metal strip to seal the sink to the countertop.

❦ **Tile-in.** Used with a tiled countertop, the sink rim is flush with the tiled surface. Grout seals the sink to the surrounding countertop area.

FAUCETS

Faucets are no longer just conduits for water. From sleek European-inspired designs to graceful gooseneck shapes, today's selections add beauty as well as function to a kitchen. An excellent example is the pot-filler faucet, which is mounted to the wall over the cooktop. Some versions have a pull-out spout; others come with a double- or triple-jointed arm that can be bent to reach up and down, or swiveled back and forth, allowing the cook to pull the faucet over to a pot on the farthest burner. Anyone who has ever had to lug a heavy pot of water from the tap to a burner will appreciate this convenience. Just remember: You'll need additional hot- and cold-water plumbing if you install one of these faucets over your range or cooktop.

State-of-the-art technology in faucets gives you not only much more control over water use but better performance and a more extensive choice for finishes as well. Some speciality features to look for include pull-out faucet heads, retractable sprayers, hot- and cold-water dispensing, single-lever control, antiscald and

Left: *This self-rimmed copper sink has a deck-mounted center-set faucet. Copper sinks require polishing to keep their patina.*

statement by mixing finishes or pair a matte, brushed, or antiqued look with one that is highly polished. Some finishes, such as chrome or enamel, are easier to care for than others—brass, for instance, which may require polishing. In terms of installation, these are the three types of faucets you'll have to choose from:

❦ *Center set.* This installation has two separate valves, one for hot, the other for cold water, and a spout. But all three pieces appear connected in one unit.

flow-control devices, a lowered lead content in brass components, and built-in water purifiers to enhance taste.

For a quality faucet, inquire about its parts when you shop. The best are those made of solid brass or a brass-base material. Both are corrosion-resistant. Avoid plastic components—they won't hold up. Ask about the faucet's valving, too. Buy a model that has a washerless cartridge; it will cost more, but it will last longer.

❦ *Widespread.* This installation features a spout with two separate valves that appear to be three distinct pieces.

❦ *Single lever.* This installation contains a spout and single lever in one piece for one-hand operation.

Besides selecting a spout type (standard, arched, gooseneck, or pull-out), you may choose between single or double levers. Pull-outs come with a built-in sprayer, if you want one. The others will require installing a separate sprayer. Until recently, a pressure-balanced faucet (one equipped with a device that equalizes the hot and cold water coming out of a faucet to prevent scalding) came only with single-lever model. Now it is available with faucets that have separate hot- and cold-water valves. You may mix your spout with one of many types of handle styles: wrist blades, levers, scrolls, geometric shapes, and cross handles.

When you design your sink and faucet area, don't be sidetracked by the good looks of a product. Think about whether it works for your application. Today, good looks come in all types. Instead, compare the size of your biggest pots and racks to see if the sink you're considering will accommodate them. If it won't and you can't install something deeper, pair the sink with a pull-out or gooseneck faucet. Always make sure it directs the flow of the water into the center of the bowl and slightly to one side. A spout that is proportionately too tall for the depth of the sink will splash water, one that is too short won't allow water to reach to the sink's corners. If you plan a double- or triple-bowl configuration, the spout should deliver enough water to each of the bowls.

Chrome, brass, enamel-coated or baked-on colors, pewter, and nickel are typical faucets finishes. Make a fashion

Thoughtful planning isn't only applied to kitchen—it works for the bath as well, which is discussed in the next chapter.

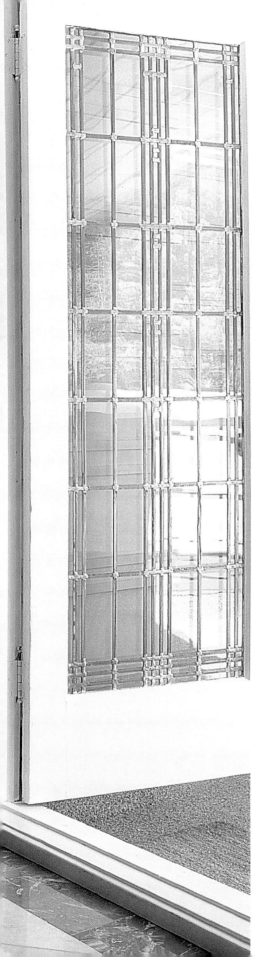

DESIGNING BATHS

Professionals know that good design in any room of the house reflects the personalities and lifestyles of the people who live there. You'll never be happy even with the most beautifully outfitted room if it is not functional and practical. A delicate hand-painted sink may be a showpiece, but it needs tender loving care to keep it beautiful. If this kind of maintenance doesn't fit into the way you live, you'll regret the day you bought that sink. Design your bath to pamper *you*, not the other way around.

Architect Louis Sullivan said, "Form follows function." That does not mean that style has to be subservient to function, but there must be a balance between the two. So even if you have a clear picture about how you want the new bathroom to look, put that thought on hold—temporarily—and think about how it will work.

Don't mislead yourself into believing that only a luxurious plan demands this kind of attention. Even if you are designing a modest bath, you can greatly increase its performance and your ultimate comfort by thoughtfully planning out every square inch of floor and wall space.

Whatever the size of your investment, you should get the most out of it. Besides, if you ever decide to sell your house, potential buyers will be put off by cramped bathrooms that look like everything was designed as an after-

Left: *Access to a private garden and hot tub indulge the owners' desire for an at-home getaway. To incorporate this luxurious addition, the owners expanded the bathroom into an adjacent small bedroom.*

thought. On the other hand, you can make a splash—and perhaps a tidy profit—if the fixtures are in good condition, the floor plan appears carefully thought out, the room looks bright, and there is ample storage.

DECIDING WHAT YOU NEED AND WANT

If you will be working with a design professional, expect to be interviewed at the beginning of the planning stage. He or she will want to get to know you and whoever else will use the new bathroom. Your designer isn't being nosy. He or she simply wants to understand your likes and habits, as well as your basic requirements and greatest expecta-

tions with respect to the new bath. The designer will also make a sketch of the existing space to get an idea of what works and what doesn't. The rough drawing may include any adjacent areas that might be considered for expansion, such as a closet, part of a hallway, or a small room.

If you will be acting as your own designer, do the same. You can't assume that you instinctively know what has to be done to transform the old bathroom into a fabulous new space just because you live there. That's acting on

Below: *Twin sinks and separate bathing areas enhance the function of a master bath. Notice how the tub, flanked by shower stalls, is the focal point of the floor plan.*

emotion. For the best result, approach the project in the same analytical manner as a professional who understands design and can be objective about what has to happen. To learn how to sketch a floor plan as if you were a professional, see the Smart Steps in Chapter Nine, on page 157.

REARRANGING AN EXISTING LAYOUT

If the existing floor plan works for you, all you have to think about is updating old fixtures, installing new tile, and perhaps replacing the cabinetry. Even so, you may want to play around with the idea of modifying the layout on paper. You may be surprised to discover, in fact, that a few minor changes in the floor plan can enhance your original arrangement. Just keep in mind: Moving plumbing fixtures in an existing bath may significantly raise costs.

SMART STEPS **ONE:** *Make a new base drawing.* As in the base drawing you made in the last chapter for the old bathroom, use a ¹/₂-inch scale. (If you haven't made a base drawing, see the Smart Steps in Chapter Nine, on page 157.) If you are using a ¹/₄-inch grid, each square represents a 6-inch square of real floor space. Begin by drawing the outer walls, and then add the windows and doors.

TWO: *Make templates of the fixtures.* Creating paper templates of fixtures and cabinets is an easy way to experiment with different layouts. You can draw the fixtures to scale on graph paper, or copy the templates in the Appendix. Then cut them out so you can move them around your plan. If you have collected pictures and spec sheets (printed product information from the manufacturer), use the dimensions given. When cutting out templates, include both the fixtures and the required front and side clearances—that way you won't get caught short. Usually, plumbing codes require a minimum clearance for each fixture. Fixture clearances are shown in the drawings on this and the next two pages. The top number of each pair indicates the minimum required by code or function. The bottom dimension allows more room between fixtures. For an efficient but convenient layout, aim for somewhere between the two numbers when you draw your plan.

THREE: *Place the fixtures.* You will use some fixtures more often than others: first the lavatory, next the toilet, then the tub or shower. An efficient plan places the lav closest to the

Bottom left and right: *When planning toilet and sink (or bidet) placement, use these dimensions to determine the necessary clearances. The bottom number is the preferred minimum clearance. If you are short on space, you can use the top dimension, which will not compromise the accessibility of the layout for most people.*

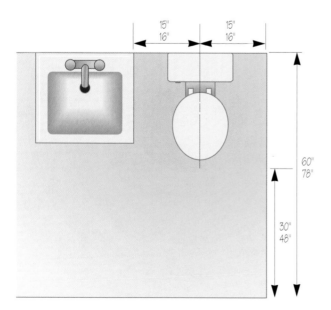

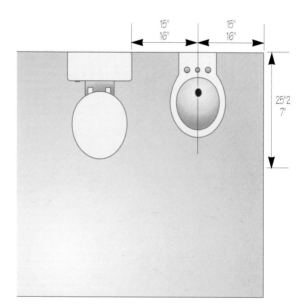

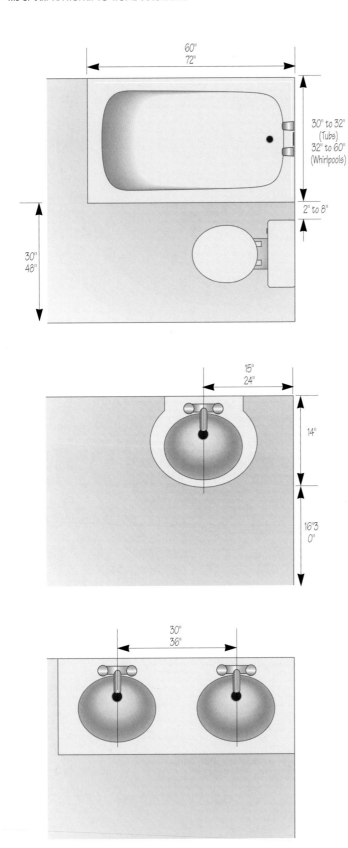

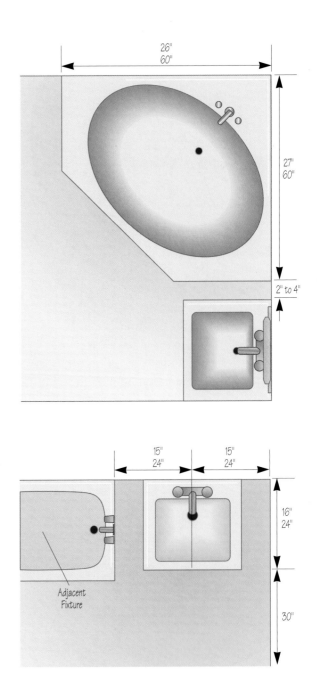

Top (left to right): *Use these clearances for rectangular tubs, whirlpools, and corner tubs. The smaller dimension is the minimum clearance required by code.*

Bottom (from middle left): *To make sure there is enough space around a lav, such as the freestanding and wall-hung units shown here, measure from the center of the basin to the wall. The minimum clearance between two lavs is 30 inches, which is measured from the center of each basin.*

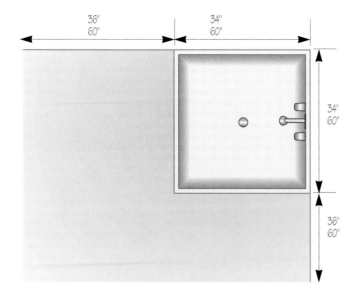

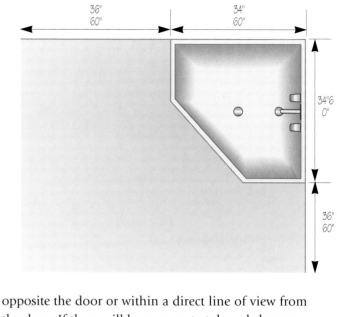

door, followed by the toilet, and finally the tub, which is located the farthest away. If there is any leeway in your plan, place the toilet so that it will not be visible when the door is open. Even in a small bathroom, the direction of the door swing can help shield the toilet from view.

Tub/Shower. Another easy way to place fixtures on your plan is to start with the largest ones. If you know you want a whirlpool bath and separate dual shower, pencil them in first. (Hint: Position the length of the tub perpendicular to the joists to distribute the weight safely. If you don't, you'll incur the costs of adding structural support to the floor.) To make the tub the focal point of the room, put it

opposite the door or within a direct line of view from the door. If there will be a separate tub and shower, locate them near each other so that they can share plumbing lines and the same sight lines. This also makes it easier to plan the space around them.

Top left and right: *Shower dimensions vary widely from the minimum usable size to the most generous. When space is tight, consider a corner unit. Don't forget to plan for clearance; the smaller dimension is the minimum clearance needed.*

Bottom left and right: *This bathroom allows full view of the toilet from outside the room. Better privacy is obtained by flopping the toilet and the sink and reversing the door swing.*

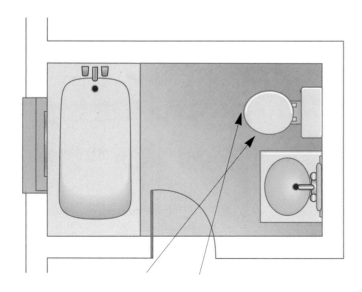

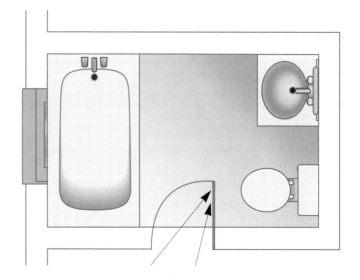

Lavatory. After placing the big items, locate your lavatory. Do you want two lavs or just one? Do you want two lavatories near each other or located on opposite sides of the room? Will two people use the room at once? Answer these questions before you pencil in the location.

If you are placing two lavatories side by side, leave enough maneuvering space and elbow room. One smart way to do this is to install storage between them. Some families install two lavatories at different heights. Not only is this more comfortable and ergonomic, it defines space as adult-designated or child-designated in a bathroom shared by all.

Toilet. Once you have the lavatories in place, go ahead and locate the toilet and bidet, if you have one. (A bidet resembles a toilet, but is actually a basinlike device for personal hygiene.) The bidet is another item you will want to keep away from the bathroom door and out of its sight line.

Extras. With the main elements penciled in, start adding the extras—the windows, doors, skylights, greenhouse, gym, sauna, and whatever other amenities you are considering. You can play with the design as long as you like, trying different ideas and placements, but make sure you take practical matters, such as pipes and codes, into consideration.

Customize. Although there are recommended guidelines for comfort and convenience, only you will be able to determine what will be most comfortable for you. If you happen to be 7 feet tall, you can probably forget about the height clearances and raise them! Likewise, if you are a small person, lower the counters. Don't worry about being able to resell your home later; another person of your height may

Right: *Chrome, glass, and white tile surfaces provide an antidote to a dark, cramped bath. The sink's tapered counter enhances maneuverability. The attached towel bar frees the wall for shelving.*

appreciate the comfort of a higher or lower surface. If the need arises, installing a new vanity with standard-height countertop is not easy, but it's not a major project either.

BASIC BATH ARRANGEMENTS

The most-common-size American bathroom measures 60x84 inches or 60x96 inches. The most common complaint about it is the lack of space. The arrangement may have suited families 50 years ago, but times and habits have changed. If it's the only bathroom in the house, making it work better becomes even more important.

When planning the layout, try angling a sink or shower unit in a corner to free up some floor space. Unlike a traditional door, which swings into the room and takes up wall space when it is open, a pocket door slides into the wall. Another smart way to add function to a small bathroom is to install a pocket door into a wall between the toilet and the sink. That way two people can use the room at the same time.

You can also make a small bathroom feel roomier by bringing in natural light with a skylight or roof window or by replacing one small standard window with several small casement units that can be installed high on the wall to maintain privacy.

If you are adding a second or possibly a third bathroom to your house, here are a few other ideas for your consideration—and inspiration.

THE POWDER ROOM

The guest bath. The half bath. It has a lot of names, and it may be the most efficient room in the house, providing just what you need often in tight quarters. A powder room normally includes nothing more than a lavatory and a toilet. You can find small-scale fixtures specifically designed for the powder room, from the tiniest lavs to unusually narrow toilets. In general, however, maintain a clearance that meets code on each side of the toilet, and include comfortable reaching room for the toilet-paper dispenser. Most powder rooms measure at least 36 inches wide by 54 to 60 inches long, depending on the layout of the space.

Keep a small powder room as light and open as possible. Plan to install good lighting because the powder room is often used for touching up makeup. (For more about planing a lighting scheme, see Chapter Three, "Light by Design," on page 44.)

Above: *When a powder room is located right off the public areas of the house, sight lines from the door are important.*

A carefully thought-out floor plan makes a difference in this usually small space. Make sure the door swings out against a wall, not inward, or use a pocket door for easy access. If it must be accessible for someone in a wheelchair, include a minimum 5-foot-diameter circle of space in the center of the room, which is just large enough for a wheelchair to turn around.

In the powder room, the vanity is often the focal point. It offers the best opportunity to showcase a decorative piece, such as a hand-painted pedestal sink or a custom-made vanity. Because the powder room is often for guests and is normally located on the ground floor near the living area, take extra care to ensure privacy. If possible, the best location is in a hallway, away from the living room, kitchen, and dining area. This room can also handle stronger wall colors—either dark or bright ones—as well as larger, bolder wallpaper patterns because it is a short-stay room.

A CHILDREN'S BATH

What should be included in a children's bath plan depends on the ages and number of children using it. If the bath will be for only one child, the design is easy. You can tailor it to him or her, taking care to plan for growing and changing needs. Anticipate the storage and lighting requirements of an older child's self-grooming habits, for example. However, if more than one child will use this bathroom, consider their genders, and whether more than two will be using the bath at the same time. How many lavatories do you really need? The answer is at least two, if not more. The best designs for growing children include compartmentalized spaces—one for the toilet, one for the bath, and one for the lavatories. If this isn't feasible given the existing space, at least try to set the toilet apart. That way the children can take turns going to the bathroom and brushing their teeth for speedier bedtimes.

Two special considerations in a kid's bath are territorial issues and safety. Children are famous for protecting their space. Rather than fight this natural tendency, plan a cabinet drawer or wall shelf for each child. For safety, you may want to install countertops and sinks lower than standard height or build a step into the vanity cabinet's toekick area.

Tubs can also be made safer for children. There are special soft covers for faucets so that children will not be hurt if they bump into them. Tub floors can be treated with anti-slipping decals or mats, plus lower grab bars help with getting in and out of the tub.

Lastly, remember what it was like to be a child. Get down to a kid's level, and design for a youngster's height

Left: *A little girl's favorite things inspired the decorations of her bathroom. The window seat offers a pleasant place to rest and provides storage space underneath for bath toys.*

Opposite: *The same designer incorporated a nautical theme into a bath shared by two boys.*

and capabilities. Consult your children about decisions regarding the room's decoration. Ask their opinions on color, wallpaper patterns, or shower curtains, for example.

THE FAMILY BATH

Compartmentalizing is the best way to start planning the family bath. But remember, when you separate the bathroom into smaller, distinct areas, you run the risk of making the room feel cramped. Try to alleviate this with extra natural light, good artificial lighting, and translucent partitions made of glass blocks or etched glass. Anything that divides with privacy while also allowing light to enter will help ease the closed-in feeling.

If separating the fixtures is not possible, include a sink in the dressing area within the master bedroom to provide a second place for applying makeup or shaving. Investigate building a back-to-back bath in lieu of one large shared room. Another popular option is to locate the bathing fixtures, both the tub and separate shower, in the center of the room; install the bidet, a toilet, and sink on either side in their own separate areas. To make the arrangement work, keep each side of the room accessible to the door.

Clockwise (from above): *This family bath makes the most of its floor space. A double vanity and lots of storage offers room for two. On the other side of the room, the shower is located across from the toilet, which has a half wall for privacy.*

Left: *This bath refrains from a closed-in look by using an interior transom-style window over the tub. The tile mosaic is functional as well as decorative: It has a built-in ledge for shampoo.*

Below: *The same bath has a large Palladian-style window over the sink, making a beautiful architectural statement. The cabinetry echoes the space-enhancing neutral color of the tiles.*

THE MASTER BATH

The concept of the master bath has come of age in the past decade. It is one of the most popular rooms to remodel and gives one of the highest returns on investment upon resale. It's where you can create that sought-after getaway—the home version of a European spa.

Some popular amenities to include in your plan are a sauna, greenhouse, exercise studio, fireplace, audio and video systems, faucets and sprayers with full massaging options, steam room, whirlpool tub, and dressing table. You are only limited by size and imagination—and some local codes.

Extras can be tempting but may require special planning. For example, you may need additional support in the floor, as well as supplemental heating and ventilation. You would not want to slip into a tub and have it fall two floors to the middle of the living room. Unfortunately, this really does happen when the weight of an oversized contemporary tub is installed on top of a 50-year-old floor. Older houses simply weren't built to accommodate the volume of water some people now use when bathing.

Some of the best floor plans for the modern adult bath also include a separate room for the toilet and bidet, a detached tub and shower, and dual sinks on opposite sides of the room with adjacent dressing rooms and walk-in closets. Modern couples want to share a master bed and bath, but they also want to have privacy and the ease of getting ready in the morning without tripping over their mates. The only way to do this harmoniously is to mingle the parts of the room that invite sharing and separate those elements that are always private.

SELECTING PRODUCTS & MATERIALS

The products you select to outfit your new bathroom will affect both your design and your budget. If you choose top-of-the-line products, expect a top-of-the-line bill. Factors that influence the cost of new fixtures, cabinetry, counter-tops, and flooring include updated technology and type of finish. The smarter the device, the more you'll pay for it. Likewise, the fancier the finish, the higher the price tag. But cost does not always reflect quality, nor does it equate necessarily with satisfaction. And quality and personal satisfaction are the most important factors to consider when making any product selection.

So, how can you make smart choices about items such as tubs and showers, tile, and cabinets? How can you tell whethera product is reliable and will endure the daily abuse of water and moisture? Are there basic differences that make one faucet or a particular toilet better than another? To find out, you can do a little research. Shop around. Visit bath designer showrooms, read books, and don't be afraid to ask questions. Otherwise, you can take your chances on buying an item that might not suit your needs. If you're not the gambling type, however, here are some steps you can take to select products and materials for your new bath with confidence.

SMART STEPS

ONE: *Separate the product from the hype.* A high price does not always mean high quality. Find out what is different about a toilet that costs $100, for example, and one that sells for $300 or even $1,000. This way you can decide whether the higher price is worth it. A knowledge-able salesperson will be able to tell you. If not, contact the manufacturer. Many have 800 numbers and Web sites set up to handle consumer questions. Sometimes the price hike is because of a feature you can't see. For example, a faucet with replaceable parts costs

Left: *Marble surfaces, such as this vanity top, are hard but porous. They require sealing to protect them from stain-damaging spills. An antique was converted into the base of the vanity.*

much more than a new faucet with parts that cannot be replaced. How much do you want to gamble that the faucet you buy won't break?

TWO: *Weigh your options.* Analyze the benefits and the risks that come with each product. Once you have that information, a decision will be easier. If you are sprucing up an old bath or adding a new one in a house you expect to sell soon, you might install a less-expensive counter-top material, for example. But if you are making a major investment in a remodeling project that you plan to live with for a long time, you might be happier in the long run with something that may cost more but gives you greater satisfaction and will be more reliable for years to come.

THREE: *Seek reliable advice.* Ask the manufacturer about the expected life of the product or its efficiency. Don't take advice from a store clerk if he or she is not an experienced remodeling professional. Talk to your contractor, who may be familiar with the product or can pass along critical feed-back from other clients who may have purchased the same item or something similar to it.

FOUR: *Don't make a choice based on style or color.* It doesn't work for cars, and it won't work for building materials. Sure, style and color are important, but it's just as easy to find a first-rate fixture that looks great in your new bathroom as it is to find one that looks fabulous but performs poorly. Opt for quality.

FIVE: *Be wary of some handmade products for the bath.* You may be tempted by a handsome unglazed sink from a chic pottery shop. Certainly, it will add a unique cachet to your design, but an unglazed sink may not meet local code. Don't buy on impulse before checking out the build-ing codes in your area. If there's any doubt in your mind, ask if you can leave a refundable deposit on the item, and then speak with your contractor, who should be familiar with the rules and can save you from a costly mistake.

SIX: *Prorate costs.* You may be dismayed by the initial sticker price, but when you divide the cost of the product or material by its anticipated longevity (how many years you

Below: *A hammered-metal basin pairs with acrylic and chrome fittings in a modern bath. A glass tile backsplash echoes the watery blue color of the tile countertop.*

expect it to last), you may be amazed at how reasonable it really is. Of course, this won't alleviate an immediate cash-flow problem, but it will ease some of the sticker shock. An expensive product that will last for 20 years may be a better choice than a cheaper one that may have to be replaced in five years. Again, weigh that decision against how long you plan to stay in the house. Are the extra benefits worth it?

SEVEN: *Inquire about guarantees and service options.* Some offers are definitely better than others. Look at the warranties that come from the manufacturer, as well as those offered by the place of purchase. A store may offer immediate replacement of the entire unit. While this may sound great, it isn't if you have to pay for labor or sched-ule time off from work for the removal and reinstallation of a fixture. Find out whether there is a better way. If all that is wrong with a faucet is a faulty washer, you may not want to yank out the entire unit. It should be your call. Find a place that offers a warranty based on the problems with the product. And always get written copies of all war-ranties from the store or your contractor.

EIGHT: *Do a reality check.* Look at your situation, and choose the best products and materials for the way you live. Don't get swept away by bells and whistles that can blow your budget. Your bottom line isn't bottomless, so compare each extra-cost feature to your real needs and lifestyle. A sumptuous shower with 18 massaging hydro-jets may be your fantasy, but if your morning routine is a race against the clock to get to work on time, invest the extra money elsewhere. Besides, multiple shower outlets, as well as large tubs, may require larger water-supply lines, and that might not be an option.

NINE: *Leave nothing to chance.* Investigate every option and every detail for the new bathroom. Don't find yourself bemoaning what you should have done when it's too late. After you sign the final check is not the time to realize you could have installed an in-line heater to keep bath water consistently warm or a steam unit in the shower. Discover everything that's out there—before getting started on the remodeling. Don't miss any of the fun stuff, and you won't have any regrets or extra charges for changes made after work has begun.

Although the trend in recent years has been to increase the size of the bathroom, most are still relatively small compared with other rooms in the house. Yet this room remains the most expensive per square foot to renovate. This behooves you to invest wisely.

FIXTURES & FITTINGS

Thirty years ago, items like tubs, toilets, and sinks were standard fare, not to mention boring. Who could have imagined they would generate the excitement they do today? As bathrooms have been elevated to symbolize status in American homes over the last couple of decades, second in prestige only to kitchens, even the most pragmatic items have become elements of design. But in addition to appearance, the workings of bathroom fixtures have become technologically more glamorous as well.

TUBS

Soakers, whirlpools, classic claw-footed models, tubs for two, spas for four, contoured shapes, ovals, squares, or rounded tubs, streamlined or sculptured models, tubs with neck rests and arm rests. Tubs in a variety of colors. Freestanding tubs. Tubs set into platforms. Tubs you step down into. It's your soak, so have it your way.

Ask yourself: How do I like to bathe? Do I prefer a long, lingering soak or an invigorating hydromassage? A popular trend is the sunk-in whirlpool tub, which comes with an array of therapeutic and relaxing options in the form of neck jets, back jets, side jets, multiple jets, or single jets that are installed in the walls behind the tub. Other options include on-off control panels that can be reached from inside the tub (as opposed to a wall timer) and an automatic turnoff that prevents motor burnout.

Left: *The rich marble platform and neoclassical columns provide a suitable setting for a glamorous jetted tub for two.*

Generally, tubs are made of one of the three following materials:

🛁 *Fiberglass* is a lightweight and moldable material. A fiberglass tub is the least expensive type you can buy. But it's prone to scratching and wear after about a dozen years. Some come with an acrylic finish, which holds up against wear longer.

🛁 *Solid acrylic* is a mid-price range product that is more durable than fiberglass and less prone to scratching because the color is solid all the way through. Whirlpool tubs are usually made of acrylic because it can be shaped easily. It's also lightweight, an important feature for large tubs that can put damaging stress on structural elements under the floor.

🛁 An enamel-coated, *cast-iron* tub will endure as long as your house stands. It's heavyweight, though, and not recommended for a large soaking tub, even if the floor has been reinforced.

The most common size for a tub that backs up against a wall is 32x60 inches, but you can find models in widths of 24 to 42 inches. If someone in the family is tall, no problem: You can purchase a standard tub that's up to 72 inches long.

SHOWERS

Spectacular spray options and spa features make showering as sybaritic as the most luxuriously appointed bath. Shower units separate from bathtubs can be prefabricated from molded fiberglass or acrylic. They come in widths of 32, 36, and 48 inches, with a standard depth of 36 inches and a height of 73 inches. Custom-built showers are typically constructed of solid-surfacing, ceramic tile, or stone. Top-of-the-line features include massaging hydrotherapy sprays, steam units, a foot whirlpool, built-in seating and storage, even a CD player. Amazing technology lets you enjoy a full body massage on a miserly amount of water. Although by law, new shower heads may not deliver more than 2.5 gallons of water per minute, you can install as many as you wish.

Above: *This custom system includes a fixed shower head and a hand-held spray, as well as a preset temperature valve, to offer a perfect shower. A built-in seat is another handy feature.*

The only thing limiting your shower is your imagination and your budget. If you want it, it's out there. Unless you're interested in a strictly no-frills unit, think about installing more than one shower head and mixing and matching devices from any or all of the following three basic spray categories.

🛁 A *fixed spray* shower head is mounted on the wall or ceiling, and it may or may not come with a massage option. New versions include a device that propels water into the air to give you a hydromassage. Other nifty models, called rain bars, let you close your eyes and pretend you're in a rain forest where gentle mists pamper you with a soft rinse. Or you can opt for a cascade of water that is delivered by a waterfall spout.

❦ A *hand-held spray* is convenient for directing water where you want it. It stores in a wall-mounted slide bar and can be adjusted up and down to accommodate the tallest or shortest bather. Combine a hand-held spray with a stationary shower head, and add a massager with as many as eight settings and a body brush, and you've created a custom shower environment that rivals any first-class away-from-home spa.

❦ *Jet sprays* are housed behind the shower walls, just as those used in whirlpool tubs are. One manufacturer offers as many as 16 with its shower unit. Jet sprays can be programmed to various settings. Get a therapeutic hydromassage to relax stiff neck muscles or a sore back, for example. If you like, select a full body massage at whatever intensity is comfortable for you.

TOILETS

Believe it or not, you do have choices when selecting a toilet for your new bathroom. Vitreous china is still the material of preference, but there's a wide range of colors and style options to suit contemporary or traditional tastes. If you like something sleek, select a European-inspired elongated bowl. Though toilet sizes vary somewhat among manufacturers, an elongated bowl will extend about 2 inches more into the room than a standard version. The typical height of a toilet seat is 15 inches, but some come as high as 18 inches, which can be more comfortable for tall or older persons.

Another option is whether your new toilet will be a one-piece, low-profile model or a two-piece unit. There are style variations within both types, including rounded bowls, long square shapes, and vintage looks. Nostalgia lovers will be happy to know that Victorian-style high-tank toilets are still manufactured. Scaled-down toilets

Above: *A sleek low-profile toilet looks contemporary in this bathroom. Its low-flush feature uses less than one-fourth the amount of water used by older toilets.*

are available, too, for condos and apartments short on space or for tiny powder rooms, such as those tucked into a stairwell or made out of an old hallway closet.

If you are still fighting in your household about whether the seat should be kept up or down, give peace a chance. Look into these new gender-friendly features: a lid that automatically lowers when the toilet is flushed or a toilet that shines a red light in the bowl when the seat is up and a green light when the lid is down.

If that isn't enough, consider a residential urinal. One type fits into the wall; another sits on the floor next to the toilet.

Besides style and type, you should be concerned about the flushing mechanism. Although appearance factors can affect cost (low-profile, one-piece, and elongated bowls being at least twice the price of standard two-piece models), the flushing mechanism may have an even bigger impact on the price tag. New toilets must conform to the government's low-flush standard, which mandates that no more than 1.6 gallons of water be used per flush. But that may change due to complaints about effectiveness. Manufacturers are working to improve flushing mechanisms. In the meantime, Congress may relax standards slightly.

There are three basic types of flushing mechanisms, listed in order of their cost, starting with the least expensive.

A *gravity-fed* mechanism is the standard device used by two-piece toilets. Press down the lever, and the force of the water that is released from the tank and into the bowl flushes waste down the drain and out through the pipes.

A *pressure-assisted* type uses water pressure in the line to compress air and, using a small amount of water, forces the bowl to empty. This is the most common type used today.

A small *electric pump* quietly pushes water and waste through the toilet. This type of mechanism is a plus for low-water pressure areas.

Manufacturers are also working on vacuum-flush toilets that would operate similarly to those on airlines and would use a miniscule amount of water. However, this type of toilet is still in the development phase and is not ready for the residential market.

BIDETS
A standard fixture in European bathrooms for decades, bidets have been slow to catch on in the American market. They are gaining in popularity, however, particularly in new construction and high-end remodeling, where they are becoming status symbols in master suites. Typically, a bidet is selected to match the toilet, and the fixtures are installed side by side.

LAVATORIES
You may find it practically impossible to select one lavatory over another because they come in so many sizes, shapes, styles, and colors. Sensuous curves, sculpted bowls, and beautiful, durable finishes can make this vessel a work of art—and an important element in your overall design. Today's lavatories can be made of vitreous china, cast iron, enameled steel, fiberglass, acrylic (solid-surfacing material), stone, faux stone, or metal. Its finish may be hand painted, contoured, beveled, brushed, or polished. A sink can be a freestanding pedestal, or it can be mounted to the wall or be part of a vanity top.

Right: *This reproduction sink and its chrome fittings suit the room's retro style. The predominately white color scheme is brightened by the delicate tile border.*

Vanity sinks, in pairs or as a single lav, are designed to be installed in one of four ways:

🐾 A *self-rimming* sink is surface-mounted. The bowl drops into the counter while the ridge forms a seal with the countertop surface. This ridge or rim can be decoratively carved or hand painted.

🐾 An *under-mounted* sink gives a tailored look. In this instance, the bowl is attached underneath the countertop for a clean, uncluttered appearance.

🐾 An *integral* sink is fabricated with a countertop from the same material—stone, faux stone, or solid-surfacing. The look is sleek, seamless, and sculptural.

🐾 Unlike a self-rimming sink, a *rimmed model* requires a metal strip to form the seal between the top of the sink and the countertop.

There are attractive, shapely lavs in every price range. Colored lavatories are usually a bit pricier, as are delicate hand-painted designs. If you will do anything at the sink besides washing your hands and face and brushing your teeth, consider choices in design and size carefully before you buy.

Something that is too shallow, for example, may not be practical for rinsing hair or hand washables. A pedestal sink may be pretty, but if you apply makeup, style your hair, or shave, this type may not provide surface storage for related grooming items. Hand-painted designs may look beautiful, but they may require special care to avoid wear, as well as more gentle cleaning—not the right option for an active family. Think before acting.

FAUCETS AND OTHER FITTINGS

Like showers, faucets are no longer just conduits for water. Today's faucet technology gives you much more control over your water. You can program an instrument for a pulsating effect or select the gentler rhythm of a babbling brook or a cascading waterfall; preset water temperature so that the water never gets hotter than you like; or protect young children, as well as disabled or elderly family members, from scalding.

For quality, inquire about the materials used for the faucet's innards. The best choices are solid brass or a brass-base metal, which are corrosion-resistant. Avoid plastic—it won't hold up. Inquire about the faucet's valving, too. Many faucets come with a washerless ceramic or nylon cartridge that lasts longer and is less prone to leaks. Ceramic is the better choice. Select finishes depending on your taste and other elements in the room that you may wish to coordinate with the fittings. Finishes include chrome, polished brass, enamel-

Left: *For an ultimately soothing bath experience, this tub's spout has a waterfall effect. The hot- and cold-water valves were placed on the outside edge of the tub—opposite the faucet—within easy reach.*

Below: *The new technology used to finish this widespread faucet set will maintain the polished-brass shine for years.*

coated colors, pewter, nickel, gold, and gold-plated. Handles may match the faucet or come in crystal, marble, or other materials.

Make a fashion statement by mixing finishes or selecting a design with inlaid stones or gems. Think of faucets as jewelry for your bathroom, and accessorize accordingly. There are three basic types of faucets for your consideration:

❦ A *center-set* faucet has two separate valves (one for hot, another for cold) and a spout that are connected in one unit.

❦ The *widespread* type features a spout with separate hot- and cold-water valves. All of the parts appear to be completely separate pieces.

❦ The *single-lever* type has a spout and a single lever in one piece for one-hand control.

Whatever your decorating motif, you can find faucets to coordinate with the look you wish to achieve. Reproduction styles in brushed-metal finishes look good in traditional décors, as do graceful gooseneck spouts. Sleek geometrical shapes with enameled or high-gloss finishes enhance contemporary designs. And don't forget baubles. Stone, faux stone, or faux gem inserts on handles provide rich-looking details in strong architecturally inspired designs.

While you're admiring all the handsome faucet styles on today's market, remember function. Cross handles are charming, but they can be difficult to grasp for the elderly, disabled persons, or the very young. Levers and wrist blades make more sense in these cases. If you like the simplicity of a single-lever faucet, install one with a hot-limit valve so that kids can't scald themselves.

GRAB BARS AND TOWEL BARS
The first thing to remember is that grab bars and towel bars are not interchangeable items. A grab bar must be installed so that it securely attaches to wall studs or

Right: *A charming old cupboard puts colorful towels on display in a bathroom with vintage style.*

blocking behind a shower or bathtub or at the toilet. (If you are remodeling your bathroom, reinforce the walls at grab bar locations.) For quality, shop for grab bars made of solid brass. For style, coordinate them with other hardware, such as the towel bars, faucets, shower heads, and cabinet pulls and handles.

Like faucets, towel bars can be likened to jewelry for the bath. Don't skimp on this detail: Look for ones with matching toilet paper holders and door and wall hooks. Shop for quality brass or chrome construction with a finish that won't rust or tarnish when exposed to moisture.

STORAGE

Undoubtedly, an important aspect of your new bath's design is storage. Besides toiletries, grooming aids, extra linens, a hamper, and cleaning supplies, you may want to store gym equipment, books, magazines, and CDs, particularly if the room will be a place you can retreat to for adult quiet time after a day at work or with the kids. To store all these items, you'll need to be creative and utilize as much space as possible.

Left *Custom-built open shelving provides storage for towels and toiletries and offers display space for plants and accessories.*

No matter what the size of the bathroom, it should contain a reasonable amount of storage. To get it, you'll have to thoroughly analyze the space and prioritize what items you must have handy, as well as any extras you'd like. Believe it or not, even a tiny 5x7-foot bathroom can accommodate spare rolls of toilet paper, additional bars of soap, a blow dryer, and curling iron, as well as a stack of clean towels, as long as you think storage issues through at the design stage of the project.

If you are working with a professional, he or she will have more than a few storage tricks to offer if you are specific about what you need. Be prepared by asking yourself some storage questions about your new bath: Is a vanity sufficient? Will it be for one or two persons? Do you require a medicine cabinet? How about a linen closet? Extra shelves? Drawers?

When you are acting on your own, think about how you intend to use the new bath. Make a list of everything you want at hand. Scale back if necessary, but start big. For example, if your children will bathe in this room, include storage for bath toys—ideally, someplace other than along the ledge of the tub. If you'll shave, groom your hair, or apply makeup at the vanity, pencil in a place—not the countertop—to keep essentials away from the sink and protected against exposure to water. If you're tired of toting dirty clothes downstairs to the basement or ground-floor laundry room, see whether your plan can accommodate a compact washer/dryer. If you're always dashing to the hallway linen closet for towels, add shelves or, if there is space, a closet in the bathroom. These are just a few of the storage-related issues that could affect your project.

In any event, it's likely that you'll want at least a vanity and a medicine cabinet in your new bath. Like fixtures and fittings, they make important statements about how the new space will look, as well as how it will function.

Smart Tips For Storage

A linen closet inside the bathroom is an amenity some home-owners think they can't afford if the space is small. If that's your dilemma, a little rethinking and reshuffling may yield the necessary room you thought you didn't have. First, reconsider the size of the bathroom fixtures you've been planning for your design. Would a smaller tub, shower unit, or vanity relieve the crunch? Second, think about building the closet into an adjoining room, if possible. Your designer may have other ideas, too.

You can't go wrong if you make good use of even the smallest pocket of space, like the toe-kick area at the bottom of the vanity, where you can install extra drawers or a slide-out step for kids who can't reach the sink yet. If there's a low-profile toilet next to the vanity, extend the countertop over the toilet. Ask your builder to suspend a drawer from underneath the extension. Don't forget to include a built-in shelf inside the shower or tub enclosure to hold soaps and shampoos. Use the wall space; install open shelves for extra towels, bars of soap, bubble bath, and the like. Better yet, think about opening up a wall between two studs and using the dead space for recessed shelving. One caution: Don't cut the studs in case it is a load-bearing wall.

Above: *A custom-painted design and handcrafted details distinguish this furniture-quality vanity. The marble countertop with arched backsplash was sealed to prevent moisture damage.*

VANITIES

Today there are many creative ways to approach the vanity. One is to treat the vanity as a decorative receptacle for a drop-in sink with just a countertop and legs and no attached cabinetry. If you can sacrifice the storage a cabinet provides, this option will add drama to your design, especially if the countertop is outfitted with handsome tile, stone, or colored concrete. But if you're limited by space and have to make the most of every inch, a vanity cabinet, which features drawers and shelves, is the wisest choice. Cabinets are available in three ways:

❧ *Stock vanities* are factory-made in a range of standard heights, sizes, and finishes. They are usually—but not always—the most economical type. Styles are limited.

❧ *Semi-custom vanities* are factory-made and outfitted with custom options upon your order. Usually midrange in price, semi-custom vanities include extras, such as pull-out bins, spin-out trays, special door styles, or custom finishes.

❧ *Custom vanities* are built-to-order to your bathroom's specifications. The cabinets can be designed by your architect, interior designer, or designer/builder. This is typically—but not always—the most expensive option.

A popular vanity trend is to retrofit a piece of fine wood furniture, such as an antique chest, with a lav, reproduction fittings, and an elegant countertop. But the wood surface has to be sealed with a protective coating that resists water and mildew. If you don't have the right piece of old furniture but want the same look, check out the new cabinet styles offered by manufacturers today. Look at designs created for the kitchen, as well as the bath. Some are interchangeable and display furniture details. Fluted pilasters, elegant moldings, and filigree patterns adorn many models that also come with beautiful hardware and finishes engineered to hold up to humidity and mildew. They wipe clean easily, too, so you don't have to worry about upkeep. Some are available with faux stone or wood laminate countertops, or granite or marble surfaces.

Whether you select a vanity style that is traditional or contemporary, with a plastic laminate, metal, or wood finish, give the vanity cabinet as much consideration as you would if it were meant for the kitchen. Top-of-the-line solid-wood construction may be too expensive for most budgets. However, a sturdy plywood frame combined with dovetail and mortise-and-tenon joinery is excellent, too. Make sure the interiors are well finished, however, and shelves aren't flimsy.

There are basically two construction styles for stock and semi-custom cabinetry: framed and frameless. Both styles are available from any American manufacturer.

 Framed cabinets feature a full frame across the face of the unit. Hinges may or may not be visible around doors and drawers.

 Frameless cabinets, often called European-style cabinets, are built without a face frame and therefore have a sleek appearance. Because the doors are mounted on the face of the box or are set into it, hinges are typically hidden inside.

MEDICINE CABINETS

You can find attractive medicine cabinets that can be wall-mounted or recessed into a non-load-bearing wall between the studs. From ultra-contemporary visions in glass and lights to designs that make bold architectural statements, there's a wide selection of stock units to match any décor or cabinet style.

When shopping for a medicine cabinet, look for one that offers room for everything from

Below: *A mirrored door conceals a medicine cabinet that is part of a bank of storage built to this bath's specifications. The wall fixtures provide extra light when applying makeup or shaving.*

toothbrushes to shaving cream and bandages. Choose one that spans the width of your van-ity or beyond it, if wall space allows. In other words, buy the largest one you can find! Look for deep shelves that accommodate objects larger than a small pill bottle. Built-in lighting, swing-out mirrors, and three-way mirrored doors are some of the other extras you may want in a medicine cabinet. In addition, some units come with a lock or a separate compartment that can be locked to keep potentially dangerous substances out of the hands of young children.

SURFACING MATERIALS

Even in well-ventilated bathrooms, steam and moisture can take their toll. So it's important to select materials for the walls, floor, and countertop that can hold up to water.

Plastic laminate and vinyl are good choices that come in different price ranges, depending on quality. Generally they are the most affordable. Ceramic tile, solid-surfacing materials, and concrete fall into the middle to high end of the spectrum. Natural stone, such as slate, granite, and marble, are at the high end of the price scale.

LAMINATE

Consider laminate for your bathroom countertops. When installed on counters, plastic laminate resists moisture superbly and is easy to maintain. Laminate is made of melamine, paper, and plastic resin bonded under heat and pressure, then glued to particle-board or plywood. It comes in so many colors, patterns, and textures that finding one to coordinate with other elements in your design—fixtures, tile, wallcovering—is easy. Want a countertop made of slate or marble, but can't afford the real thing? Does buttery leather, cool glass, or warm wood appeal to you? A faux version in laminate may be the answer. Besides giving you a price break, plastic laminate offers a practical alternative to some natural materials that would be too delicate for such an installation. In that sense, it is versatile and practical. Plastic laminate countertop material comes in various grades. It is generally affordable, so don't skimp by purchasing the cheapest one you can find. To get your money's worth, select the highest quality, which won't chip easily and stays looking good longer. At the very top of the line is "color-through" laminate. As opposed to laminate with color on the surface only, this type will not show a brown seam line at the edge.

With regard to flooring, the latest laminate products boast easy care, as well as moisture and stain resistance. Manufacturers now offer literally dozens of designs that are dead ringers for real wood or stone. These come in either tongue-and-groove planks or as tiles. Like sheet laminate used for

Left: *One of the benefits of solid-surfacing materials is their potential for creating carved or beveled effects, such as along this countertop's edge and basin rim.*

Right: *Mixing raised-pattern, hand-painted, and roped accent strip tiles adds a three-dimensional look to a countertop design.*

countertops, laminate flooring is more economical than the natural materials it portrays, and in more cases, it installs right over old flooring.

CERAMIC TILE

Besides its practical attributes, such as imperviousness to water, durability, and easy maintenance, ceramic tile offers the greatest opportunity to bring style and personality to your bathroom. Use it to add color, pattern, and texture to the wall, floor, or countertop. Enclose a tub or shower with it. Tile is versatile. It comes in a variety of shapes, sizes, and finishes. Use decorative tiles with hand-painted finishes or raised-relief designs to create a mural or mosaic. You're only limited by your imagination. Hand-painted tile is expensive, but it allows you to do something truly unique. If cost is a factor, accent standard tiles with a few hand-painted designs. Or achieve a similar look at less cost by using mass-produced tiles with silk-screened designs. Visit a tile showroom in your area or the design department of a nearby home center to get ideas. Mix and match embossed tiles, accent and trim strips, edges, and a contrasting colored grout (the compound that fills the joints). For long-lasting wear and easy maintenance, always apply a grout sealer in areas exposed to water, such as the countertop or tub surround.

Consider the finish when you're shopping for tile. There are two kinds: glazed and unglazed. Unglazed tiles are not sealed and always come in a matte finish. If you want to use them in the bathroom, you will have to apply a sealant. Glazed tiles are coated with a sealant that makes them impervious to water. This glaze can be matte finish or one that is highly polished. Highly glazed tile, however, can be a hazard on the floor. Instead, opt for a soft-glazed tile intended for floor installation. When shopping, inquire about the manufacturer's slip-resistance rating for the tile

you are considering. It's also a good idea to make sure any tile selected for a countertop installation can handle the spills and knocks that occur typically around the sink and on the countertop surface.

SOLID-SURFACING MATERIAL

An extremely durable, easily maintained synthetic made of polyester or acrylic, solid-surfacing material is used to fabricate countertops, sinks, shower enclosures, and floors. It's not cheap, costing almost as much per linear foot as granite or marble, but it wears long and well. It is

Right: *Prefabricated cabinetry and a laminate countertop offer beauty without lots of mainte-nance. The countertop also features an inte-grated laminate sink.*

completely impervious to water, and any dents or abrasions that may occur over time are repaired easily with a light sanding. At first, solid surfacing was available only in shades of white or pastel colors, but now its color palette has greatly expanded and includes faux-stone finishes, too.

STONE AND CONCRETE

Granite, marble, and slate are probably the most expensive materials you can choose for a countertop. They are all extremely durable and rich looking. Two other stone materials, limestone and concrete, are find-ing their way into the creative hands of designers today, too. Unlike granite, marble, and slate, limestone has more of a primi-tive, textured appeal. Concrete offers flexi-bility, but it cracks easily. It can be colored, shaped, carved, and inlaid with objects, such as pieces of tile, glass, or shells, for a sophisticated effect.

As countertop material, any one of these materials introduces a dramatic element to the room. The only thing you have to worry about is sealing your natural counter-top properly against moisture.

These materials are also heavy, so beware if you plan to use them to fabricate a tub or shower. Check with your builder or a structural engineer to find out whether you'll need additional support under the floor to carry the extra weight.

When considering any one of these options for flooring, however, remember that they are cold underfoot and unforgiving—anything you drop that is delicate will break. Stone may pose a safety hazard on the floor, too, because it gets slick when wet. A fall on a stone floor can cause serious injury. Older persons and children are at particular risk. If you choose one of these materials, use slip-resistant carpeting over it. Also, the task of installing a stone or concrete floor is not easy. Leave the laying, cutting, and fitting stone or pouring concrete to a professional.

WOOD

Wood has typically been taboo in the bathroom because of its susceptibility to water damage, mildew, and warping. However, if you seal it properly with one of today's sophisticated, high-tech finishes you can use it safely. This should come as good news to homeowners who like the incomparable warmth offered by real wood. On walls or countertops, wood requires a urethane finish. Some kinds of wood, such as teak, hold up better than other softer, porous types, such as pine.

DEFINING YOUR STYLE

Before locking yourself into one rigid style when choosing products for your bath, remember the first rule of thumb about decorating: Please yourself. While you may want to emulate a certain look, don't become a slave to it and squash your creative spirit. The key is to build a room around a theme or a mood while carefully incorporating your personality. A favorite color is a good starting point, as is a repeated motif or an attractive pattern.

When considering style, everyone needs a little inspiration. Think about rooms you have admired and what attracted you. Was it a painted finish? A pretty fabric? Elegant cabinetry? How did the room make you feel? Restful? Energetic? Cheer? Nostalgic?

You can also take a cue from the rest of your home. Look at the style of the architecture. Is it contemporary? Colonial? Even if the architecture is nondescript, you can introduce a period flavor with reproduction fixtures, wallcoverings, molding, and accessories. You can build on these preferences in the new bathroom or

depart from them entirely. Find one transitional element, such as the floor treatment or a wallcovering, to create a visual bridge from room to room.

Whatever you do, your approach to decorating the new bath should be deliberate. Let it evolve over time; don't rush your choices. Remember to let your own preferences guide you in the end.

Right: *A protective urethane finish makes the wood paneling, cabinetry, and parquet floor of this bathroom a stylish surface option.*

PRODUCT SHOPPING LIST

It's a good idea to keep a record of what products you are buying for the new bath, what they cost, plus each one's style name or number, size, color, quantity, and the manu-

facturer's name, plus the cost. It's too easy to lose notes jotted down on scraps of paper, however. To make that task simple, here's a list of the typical purchases involved in a new bath. You can use the list to do your shopping and to keep a permanent record of your expenditures.

Description	Style	Size	Color	Qty.	Mfr.	Total Price
Permanent Fixtures						
Bidet						
Door						
Pedestal lavatory						
Shower door (if separate)						
Shower stall						
Standard tub						
Toilet						
Vanity lavatory						
Whirlpool tub						
Window						
Fittings						
Grab bars						
Hand-held sprayers						
Lavatory faucet set						
Shower curtain rod						
Soap dish						
Standard towel bars						
Shower faucet set						
Toilet-paper holder						
Toothbrush holder						
Tub faucet set						

Description	Style	Size	Color	Qty.	Mfr.	Total Price
Storage						
Cabinets						
Medicine cabinet						
Open shelves						
Vanity						
Surfacing products						
Countertop						
Floor tile						
Other flooring						
Paint						
Wall tile						
Paneling						
Wainscot						
Wallpaper						
Lighting and electrical						
Ceiling fixtures						
Exhaust fan						
Exhaust fan with light						
Fluorescent strips						
Heat lamp						
Heated towel bars						
Mini light strips						
Mini spotlights						
Miscellaneous						
Recessed canisters						
Track lights						
Wall sconces						

BRINGING STYLE OUTDOORS

Outdoor areas like decks and porches that are comfortable and practically designed increase the living space of your home the minute warm weather arrives. They are among life's pleasant bonuses and can easily become your favorite "rooms." Outdoors, you've also got a leg up in terms of design because Mother Nature has handed you a gorgeous color scheme with which to work.

There are two types of outdoor spaces: those totally or partially protected from the elements, such as sun rooms, porches, or gazebos, and those areas open to the elements, such as decks, patios, or garden hideaways.

Coordinate your outdoor spaces with the exterior of your house, especially if it is located in front or on the side of the house in full view of passersby. Look at the space from the outside toward the house. Consider the scale of furnishings. Indoor/outdoor furniture comes in a variety of sizes and styles: some sleek and space-saving, some designed to visually fill up an area. Think about the difference between a folding metal bistro chair and a chair with hefty, oversized wicker arms and back, for example. The bistro chairs may look skimpy on a large deck, while a grouping of oversized wicker furniture can crowd a small porch.

Look at your outdoor space through windows and doors, and consider extending the interior style to the outside space. Bright colors will stop your eyes at

Left: *Blending with the brick exterior of the house and the lush foliage, wicker in a natural finish is the right choice for this peaceful porch.*

the porch, while muted ones will allow you to focus first on garden focal points, such as a magnificent bush, tree, or flower bed. Plan outside furnishings so that they augment a good view instead of blocking it.

Once you have a furniture style in mind, develop a plan that defines the function of the space and determines the furniture pieces you'll need. Consider, for instance, what's needed for conversational sitting, entertaining, cooking, playing (for children), sleeping, and sunbathing.

SHELTERED SPACES: SUN ROOMS & PORCHES

Attached outdoor spaces that provide total or partial shelter should be considered an extension of the home's interior design. In most cases these areas embrace an entrance or serve to join two interior areas—a breezeway, for example. Traffic patterns figure importantly in overall furniture arrangements, as does the selection of furniture, durable fabrics, and other elements.

ONE: *Document your ideas.* Keep a folder full of your inspirations. Photograph the area you want to decorate from both inside the house and facing toward it. Keep clippings of similar spaces and furnishings, shades, and lighting that you like from magazines and product brochures; collect paint color chips and samples of fabric and flooring, too. Don't forget plantings, including window boxes and potted plants, and anything else influencing the design. Consider all the seasons the space is used. Will you want to add curtains to a sun room for insulation come winter so that you can continue to use it? Will blinds or curtains add to a porch's comfort by blocking spring and fall winds?

TWO: *Make a floor plan.* Use the same steps for developing a grid and cutting out representative furniture pieces as recommended for inside rooms. (See Chapter One, "Understanding and Arranging Space," on page 12.) Add special features unique to your space, such as notations indicating good and bad views. You will want to arrange furniture to take advantage of a good view or to face away from an ugly one.

Indicate the sun's exposure throughout the day, and note whether it should influence furniture placement. For instance, you may need shades for the southern side of a porch, or you may want to group furniture to face fabulous sunsets in the west.

THREE: *Make furniture templates.* Make templates of the furniture you plan to use, as well as of other elements, that require clearance space, such as planters, window boxes, or blinds. You can also use the furniture templates in the Appendix on page 236. Group them on the floor plan; try different configurations to see which is best.

FOUR: *Factor in traffic patterns.* Indicate pathways to and from the house. Take into account the swing of each door because you cannot place furniture in its way. For sliding glass doors, indicate which side is the entrance.

Arrange furniture so that conversational areas are not interrupted by traffic to and from the house. For instance, a common problem is a porch with a central door and a stepped entrance directly opposite the door. Rather than arranging furniture in one big grouping, create smaller areas at

each end of the porch. Suggestions include a table with chairs on one side and a conversational grouping on the other. A table just outside the door can double as a buffet table.

Plot any other traffic aisles, and make sure that you have not blocked passages to the cords for adjusting blinds or for watering plants.

FURNISH WITH CARE

Furniture for outdoor use spans the designs made popular through the centuries. You can select benches similar to those used in Versailles, Adirondack chairs, antebellum wrought iron

Clockwise (from far left): *In this living room and sun room combination, the furniture is arranged to visually divide the two areas. The yellow-and-green color scheme coordinates both spaces and ties in with the verdant view. The upholstered sofa is appropriate for an enclosed room; the white wicker adds an outdoorsy element.*

Left: *Wood furniture, painted here in fresh white and sunny yellow, is one weather-resistant option for porches.*

Inset: *Throw pillows, area rugs, potted plants, and other accessories add to the comfort and beauty of an outdoor setting.*

Wicker and Rattan. Check that the frame is weather resistant, such as aluminum with a baked-on finish. If the location is protected, some bamboo frames are porch-suitable. Synthetic wicker and special finishes on natural wicker materials offer various levels of resistance to sun and rain.

Iron. Its weight makes this metal a good choice for windy areas, but it is heavy and difficult to rearrange. Either cast or wrought iron will rust unless treated with special rust-retarding paint and touched up or repainted over the years.

Aluminum. From budget tubular furniture to wrought- or cast-aluminum frames, this modern material is rustproof and lightweight. Pieces designed to look like ironwork often have a baked-on enamel or textured finish. Look for finishing details such as smooth seams on welded parts. Cast-aluminum pieces and those of thick, heavy-gauge alloys are top of the line in aluminum.

Plastic and fiberglass furniture. Buy the best quality you can afford, because inexpensive pieces that break easily will decorate the dump for decades to come. Warranties are a guide, but test pieces by sitting on them and rocking around. Tubular parts made of PVC (polyvinyl chloride) can sometimes be disassembled for storage, depending upon how they are joined. Resin pieces are molded into a variety of shapes. Both come in a range of colored plastics; some are not able to withstand direct sunlight without discoloring.

FILLING IT OUT

Pillows, upholstery, slipcovers, shades and blinds, lighting, flooring, and rugs all make a sun room or a porch lush and comfortable. What you can use depends on how rigorous the weather is on the furnishings. In a relatively moisture-free hot climate, for instance, sun resistance is the

inspired by Victorian New Orleans, and myriad other choices. A word of caution: Just as decorative birdhouses won't last outdoors, some furniture with outdoor looks may not stand up to weather. Check warranties, and read directions on the furniture for care and maintenance. Then match your choices to the possible weather exposure of the furniture itself. It may be made of one or more materials.

Wood. Naturally weather-resistant woods, such as cypress, teak, or redwood, require little upkeep and don't need staining or preservative coatings. Pressure-treated wood is decay resistant and has a greenish-brown color; it can be painted, stained, or coated with a clear waterproofer. Other wood should be treated with a moisture-resistant preservative, either clear or pigmented.

quality you want to look for, but mildew resistance is not essential. In other areas, both sun and moisture (caused by dew at night) can damage the goods. Select products specifically resistant to mold and mildew and ultraviolet rays. Choices abound for products that work well in a protected outdoor environment. Here's some guidance on which are suitable for the outdoors.

Shades and blinds. Simple matchstick or rattan rollups can protect furnishings from some rain and sun. Other treatments might include fabulous see-through screens and blinds that block ultraviolet rays while allowing breezes to waft through the space. Shower curtains or simply made fabric curtains are decorative solutions that add privacy as well as beauty. (Bed sheets are an inexpensive alternative to fabric.) Remember, however, if the fabric isn't sun resistant, the curtains will fade over time.

Flooring and rugs. Tile, slate, cement, and weatherproof painted wood are floor choices that require minimal care. Soften the look and the feeling underfoot with natural-fiber rugs, such as sisal or hemp, which resist moisture damage by nature; this type of floor covering works best in sheltered outdoor spaces. Another possibility is indoor-outdoor carpeting, which can be left outside all year long.

Below: *The fabric for the billowing, pale blue curtains on this enclosed porch was chosen for its sun resistance.*

Fabrics. Cushions and pillows with fillings that allow water to drain through them take very little care. Add to this a wide range of new fabrics—acrylics, woven vinyl-coated polyester, laminated cotton that feels like uncoated fabric—and almost anything is possible. Look for these fabrics at tent, awning, or fabric stores, as well as the porch and patio sections of department stores and pool-supply stores. Don't overlook clear plastic to protect some fabrics, and go ahead and use conventional fabrics that catch your fancy if the area is protected. Store pillows when the weather turns foul. Fabrics treated for stain resistance are more expensive but wear better.

Clockwise (from top left): *This porch is situated in a particularly shady location, so the homeowners opted not to hang blinds. The summery-colored pillows on these rocking chairs are stuffed with easily drained fillings, in case they get wet. Sun rooms are also handy as impromptu guest rooms; this sleigh bed can be used for sitting or sleeping. Indoor lighting, such as the table lamp, is safe to use in enclosed spaces like this sun room, but is not recommended for outdoor decks or porches.*

Lighting. Outdoor ground-fault circuit interrupters, built-in lighting, and fans make all the difference for nighttime use of porches and sun rooms. Avoid conventional indoor lighting unless your space is attached to the house. And be kind to your neighbors: Be sure lighting does not encroach on their space. (The same goes for any noise you create, such as from a television, radio, or stereo system.) Don't over-light, but do provide adequate transitional lighting from inside to outside, allowing eyes to adjust.

WIDE OPEN SPACES: PATIOS, DECKS & GAZEBOS

Free-standing outdoor spaces, such as gazebos or other garden structures, differ from sheltered spaces in several ways. Generally, they are not seen from the front of the house and are usually integrated with the landscape. Gazebos provide a wonderful opportunity to let loose a little and give in to your more fanciful side.

First, consider how you will use your outdoor room. Will it be for dining and barbecues? As a place for the kids to muck about in a wading pool and sandbox? As a quiet spot to read and relax? For warm-weather parties? Or will it be all of these things? Also consider how much privacy you want.

Decks, patios, and terraces usually exist next to a wall of the house or adjoin a porch. Attached areas call for making the most efficient use of existing doors, windows, and steps. A deck or patio might also be a short walk from the protection of the dwelling or alongside a pool, pond, or playground area. In that case, you have the luxury of developing your own entrances and traffic patterns.

As with porches and sun rooms, make a plan before you start work on your patio or deck. Use the Smart Steps for porches and sun rooms as a guide in developing ideas. (See page 222.) Creating workable traffic patterns is important, as you will sometimes be carrying trays full of food, entertainment equipment, and games and toys through the space. You have to organize furnishings so that access is easy, trips to and from the house are no longer than necessary, and you can maneuver easily through the space.

Below top: *Entering and leaving this gazebo is easy because the doorways flank the middle section, where the seating is located.*

Below bottom: *Drapery in primary colors boldly announces that this space is independent of the main house.*

In most instances, you will want to make the patio or deck as large as possible so that it can function as a combination outdoor family room, cooking and dining area, and even a play area for kids. If space is restricted, you might consider creating an intimate area, with a small table and a pair of

Above: *This long and narrow pergola-covered deck is used for conversation and dining. To keep the traffic flow smooth, a pathway was left between the two areas.*

bistro chairs, that serves as a breakfast nook or even as a place to do paperwork in the sun.

To figure out traffic patterns, think about how you will enter this outdoor room. Will it be mostly from the house? Is the approach a path from the house or porch? Are there other areas, such as garden beds, potting sheds, bird baths, or lawn seating, that should determine exits from the patio or deck? It can be irritating to have to circumvent a deck rail or hedge to get to a frequently used destination, such as the potting shed or the barbecue

grill. Figuring out potential trouble spots in advance will save you time and aggravation.

Most open spaces look best when they are defined by either hedges or fencing. Low plantings provide definition without impeding the view. Choices are nearly endless, ranging from clipped boxwood and privet hedges to low-growing junipers to a flower border of perennials or annuals. Consider what colors and fragrances you would like to have. (To learn about arranging your garden, see "Landscape Basics" on page 232.)

For even greater privacy—or to formalize the boundaries of a deck or patio—opt for fencing. Height depends upon your situation. A low slatted fence is a good choice for containing small children without blocking the view or interfering with the flow of air. Taller options that also allow air to flow and only partially block the view include lattice panels and alternating-board fences. Deck railing and fencing are often designed with built-in seating, consisting of attached uprights, rails, and benches that may contain storage underneath.

Lighting defines spaces at night. It is also a safety factor. Both on-deck and in-ground systems with low voltage can be easily installed by a do-it-yourselfer. Other systems can be intricate and costly and may require a licensed electrician. Features may include fixtures for highlighting plantings or other yard features and timed sequencing that turns on and off automatically or when triggered by motion.

THE FAMILY ROOM/CONVERSATION AREA
A deck or patio is used most often as a fair-weather family room. Comfortable seating comes first, arranged for conversation as it would be in an indoor room. Add to this an area for snacking and outdoor recreation. Consider the activities

mine how much sun it gets. Awnings, umbrellas, pergolas, and even built-in trellises are good choices for sun protection on decks and patios, which is an increasingly important consideration for many.

When the same space is used for large parties, it is likely that most of the furniture will be pushed to the perimeters and more furniture will be added so that guests can mingle. Replot your traffic patterns and do a walk-through before the party to make sure everything is convenient for your guests.

SMART STEPS **ONE:** *Provide storage.* Make your own bin with a lift-up top large enough to contain the pillows and other nonwaterproof accessories you like to have on hand, or purchase a ready-made unit designed for this purpose. A bin can keep things dry during rainstorms, but don't

of your household, how and who you entertain, what your hobbies are, the age of your family members, and other factors that define your needs. Remember that this is an outdoor room: The more components that can remain in place in inclement weather, the easier for you.

Decide up front whether you need shaded areas, as well as those exposed to the sun. Where you position your space in relation to the shade provided by your house, trees, or other buildings will deter-

Above: *Some shade is usually desirable for outdoor dining. Here, the slatted pergola provides a pleasing combination of sun and shade over a café table and metal chairs.*

Right: *This Southwestern outdoor kitchen has a built-in grill and sink, as well as ample storage for any table-setting accessories.*

count on it to replace permanent storage during winter. It may not be weather resistant enough to protect outdoor furnishings. Keep ease of winter storage in mind when you are deciding on furniture, cushions, umbrellas, extra folding tables, and the like.

TWO: *Invest in coverups.* Vinyl slipcovers and protective cloths are available to place over large-sized pieces of cushioned furniture, and you will not have to move the cushions. They are not expensive and are easy to store.

THE KITCHEN/DINING AREA

Some people set up complete, permanent cooking centers as the focus of their outdoor spaces. Others content themselves with a simple grill. In either case, practical planning makes outdoor

Clockwise (from top left): *Wisely situated away from the dining table, a brick grill is the centerpiece of a well-equipped outdoor kitchen. Dining outdoors doesn't require an elaborate setup, as long as there is easy access into the house. Raised up a few steps, this gazebo provides a clear view for watching children who are playing in the garden.*

Below: *If there is no room for a storage bin, opt for vinyl slip-covers to protect outdoor furnishings, such as this cushioned lounge chair. Also, if you live in a rainy area, check whether or not the cushion's fabric is mildew resistant.*

number of accessories, such as rotisseries, side burners, smoke ovens, and warming racks.

Then choose a site for the cooking area. It can be placed either nearby or far away from the house. Both ways have their advantages. A cooking area that is near the house benefits from easy access to the indoor kitchen, but one that is positioned away from the house keeps heat and smoke from diners. Remember, elaborate outdoor kitchens need gas, electric, and plumbing lines; it is easier and less expensive to run lines when the cooking area is near the house.

In general, when arranging any outdoor cooking area, make sure that all accouterments—including serving platters, a spatula, a knife, and a pair of tongs—are readily at hand for the cook by providing plenty of surfaces and shelving. You need to accommodate both raw food and the finished product; a roll-around cart may suffice. Keep the pathway clear from the kitchen to the cooking area. A fire extinguisher nearby is an excellent precaution.

Any countertop material should be able to withstand varying weather conditions. Rain, snow, and bright sunlight will fade, pit, and rot some surfaces, so choose carefully. Tile, concrete, or natural materials, such as stone or slate, are good options. (Seal porous stone to prevent grease stains.) Avoid using a laminated countertop, unless it's in a well-protected area—an enclosed porch, for instance—because exposure to the weather causes the layers to separate. Solid surfacing is more durable, but may also need to be in a sheltered location. Think twice about using teak or other decay-resistant woods for a countertop, as they stain easily and may harbor bacteria.

cooking efficient and more enjoyable, whether it is for the family or a host of guests.

Decide exactly what features you want in the cooking area. Aside from the grill, do you want an elaborate setup with a sink or a refrigerator? Perhaps a dishwasher? If so, these appliances need to be protected from the elements; place the cooking center in a sheltered location. If you prefer to keep it simple with just a grill, this option still requires some decision making. Do you want a charcoal, liquid propane (LP), or natural-gas grill? Charcoal grills are the least expensive; natural gas ones are the most expensive. The number of burners and features, such as a push-button ignition, increase the cost, too. You can also choose from a

Decay-resistant wood, such as redwood, cedar, teak, or mahogany, is the right choice for cabinetry, however. Other types of wood should be sealed and stained or painted. Oriented-strand board (OSB), which is made of bonded wood fiber, is also weatherproof enough for outdoor cabinetry.

LANDSCAPE BASICS

No outdoor living space is completely successful until it is integrated with the surrounding landscape. Just as there are principles for designing interior spaces, there are also guidelines for exterior ones. If you are choosing a site for a gazebo or a patio, it is one of the most important landscape design decisions you'll make. If the structure already exists, you can enhance it by assessing and changing the landscape. For instance, you may want to plan a garden around a gazebo, planting shrubs and flowers to highlight the beauty of the site. Or you may want to treat the gazebo as a secluded retreat. Achieving either goal takes careful planning of the site and surrounding plantings.

ONE: *Evaluate the site.* The landscape design should provide a framework for your outdoor living space. The views, lines, property configuration, and traffic patterns need to work together. Spend some time getting acquainted with your site and noting any special features. What are the site's assets? Are there beautiful views? Are there natural features, such as trees or streams? Consider the size and shape of your lot, the style of the house itself, as well as your own lifestyle needs and preferences.

TWO: *Balance the elements.* This is the process of arranging various site elements so that they are resolved and balanced. A visually heavy or large object can be balanced by a visually lighter or smaller object on the site if the smaller object is darker in color value, is unusually or irregularly shaped, has a contrasting texture, or is more elaborately detailed. All of these strategies will help to

draw attention to the smaller object and thereby visually balance it with the larger object. For example, let's say you have a large clump of pine trees on one side of your yard. To visually balance the trees you might plant smaller, more colorful ornamental trees on the other side of the yard, or you might use a man-made object such as a gazebo.

THREE: *Create a cohesive design.* Harmony can be achieved by selecting and using elements that share a com-

mon trait or characteristic. By using elements that are similar in size, shape, color, material, texture, or detail, you can create a cohesive feeling and relation among the various elements on the site. An example of this might be using a shape, such as a square. Imagine having a square concrete patio scored in a square (or diamond) pattern with a square table covered in a checkered tablecloth. The results can be extremely pleasing and harmonious.

FOUR: *Add interest.* While both balance and harmony are used to achieve unity, too much unity can be, well, boring. That's where variety and contrast come in handy. By varying the size, shape, color, material, texture, and detail, you can introduce a note of interest or a focal point into the total composition. For instance, placing a round wooden planter onto the square-patterned patio discussed in Step Three will provide a pleasing contrast of both shape and material. The contrasting object (the round wooden planter) will draw attention to itself and provide visual relief and interest to the total setting.

FIVE: *Establish visual rhythm.* In design terms, rhythm—or how elements are spaced relative to similar elements—can create another type of unity in a composition. Rhythm helps to establish a visually satisfying progression or sequence to a site design. For example, you can create a regular rhythm on a walkway if you place a band of decorative brick at 4-foot intervals. On the other hand, a song composed of only one sequence of notes is boring. Vary such things as the interval, color, size, shape, texture, or material of the elements.

SIX: *Emphasize an element.* This point assumes that within your site some of the elements have more significance than the rest and that these special elements should be emphasized. This is probably starting to sound familiar to you by now, but a special element is given its due emphasis by making it larger; by giving it a different shape (round versus square); by using a singular color, texture, or material; by shifting or rotating its orientation; by centering it within a circle or at the end of walkway; or by lighting it at night. However, if you emphasize too much, you may end up with a visually confusing design.

Clockwise (from top left): *To visually balance this deck arrangement, a dining table and chairs were placed opposite a chaise longue and grouping of potted plants. A repeating check motif links together the seat cushions, painted floor, and table setting on this deck. Make one element a focal point in your landscape, such as this teak bench, to give your outdoor setting a dramatic touch.*

SEVEN: *Let simplicity be your guide.* Simplicity is one of the hardest things to achieve in a design because there is a tendency to use all available tools and elements. The most elegant site designs are those that begin and end with simplicity as their guiding design principle. The Zen rock gardens of Japan are a good example.

CONCLUSION

I nterior design adds value to a house, but what's more important is how it enhances living. It creates atmosphere, comfort, and functionality, and allows a very personal means of self expression. It also seems to satisfy something very basic to human nature, for even our earliest ancestors decorated their primitive abodes. Perhaps they, like us, understood that there really is no place like home.

You don't have to spend a lot of money, nor do you have to inherit priceless antiques to make the place you call home a comfortable, beautiful retreat. You don't even have to hire a professional to achieve it. What is required is that you care, that you take the time to think about your surroundings and what you might do to enrich them.

Many people just fill up space willy-nilly and then complain that they don't have a knack for decorating. In a world that is teeming with technological splendors, too little attention is given to aesthetics. Your world, your home, is the place where you have the power to change that. Educating yourself will help. Following a logical plan of action will, too. If you get into a jam, don't be afraid to consult an interior designer. Above all, take the time to look and to consider, then let your creativity take it from there. Winston Churchill once said, "We shape our dwellings, and afterwards, our dwellings shape us." With forethought, patience, and a newly acquired design sense, yours will be nurturing and uplifting.

Left: *Truly beautiful rooms are the result of someone's effort; they don't just happen, and they aren't always expensive.*

A P P E N D I X

Window and Door Templates

Windows

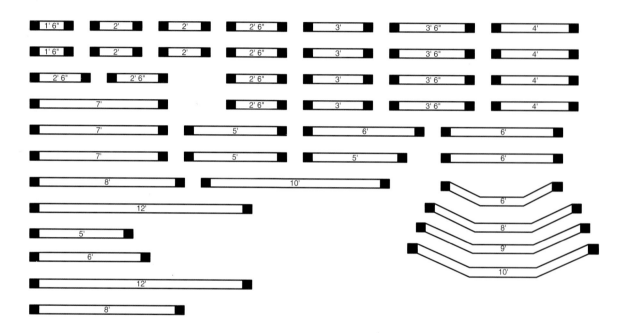

Doors

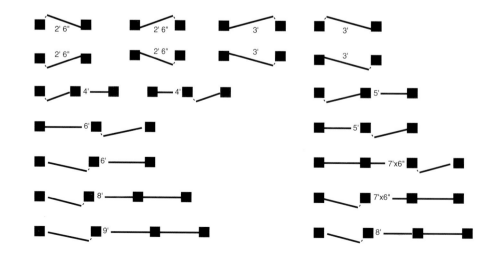

Appendix: Furniture Templates

Sofas, Love Seats and Sofa Beds

Beds

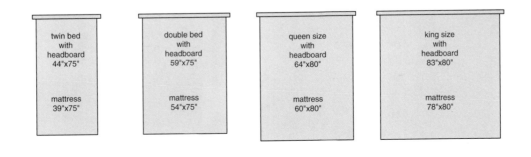

Appendix: Furniture Templates

Chairs and Ottomans

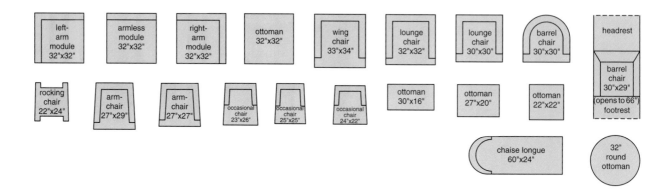

End Tables

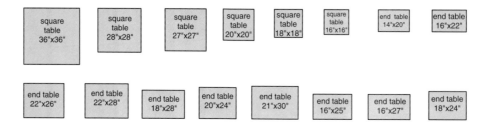

Coffee Tables and Desks

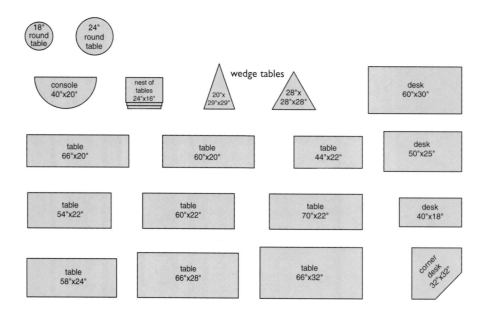

Appendix: Furniture Templates

Accessories

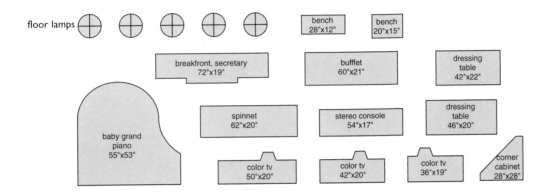

floor lamps

bench
28"x12"

bench
20"x15"

breakfront, secretary
72"x19"

bufffet
60"x21"

dressing
table
42"x22"

baby grand
piano
55"x53"

spinnet
62"x20"

stereo console
54"x17"

dressing
table
46"x20"

color tv
50"x20"

color tv
42"x20"

color tv
36"x19"

corner
cabinet
28"x28"

Appendix: Kitchen Templates

Dining and Café Tables

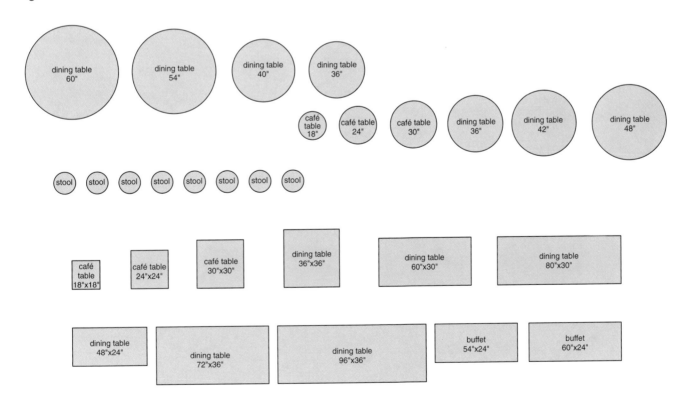

dining table
60"

dining table
54"

dining table
40"

dining table
36"

café
table
18"

café table
24"

café table
30"

dining table
36"

dining table
42"

dining table
48"

stool stool stool stool stool stool stool stool

café
table
18"x18"

café table
24"x24"

café table
30"x30"

dining table
36"x36"

dining table
60"x30"

dining table
80"x30"

dining table
48"x24"

dining table
72"x36"

dining table
96"x36"

buffet
54"x24"

buffet
60"x24"

Appendix: Kitchen Templates

Countertops

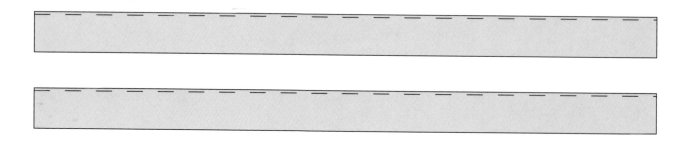

Base Cabinets

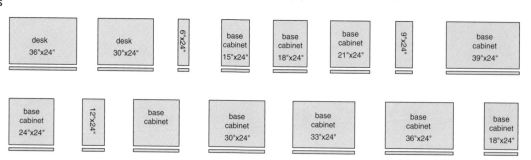

desk 36"x24"

desk 30"x24"

6"x24"

base cabinet 15"x24"

base cabinet 18"x24"

base cabinet 21"x24"

9"x24"

base cabinet 39"x24"

base cabinet 24"x24"

12"x24"

base cabinet

base cabinet 30"x24"

base cabinet 33"x24"

base cabinet 36"x24"

base cabinet 18"x24"

Islands and Appliances

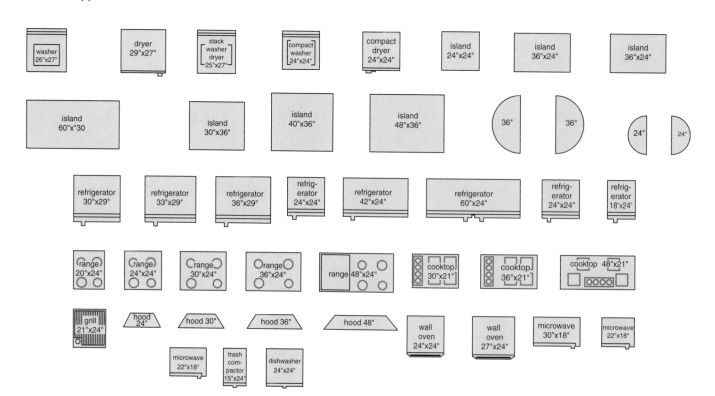

washer 26"x27"

dryer 29"x27"

stack washer dryer 25"x27"

compact washer 24"x24"

compact dryer 24"x24"

island 24"x24"

island 36"x24"

island 36"x24"

island 60"x"30

island 30"x36"

island 40"x36"

island 48"x36"

36"

36"

24"

24"

refrigerator 30"x29"

refrigerator 33"x29"

refrigerator 36"x29"

refrig-erator 24"x24"

refrigerator 42"x24"

refrigerator 60"x24"

refrig-erator 24"x24"

refrig-erator 18"x24"

range 20"x24"

range 24"x24"

range 30"x24"

range 36"x24"

range 48"x24"

cooktop 30"x21"

cooktop 36"x21"

cooktop 48"x21"

grill 21"x24"

hood 24"

hood 30"

hood 36"

hood 48"

wall oven 24"x24"

wall oven 27"x24"

microwave 30"x18"

microwave 22"x18"

microwave 22"x18"

trash com-pactor 15"x24"

dishwasher 24"x24"

Appendix: Kitchen Templates

Sinks

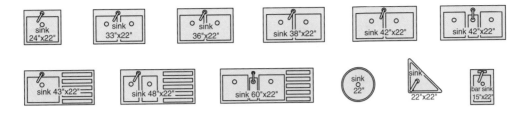

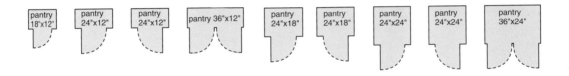

Pantries

Appendix: Bathroom Templates

Lavatories

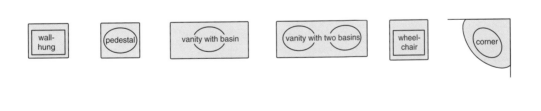

Toilets

Tubs and Shower

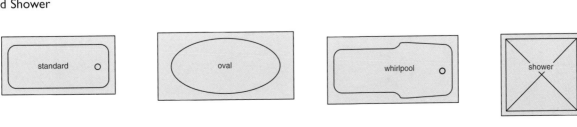

Appendix: Bathroom Symbols

Hardware

Appendix: Landscape Symbols

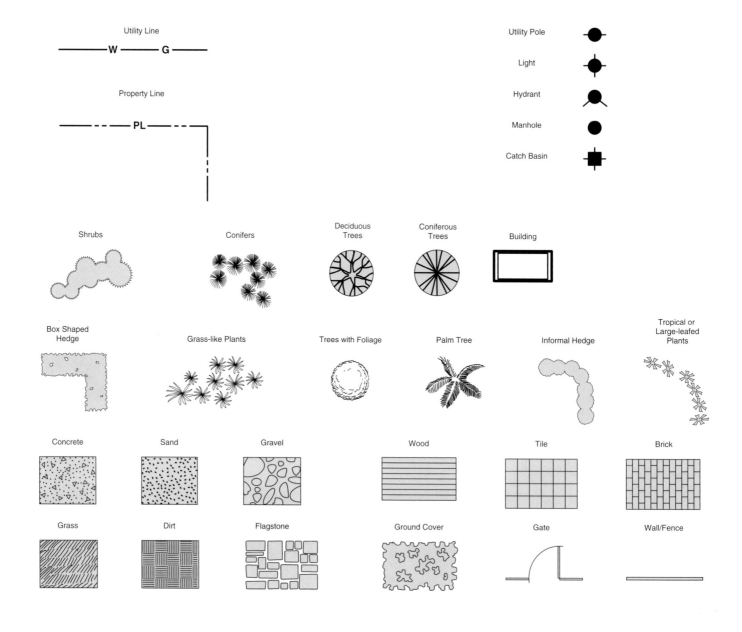

Scale: 1 square = 1 foot

G L O S S A R Y

Accent Lighting: A type of lighting that highlights an area or object to emphasize that aspect of a room's character.

Accessible Designs: Those that accommodate persons with physical disabilities.

Adaptable Designs: Those that can be easily changed to accommodate a person with disabilities.

Analogous Scheme: See Harmonious Color Scheme.

Ambient Lighting: General illumination that surrounds a room. There is no visible source of the light.

Armoire: A large, ornate cupboard or wardrobe that is used for storage.

Art Deco: A decorative style that was based on geometric forms. It was popular during the 1920s and 1930s.

Art Nouveau: A late-nineteenth-century decorative style that was based on natural forms. It was the first style to reject historical references and create its own design vocabulary, which included stylized curved details.

Arts and Crafts Movement: A decorative style that began in England during the late nineteenth century, where it was known as the Aesthetic Movement. Lead by William Morris, the movement rejected industrialization and encouraged fine craftsmanship and simplicity in design.

Backlighting: Illumination coming from a source behind or at the side of an object.

Backsplash: The vertical part at the rear and sides of a countertop that protects the adjacent wall.

Base Cabinet: A cabinet that rests on the floor and supports a countertop.

Box Pleat: A double pleat, underneath which the edges fold toward each other.

Broadloom: A wide loom for weaving carpeting that is 54 inches wide or more.

Built-In: Any element, such as a bookcase or cabinetry, that is built into a wall or an existing frame.

Cabriole: A double-curve or reverse S-shaped furniture leg that leads down to an elaborate foot (usually a ball-and-claw type).

Candlepower: The luminous intensity of a beam of light (total luminous flux) in a particular direction, measured in units called candelas.

Casegoods: A piece of furniture used for storage, including cabinets, dressers, and desks.

Chaise Longue: A chair with back support and a seat long enough for outstretched legs.

Clearance: The amount of space between two fixtures, the centerlines of two fixtures, or a fixture and an obstacle, such as a wall. Clearances may be mandated by codes.

Code: A locally or nationally enforced mandate regarding structural design, materials, plumbing, or electrical systems that state what you can or cannot do when you build or remodel. Codes are intended to protect standards of health, safety, and land use.

Colonial Style: An early-American architectural and decorative style during the Colonial period that was influenced by design ideas brought by settlers from Europe, particularly England. This basic and functional style initially featured a minimum of ornament but became more elaborate with the prosperity of the Colonies.

Color Wheel: A pie-shaped diagram showing the range and relationships of pigment and dye colors. Three equidistant wedge-shaped slices are the primaries; in between are the secondary and tertiary colors into which the primaries combine. Though represented as discrete slices, the hues form a continuum.

Complementary Colors: Hues directly opposite each other on the color wheel. As the strongest contrasts, complements tend to intensify each other. A color can be grayed by mixing it with its complement.

Contemporary: Any modern design (after 1920) that does not contain traditional elements of the past.

Cove: 1. A built-in recess in a wall or ceiling that conceals an indirect light source. 2. A concave recessed molding that is usually found where the wall meets the ceiling or floor.

Daybed: A bed made up to appear as a sofa. It usually has a frame that consists of a headboard, a footboard, and a sideboard along the back.

Dimmer Switch: A switch that can vary the intensity of the light it controls.

Distressed Finish: A decorative paint technique in which the final paint coat is sanded and battered to produce an aged appearance.

Dovetail: A joinery method in which wedge-shaped parts are interlocked to form a tight bond. This joint is commonly used on furniture parts, such as drawers.

Dowel: A short cylinder, made of wood, metal, or plastic, that fits into corresponding holes bored in two pieces of wood, creating a joint.

Étagère: Free-standing or hanging shelves for displaying small objects.

Faux Finish: A decorative paint technique that imitates a pattern found in nature, such as marble or wood.

Federal: An architectural and decorative style popular in America during the early nineteenth century, featuring delicate ornamentation, usually of swags and urns, and symmetrically arranged rooms.

Fittings: The plumbing devices that bring water to the fixtures. These can include faucets, spouts, and drains, etc.

Fluorescent Lighting: A glass tube coated on the interior with phosphor, a chemical compound that emits light when activated by ultraviolet energy. Air in the tube is replaced with a combination of argon gas and a small amount of mercury.

Gateleg Table: A drop-leaf table supported by a gate-like leg that folds or swings out.

Georgian: An architectural and decorative style popular in America during the late eighteenth century, with rooms characterized by the systematic use of paneling, other classically inspired woodwork, and bold colors.

Gothic Revival: An architectural and decorative style popular in America during the mid-nineteenth century. It romanticized the design vocabulary of the medieval period, using elements such as pointed arches and trefoils (three-leaf motifs).

Greek Revival: An architectural and decorative style that drew inspiration from ancient Greek designs. Its dignified motifs, such as the Greek key and acanthus, and classical elements, such as pediments and columns, became popular in America as symbols that embodied the idea of democracy.

Ground-Fault Circuit Interrupter (GFCI): A safety circuit breaker that compares the amount of current entering a receptacle with the amount leaving. If there is a discrepancy of 0.005 volt, the GFCI breaks the circuit in a fraction of a second. GFCIs are required by the National Electrical Code in areas of the house that are subject to dampness.

Grout: A cement mortar that is used to fill holes, commonly used as an adhesive for setting tiles.

Hardware: Wood, plastic, or metal plated trim found on the exterior of furniture, such as knobs, handles, and decorative trim.

Harmonious Color Scheme: Also called analogous, a combination focused on neighboring hues on the color wheel. The shared underlying color generally gives such schemes a coherent flow.

Focal Point: The dominant element in a room or design, usually the first to catch your eye.

Footcandle: A unit that is used to measure brightness. A footcandle is equal to one lumen per square foot of surface.

Framed Cabinet: A cabinet with a full frame across the face of the cabinet box.

Frameless Cabinet: A cabinet without a face frame. It may also be called a "European-style" cabinet.

Frieze: A horizontal band at the top of the wall or just below the cornice.

Full-Spectrum Light: Light that contains the full range of wavelengths that can be found in daylight, including invisible radiation at the end of each visible spectrum.

Hue: Another term for specific points on the pure, clear range of the color wheel.

Incandescent Lighting: A bulb (lamp) that converts electric power into light by passing electric current through a filament of tungsten wire.

Indirect Lighting: A more subdued type of lighting that is not head-on, but rather reflected against another surface such as a ceiling.

Inlay: A decoration, usually consisting of stained wood, metal, or mother-of-pearl, that is set into the surface of an object in a pattern and finished flush.

International Style: A post–World War II architectural and decorative style that emphasized simplicity and lacked ornamentation. Smooth surfaces, an extensive use of windows, and white walls are hallmarks of this pared-down style.

Lambrequin: Drapery that hangs from a shelf, such as a mantel, or covering the top of a window or a door. This term is sometimes used interchangeably with valance.

Laminate: To bond one or more thin layers of durable plastic to a fabric or a material—Formica, for example.

Love Seat. A sofa-like piece of furniture that consists of seating for two.

Lumen: The measurement of a source's light output—the quantity of visible light.

Lumens Per Watt (LPW): The ratio of the amount of light provided to the energy (watts) used to produce the light—measurement of the bulb's efficacy.

Modular: Units of a standard size, such as pieces of a sofa, that can be fitted together in a number of ways.

Molding: An architectural band that can either trim a line where materials join or create a linear decoration. It is typically made of wood, but metal, plaster, or polymer (plastic) is also used.

Mortise-and-Tenon Joinery: A hole (mortise) cut into a piece of wood that receives a projecting piece (tenon) to create a joint. It is often used in fine furnituremaking.

Neoclassic: Any revival of the ancient styles of Greece and Rome, particularly during the late eighteenth and early nineteenth centuries. The shapes and ornaments of ancient architecture were applied (incorrectly) to furniture design.

Occasional Piece: A small piece of furniture for incidental use, such as end tables, coffee tables, or extra chairs.

Orientation: The placement of any object or space, such as a window, a door, or a room, and its relationship to the points on a compass.

Panel: A flat, rectangular piece of material that forms part of a wall, door, or cabinet. Typically made of wood, it is usually framed by a border and either raised or recessed.

Parquet: Inlaid woodwork arranged to form a geometric pattern on a floor. It consists of small blocks of hardwood, which are often stained in contrasting colors.

Pattern Matching: To align a repeating pattern when joining together two pieces of fabric or wallpaper.

Pediment: A triangular piece found over doorways, windows, and occasionally mantles. It also refers to a low-pitched gable on the front of a building that is either from or inspired by ancient Greece.

Peninsula: A countertop, with or without a base cabinet, that is connected at one end to a wall or another counter and extends outward, providing access on three sides.

Post-Modernism: A term used to define the developments in architecture and interior design that originated in modernism but began to diverge from that style. Unlike modernism, it includes ornamentation and uses historical references that are whimsically out of context.

Primary Color: Red, blue, or yellow that can't be produced in pigments by mixing other colors. Primaries plus black and white, in turn, combine to make all the other hues.

Secondary Color: A mix of two primaries. The secondary colors are orange, green, and purple.

Sectional: Furniture made into separate pieces that coordinate with each other. The pieces can be arranged together as large unit or independently. Examples include L-shaped sofas, bookcases, and desk furniture.

Slipcover: A fabric or plastic cover that can be draped or tailored to fit over a piece of furniture.

Stud: A vertical frame element made of wood or metal that is used in the construction of walls and partitions to add support.

Task Lighting: Lighting that concentrates in specific areas for tasks, such as preparing food, applying makeup, reading, or doing crafts.

Tone: Degree of lightness or darkness of a color.

Tongue-and-Groove Joinery: A joinery technique in which a protruding end (tongue) fits into a recess (groove), locking the two pieces together.

Track Lighting: Lighting that utilizes a fixed band that supplies a current to movable light fixtures.

Trompe L'oeil: Literally meaning "fool the eye"; a painted mural in which realistic images and the illusion of more space are created.

Tufting: The fabric of an upholstered piece or a mattress that is drawn tightly to secure the padding, creating regularly spaced indentations.

Turning: Wood that is cut on a lathe into a round object with a distinctive profile. Furniture legs, posts, rungs, etc., are usually made in this way.

Uplight: Also used to describe the lights themselves, this is actually the term for light that is directed upward toward the ceiling or the upper part of walls.

Valance: Short drapery that hangs along the top part of a window, with or without a curtain underneath. It can also be made of wood or metal that is painted or covered with fabric.

Value: In relation to a scale of grays ranging from black to white, this is the term to describe the lightness (tints) or darkness (shades) of a color.

Veneer: High-quality wood that is cut into very thin sheets for use as a surface material.

Wall Cabinet: A cabinet, usually 12 inches deep, that's mounted on the wall a minimum of 12 inches above a countertop.

Welt: A cord, often covered by fabric, that is used as an elegant trim on cushions, slipcovers, etc.

Work Triangle: The area bounded by the lines that connect the sink, range, and refrigerator.

INDEX

PHOTO CREDITS

p. 1: *Photographer:* Nancy Hill. **p. 2:** Gordon Beall. **p. 6:** Mark Lohman. **p. 8:** *Photographer:* Mark Samu. **p. 10–11** (clockwise, from above): *Photographer:* Sam Gray; *Designer:* Bierly-Drake Associates, Inc. *Photographer:* Nancy Hill. *Photographer:* Nancy Hill. *Photographer:* Tria Giovan. *Photographer:* Tria Giovan. *Photographer:* davidduncanlivingston.com. **p. 12–13:** *Photographer:* Beth Singer. **p. 14–15** (clockwise from left to right): *Photographer:* Tria Giovan. *Photographer:* Norman McGrath. *Photographer:* Kari Haavisto. **p. 16:** *Photographer:* Sam Gray. **p. 17:** *Photographer:* Bob Greenspan; *Stylist:* Susan Andrews. **p. 18:** *Photographer:* Sam Gray. **p. 19:** *Photographer:* Nancy Hill. **p. 21:** *Photographer:* Gordon Beall. **p. 22–23** (clockwise, from top): *Photographer:* Melabee M Miller. *Photographer:* Bob Greenspan; *Stylist:* Susan Andrews. *Photographer:* Mark Samu. **p. 24:** *Photographer (top and bottom):* Melabee M Miller. **p. 25:** *Photographer:* davidduncanlivingston.com. **p. 26:** *Photographer:* Alan Shortall. **p. 27:** *Photographer (top):* davidduncanlivingston.com. *Photographer (bottom):* Mark Samu. **p. 28–29:** *Photographer:* Jessie Walker; *Designer:* Eileen Hare Int. **p. 30:** *Photographer:* Mark Samu, reprinted with permission from *House Beautiful Kitchen/Baths, 1998/The Hearst Corporation; Stylist:* Margaret McNicholas; *Designer:* Lucianna Samu. **p. 32:** *Photographer:* Holly Stickley. **p. 33:** *Photographer:* Bob Greenspan; *Stylist:* Susan Andrews; *Designer:* Kelee Kattilac. **p. 34:** *Photographer:* Jessie Walker; *Designer:* Jane Hopper, Inc. **p. 35:** *Pho-*

tographer: Kari Haavisto. **p. 36:** *Photographer:* Sam Gray. **p. 37:** *Photographer:* davidduncanlivingston.com. **p. 38:** *Photography (Chintz):* Courtesy of Thibaut. *Photographer (Damask):* Pat Leighty/Springs Window Fashions. *Photography (Gingham):* Courtesy of Country Curtains. *Photography (Muslin):* Courtesy of Country Curtains. *Photography (Toile de Jouy):* Courtesy of Scalamandre. **p. 39:** *Photographer:* davidduncanlivingston.com. **p. 40–41** (clockwise, from right): *Photographer:* Tria Giovan. *Photographer:* Jessie Walker. *Photographer:* Tria Giovan. *Photographer:* Tria Giovan. **p. 42:** *Photographer:* Jessie Walker. **p. 42–43:** *Photographer:* Mark Samu. **p. 44–45:** *Photographer:* Sam Gray; *Designer:* Christopher Benson Interiors. **p. 46:** *Photographer:* Mark Samu, reprinted with permission from *Good Housekeeping "Do It Yourself", 1998/The Hearst Corporation; Stylist:* Margaret McNicholas; *Designer:* Lucianna Samu. **p. 47:** *Photographer:* Mark Samu; *Designer:* Steven Goldgram Design. **p. 48–49** (clockwise, from left to right): *Photographer:* Gordon Beall; *Designer:* Skip Sroka. *Photographer:* Sam Gray; *Designer:* Bierly-Drake Associates, Inc. *Photographer:* Brian Vanden Brink; *Designer:* Tom Catalano. *Photographer:* Brian Vanden Brink; *Designer:* Jack Silverio. **p. 50:** *Photographer:* Tria Giovan. **p. 52–53** (clockwise, from left to right): *Photographer:* Gross & Daily. *Photographer:* Tria Giovan. *Photographer:* Mark Samu, reprinted with permission from *House Beautiful Kitchens/Baths, 1998/The Hearst Corporation. Stylist:* Margaret McNicholas. *Photographer:* Brian Vanden Brink; *Designer:* John Morris. **p. 54:** *Pho-*

tographer: Mark Samu; *Designer:* Tom Edwards Design. **p. 55:** *Photographer:* Mark Samu, reprinted with permission from *House Beautiful Kitchens/Baths, 1998/The Hearst Corporation; Stylist:* Margaret McNichols; *Designer:* Peter Cook, A.I.A. **p. 56:** *Photographer:* Brian Vanden Brink. **p. 57:** *Photographer:* Gordon Beall; *Designer:* Sarah Jenkins. **p. 58–59:** *Photographer:* Gordon Beall; *Designer:* Carey Kirk. **p. 59:** *Photographer:* Gordon Beall; *Designer:* Carey Kirk. **p. 60–61** (clockwise, from left to right): *Photographer:* Sam Gray; *Designer:* Bierly-Drake Associates, Inc. *Photographer:* J.B. Grant; *Designer:* Friedes Associates. *Photographer:* Alan Shortall. *Photographer:* Beth Singer. *Photographer:* davidduncanlivingston.com. **p. 62–63:** *Photographer:* Mark Lohman. **p. 64:** *Photographer:* Beth Singer; *Designer:* Brian Killian & Company. **p. 65:** *Photographer:* Mark Samu, reprinted with permission from *Good Housekeeping "Do It Yourself", 1998/The Hearst Corporation; Stylist:* Margaret McNicholas; *Designer:* EJR Architect. **p. 66:** *Photographer:* Mark Samu, reprinted with permission from *House Beautiful Home Remodeling & Decorating, 1997/The Hearst Corporation; Stylist:* Margaret McNicholas; *Designer:* Austen Patterson Disston Architects. **p. 67:** *Photographer:* Tria Giovan. **p. 68:** *Photographer (top):* Holly Stickley. *Photographer (bottom):* Beth Singer. **p. 69:** *Photographer:* Norman McGrath. **p. 70:** *Photographer:* Al Teufen. **p. 71:** *Photographer:* Bob Greenspan; *Stylist:* Susan Andrews. **p. 72:** *Photographer:* davidduncanlivingston.com. **p. 72–73:** *Photographer:* Anne Gummerson; *Designer:* Kerry Whitaker Townsend. **p. 74:** *Photographer:* Mark Samu, reprinted with permission from *House Beautiful Home Remodeling & Decorating, 1998/The Hearst Corporation; Stylist:* Margaret McNicholas. **p. 75:** *Photographer:* Alan Shortall. **p. 76–77:** *Photographer:* Tria Giovan. **p. 78:** *Photographer:* Bob Greenspan. *Stylist:* Susan Andrews; *Designer:* Carol Briscoe. **p. 79:** *Photographer:* Jessie Walker. **p. 80:** *Photographer (left):* Jessie Walker; *Designer:* Lisbon Int. *Photographer (technique):* George Ross. **p. 81:** *Photographer (right):* Jessie Walker; *Designer:* Suzanne Murphy. *Photographer (techniques):* George Ross. **p. 82:** *Photographer (top):* Jessie Walker; *Designer:* Adele Lampert. *Photographer (techniques):* George Ross. **p. 83:** *Photographer (left):* Woody Cady. *Photographer (technique):* George Ross. **p. 84:** *Photographer:* Jessie Walker; *Designer:* Carol Knott Int.; *Trompe l'oeil:* Simes Studios. **p. 85:** *Photographer (right):* Bob Greenspan. *Stylist:* Susan Andrews; *Designer:* Charlie MacKaman. *Photographer (techniques):* George Ross. **p. 86:** *Photographer:* Gordon Beall. **p. 78:** *Photographer:* Mark Lohman. **p. 88:** Photographers (left): Gramercy. **p. 88–89:** *Photographer:* Mark Lohman; *Designer:* Janet Lohman Interior Design. **p. 89:** *Photographer (right):* Mark Lohman; *Designer:* Janet Lohman Interior Design. **p. 90:** *Photographer:* Tria Giovan. **p. 91:** *Photographer (top):* davidduncanlivingston.com. *Photographer (bottom):* Bob Greenspan. *Stylist:* Susan Andrews; *Designer:* Glenna Walton/Walton Design. **p. 92:** *Photographer (top):* Jessie Walker; *Designer:*

Suzanne Murphy. *Photographer (bottom):* Roy Inman. *Stylist:* Susan Andrews; *Designer:* Kelee Kattilac. **p. 93** (both photos): *Photographer:* Bob Greenspan. *Stylist:* Susan Andrews; *Designer:* Kelee Kattilac. **p. 94:** *Photographer (top & inset):* Mark Lohman; *Designer:* Debra Jones. **p. 95:** *Photographer (top):* Mark Lohman; *Designer:* Janet Lohman Interior Design. *Photographer (bottom):* Bob Greenspan. *Stylist:* Susan Andrews; *Designer:* Kelee Kattilac. **p. 96–97** (clockwise, from top right): *Photographer:* Bob Greenspan. *Stylist:* Susan Andrews. *Photographer:* Sam Gray; *Designer:* Mary McGee Interiors. *Photographer:* Bob Greenspan. *Stylist:* Susan Andrews; *Designer:* Kelee Kattilac. *Photographer:* Jeremy Samuelson. **p. 98–99** (clockwise, from left to right): *Photographer:* Mark Samu. *Photographer:* Gordon Beall; *Designer:* Joan Bixler. *Photographer:* Anne Gummerson. *Photographer:* Mark Samu. *Photographer:* Bob Greenspan; *Stylist:* Susan Andrews; *Designer:* Nikki Diamantis. **p. 100–101:** *Photographer:* Steve Gross & Susan Daley. **p. 102:** *Photographer:* Nancy Hill; *Designer:* Karyne Johnson, Pananche Interiors. *Photographer:* Nancy Hill. **p. 103:** *Photographer:* Alan Shortall. *Photographer:* Mark Samu, reprinted with permission from The Hearst Corporation. **p. 104–105:** *Photographer:* davidduncanlivingston.com. *Photographer:* Mark Lohman. **p. 106:** *Photographer:* Holly Stickley. **p. 107:** *Photographer:* Gordon Beall. *Photographer:* Tria Gordon. **p. 108:** *Photographer:* Gordon Beall. **p. 109** (clockwise, from the right): *Photographer:* Lilo Raymond. *Photographer:* Gordon Beall. **p. 110:** *Photographer:* J.B. Grant. *Photographer:* davidduncanlivingston.com. *Photographer:* Alan Shortall. **p. 111:** *Photographer:* Alan Shortall. *Photographer:* Terry Wild Studio. **p. 112:** Mark Lohman. **p. 113:** *Photographer:* Sam Grey. *Photographer:* Lilo Raymond. *Photographer:* Mark Lohman. **p. 114–115:** *Photographer:* Roy Inman; *Stylist:* Susan Andrews. *Photographer:* Tria Giovan. **p. 117:** *Photographer:* Steven Mays. **p. 118–119:** *Photographer:* davidduncanlivingston.com. **p. 120:** *Photographer:* Steve Gross & Susan Daley. **p. 121:** *Photographer:* Jeremy Samuelson. **p. 122:** *Photographer:* Sam Gray. **p. 123:** *Photographer:* Mark Lohman. **p. 124:** *Photographer (top):* Steve Gross & Susan Daley. *Photographer (bottom):* Jessie Walker. **p. 125** (all photos): *Photographer:* Brian McNeill. **p. 126:** *Photographer:* davidduncanlivingston.com. **p.** 127: *Photographer:* Tria Giovan. **p. 128–129** (clockwise, from left to right): *Photographers:* Steve Gross & Susan Daley. *Photographer:* Mark Lohman. *Photographer:* Alan Shortall. *Photographer:* Beth Singer. **p. 132:** *Photographer:* Lilo Raymond. **p. 133:** *Photographer (top):* Jessie Walker. *Photographer (bottom):* Gordon Beall. **p. 134:** *Photographer:* davidduncanlivingston.com. **p. 135:** *Photographer:* Jessie Walker. **p. 136–137:** *Photographer:* Tria Giovan. **p. 138:** *Photographer:* Sam Gray; *Designer:* Bierly-Drake Associates, Inc. **p. 139:** *Photographer:* Mark Lohman; *Designer:* Debra Jones. **p. 140:** *Photographer (top & bottom):* Mark Lohman; *Designer:* Debra Jones. **p. 141:** *Photographer:* Mark Lohman; *Designer:* Lynn Pries Inte-

rior Design. **p. 142:** *Photographer:* Anne Gummerson; *Designer:* Sarah Schweizer. **p. 143:** *Photographer (top & bottom):* Tria Giovan. **p. 144:** *Photographer:* Tria Giovan. **p. 145:** *Photographer:* Kari Haavisto. **p. 146:** *Photographer:* Roy Inman; *Stylist:* Susan Andrews; *Designer:* Mary Ann Dunham, A.S.I.D. **p. 147:** *Photographer (top & bottom):* Steven Mays. **p. 148:** *Photographer (top & bottom):* Melabee M Miller; *Designer:* Linda Daly, A.S.I.D. **p. 149:** *Photographer (top & bottom):* davidduncanlivingston.com. **p. 150–151** (clockwise, from top left): *Photographer:* Nancy Hill. *Photographer:* Mark Lohman. *Photographer:* davidduncanlivingston.com. *Photographer:* davidduncanlivingston.com. **p. 152:** *Photographer:* Kari Haavisto. **p. 153:** *Photographer (top & bottom):* Bruce McCandless; *Designer:* Higher Limit Design. **p. 154–155** (clockwise, from left): *Photographer:* Mark Samu, reprinted with permission from *Good Housekeeping "Do It Yourself",* 1998/The Hearst Corporation; *Stylist:* Margaret McNicholas; *Designer:* EJR Architect. **p. 156–157** (clockwise, from below): *Photographer:* Mark Lohman; *Designer:* Lynn Pries Interior Design. **p. 158–159** (clockwise, from left): *Photographer :* Bob Greenspan; *Stylist:* Susan Andrews; *Designer:* Gelenna Walton & Lisa Mermis. **p. 160–161:** *Photographer:* Mark Samu, reprinted with permission from *House Beautiful Kitchen/Baths,* 1998/The Hearst Corporation; *Stylist:* Margaret McNicholas; *Designer:* Lucianna Samu. **p. 162:** *Photographer:* Alan Shortall. **p. 163:** *Photographer:* John Schwartz. **p. 171:** *Photographer:* Melabee M Miller. **p. 172–173:** *Photographer:* John Schwartz. **p. 173:** *Photographer:* davidduncanlivingston.com. **p. 174–175** (clockwise, from left to right): *Photographer:* davidduncanlivingston.com. *Photographer:* Mark Samu, reprinted with permission from *House Beautiful Kitchen/Baths,* 1997/The Hearst Corporation; *Stylist:* Margaret McNicholas; *Designer:* Shaver Melahn Studios. *Photographer:* Mark Samu, reprinted with permission from *House Beautiful Kitchen/Baths,* 1997/The Hearst Corporation; *Stylist:* Margaret McNicholas; *Designer:* Shaver Melahn Studios. **p. 176–177** (all photos): *Photographer:* Nancy Hill; (bottom middle & right): *Designer:* Mary Fisher Designs. **p. 178–179** (all photos): *Photographer:* Andrew McKinney; *Designer:* Lu Ann Bauer. **p. 180:** *Photographer (left):* Grey Crawford. *Photographer (right):* Mark Samu, reprinted with permission from *House Beautiful Kitchen/Baths,* 1997/The Hearst Corporation; *Stylist:* Margaret McNicholas; *Designer:* Shaver Melahn Studios. **p. 181:** *Photographer (top):* davidduncanlivingston.com. *Photographer (bottom):* Tria Giovan. **p. 182:** *Photographer:* Nancy Hill. **p. 183:** *Photographer:* Brian Vanden Brink. **p. 184–185** (clockwise, from left to right): *Photographer:* Philip Clayton-Thompson. *Photographer:* Jessie Walker. *Photographer:* Mark Samu. **p. 186:** *Photographer (top):* davidduncanlivingston.com. *Photographer (bottom):* Mark Samu, reprinted with permission from The Hearst Corporation; *Designer:* Meredith Hutchinson Interiors. **p. 187:** *Photographer (top):* Mark Samu. *Photographer (bottom):* Nancy Hill. **p. 188:** *Photographer:* Mark Samu, reprinted with permission from *House Beautiful Kitchen/Baths,* 1998/The Hearst Corporation;

Stylist: Margaret McNicholas; *Designer:* Peter Cook, A.I.A. **p. 189:** *Photographer:* davidduncanlivingston.com. **p. 190–191:** *Photographer:* Mark Samu, reprinted with permission from *House Beautiful Kitchen/ Baths,* 1997/The Hearst Corporation; *Designer:* Carolyn Miller. **p. 192:** *Photographer:* Rob Melnychuk. **p. 196:** *Photographer:* Rob Melnychuk. **p. 197:** *Photographer:* Melabee M. Miller; *Designer:* Pat McMillan. **p. 198–199:** *Photographer:* Leonard Lammi; *Designer:* Cheryl Casey Ross. **p. 200** (all photos): *Photographer:* Jessie Walker. **p. 201:** *Photographer (top & bottom):* Mark Samu, reprinted with permission from *House Beautiful Kitchens/Baths,* 1997/The Hearst Corporation. **p. 202:** *Photographer:* Stephen Cridland. **p. 203:** *Photographer:* Holly Stickley. **p. 204:** *Photographer:* Marc Samu; *Designer:* Lee Najman Designs. **p. 205:** *Photographer:* davidduncanlivingston.com. **p. 206:** *Photographer:* Mark Samu. **p. 207:** *Photographer:* Nancy Hill. **p. 208–209:** *Photographer:* Mark Lohman; *Designer:* Janet B. Lohman. **p. 209:** *Photographer:* Philip Clayton-Thompson. **p. 210:** *Photographer:* Nancy Hill. **p. 211:** *Photographer:* Nancy Hill. **p. 212:** *Photographer:* davidduncanlivingston.com. **p. 213:** *Photographer:* Jessie Walker. **p. 214:** *Photographer:* Melabee M Miller. **p. 215:** *Photographer:* davidduncanlivingston.com. **p. 216:** *Photographer:* davidduncanlivingston.com; *Designer:* Neil Kelly. **p. 217:** *Photographer:* Mark Samu; *Designer:* Carolyn Miller. **p. 220–221:** *Photographer:* Mark Lohman. **p. 222–223** (clockwise, from far left): *Photographer:* Mark Lohman; *Designer:* Janet Lohman Interior Design. **p. 224:** *Photographer (both photos):* Lilo Raymond. **p. 225:** *Photographer:* Kari Haavisto. **p. 226– 227** (clockwise, from top left): *Photographer:* Jeremy Samuelson. *Photographer:* Mike Moreland. *Photographer:* davidduncanlivingston.com. *Photographer:* Alan Shortall. **p. 227:** *Photographer (top & bottom):* Mark Samu; *Designer:* Patrick Falco Design. **p. 228:** *Photographer:* Jeremy Samuelson. **p. 229:** *Photographer (top & bottom):* Jeremy Samuelson.

p. 230 (clockwise, from top left): *Photographer:* Jeremy Samuelson. *Photographer:* Mark Lohman. *Photographer:* Jack Parsons; *Designer:* Maurice Dixon. **p. 231:** *Photographer:* Jeremy Samuelson. **p. 232:** *Photographer:* Woody Cady. **p. 233:** *Photographer (top):* Jessie Walker. *Photographer (bottom):* Lilo Raymond. **p. 234–235:** *Photographer:* Bob Greenspan; *Stylist:* Susan Andrews. **p. 245:** *Photographer:* Jessie Walker; *Designer:* Jane Hopper, Inc. **p. 246:** *Photographer:* Mark Lohman; *Designer:* Debra Jones. **p. 247:** *Photographer:* Sam Gray. **p. 248:** *Photographer:* Mark Samu, reprinted with the permission of The Hearst Corporation. **p. 249:** *Photographer:* Anne Gummerson. **p. 254:** *Photographer:* J. B. Grant; *Designer:* Friedes Associates. **p. 255:** *Photographer:* Jeremy Samuelson. *Photographer:* davidduncanlivingston.com.

S O U R C E S

Photographers & Stylists

Susan Andrews, Stylist, Overland Park, KS; 913/649-2926. *Gordon Beall,* Chevy Chase, MD; 301/718-3080. *Brian Vanden Brink,* Rockport, ME; 207/236-4035. *Woody Cady,* Bethesda, MD; 301/656-0009. *Stephen Cridland,* Portland, OR; 503/274-0954. *Tria Giovan,* New York, NY; 212/533-6612. *J.B. Grant,* West New York, NJ; 212/714-7152. *Sam Gray,* Boston, MA; 617/237-2711. *Bob Greenspan* (contact Susan Andrews). *Steve Gross & Susan Daley,* New York, NY; 212/679-4606. *Anne Gummerson,* Baltimore, MD; 410/276-6936. *Kari Haavisto,* New York, NY; 212/807-6760. *Nancy Hill,* Ridge Field, CT; 203/431-7655. *Roy Inman* (contact Susan Andrews). *David Duncan Livingston,* Mill Valley, CA; 415/383-0898. *Mark Lohman,* Los Angeles, CA; 213/933-3359. *Steven Mays,* New York, NY; 212/627-0669. *Bruce McCandless,* White Plains, NY; 914/948-2948. *Norman McGrath,* New York, NY; 212/799-6422. *Brian McNeill,* Hatfield, PA; 215/368-3326. *Rob Melnychuk,* Vancouver, BC, Canada; 604/736-8066. *Melabee M Miller,* Hillside, NJ; 908/527-9121. *Mike Moreland,* Roswell, GA; 404/993-6059. *Jack Parsons,* Santa Fe, NM; 505/984-8092. *Lilo Raymond,* Eddyville, NY; 914/338-8861. *Mark Samu,* Bayport, NY; 212/754-0415. *Jeremy Samuelson,* Los Angeles, CA; 213/937-5964. *Alan Shortall,* Chicago, IL; 773/252-3747. *Beth Singer,* Franklin, MI; 248/626-4860. *Holly Stickley,* Tigard, OR; 503/639-4278. *Al Teufen,* Medina, OH; 216/723-3237. *Philip Clayton-Thompson,* Portland, OR; 503/234-4883. *Jessie Walker,* Glencoe, IL; 847/835-0522.

Designers, Architects & Manufacturers

Austen Patterson Disston Architects, Southport, CT; 203/255-4031. *Christopher Benson Interiors,* Boston, MA; 617/536-0285. *Bierly-Drake Associates, Inc.,* Boston, MA; 617/247-0081. *Joan Bixler,* VA. *Carol Briscoe. Tom Catalano, Architect,* Boston, MA; 617/338-7447. *William Cohen,* New York, NY; 212/686-7281. *Peter Cook, A.I.A.,* Southampton, NY; 516/283-0077. *Country Curtains,* Stockbridge, MA; 800/937-1237. *Linda Daly, ASID,* Ivyland, PA; 515/598-3345. *Nikki Diamantis,* Omaha, NE; 402/333-7000. *Maurice Dixon,* Santa Fe, NM. *Mary Ann Dunham, A.S.I.D.,* Kansas City, MO; 816/452-1177. *Tom Edwards Design,* New York, NY; 212/421-6666. *EJR Architect,* Oyster Bay Cove, NY; 516/922-2479. *Patrick Falco Design,* NY; 516/737-9213. *Mary Fisher Designs,* Scottsdale, AZ; 480/473-0986. *Friedes Associates,* New York, NY; 212/777-4999. *Steven Goldgram Design,* Blue Point, NY; 516/363-6186. *Eileen Hare Int.,* Himsdale, IL; 630/323-5153. *Higher Limit Design,* Hohokus, NJ; 201/445-0978. *Jane Hopper, Inc.,* Winnetka, IL; 847/441-6289. *Meredith Hutchinson Interiors,* West Port, CT; 203/226-0553. *Sarah Jenkins,* Chevy Chase, MD; 301/951-3880. *Debra Jones,* Los Angeles, CA; 310/476-9597. *Kelee Kattilac,* Kansas City, MO; 816/931-3496. *Brian Killian & Company,* Birmingham, MI; 248/645-9801. *Carey Kirk,* Anapolis, MD; 410/263-8660. *Carol Knott Int. Design.,* Kennelworth, IL; 847/256-6676. *Adele Lampert, Page One Int.,* Barrington, IL; 847/382-1001. *Lisbon Int.,* Lake Forest, IL; 847/295-1444. *Janet Lohman Interior Design,* Los Angeles, CA; 310/471-3955. *Charlie MacKaman,* Kansas City, MO. *Mary McGee Interiors,* Boston, MA; 617/267-7979. *John Morris, Architect,* Camden, ME; 207/231-8321. *Suzanne Murphy,* Glencoe, IL. *Lynn Pries Interior Design,* Newport Beach, CA; 714/721-0356. *Lucianna Samu,* Blue Point, NY; 516/363-5902. *Scalamandre,* Long Island City, NY; 718/361-8500. *Sarah Schweizer, Architect,* Baltimore, MD; 410/329-3765. *Jack Silverio, Architect,* Lincolnville, ME; 207/763-3885. *Simes Studios,* Chicago, IL; 312/327-7101. *Thibaut, Inc.,* Newark, NJ; 973/643-1118. *Kerry Whitaker Townsend,* Baltimore, MD; 410/472-4222. *Glenna Walton & Lisa Mermis, Walton Design,* Olathe, KS; 913/764-3011.

Have a home decorating, improvement, or gardening project? Look for these and other fine **Creative Homeowner books** wherever books are sold.

Design advice and industry tips for choosing window treatments. Over 225 illustrations. 176pp., 9"x10"
BOOK # 279431

How to create kitchen style like a pro. Over 150 color photographs. 176 pp.; 9"x10"
BOOK #: 279935

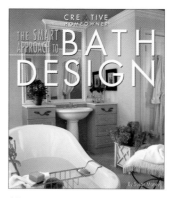

All you need to know about designing a bath. Over 150 color photos. 176 pp.; 9"x10"
BOOK #: 287225

Master stenciling, sponging, glazing, marbling, and more. Over 300 illustrations. 272 pp.; 9"x10"
BOOK #: 287225

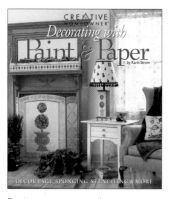

Projects to personalize your rooms with paint and paper. 300 color photos. 176 pp.; 9"x10"
BOOK #: 279723

Learn how to make the most of color. More than 150 color photos. 176 pp.; 9"x10"
BOOK #: 287264

Interior designer Lyn Peterson's easy-to-live-with decorating ideas. Over 350 photos. 304 pp.; 9"x10"
BOOK #: 279382

Original ideas for decorating and organizing kids' rooms. Over 200 illustrations. 176 pp.; 9"x10"
BOOK #: 279473

Covers everything from design to construction projects; more than 600 photos. 320 pp.; 9"x10"
BOOK #: 274615

For beginning and experienced gardeners. Over 500 color photos and illustrations. 208 pp.; 9"x10"
BOOK #: 274032

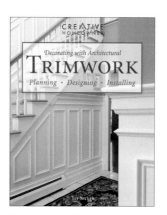

How to use trimwork to transform a home. Over 400 photos and illustrations. 208 pp.; $8^1/_2$"x$10^7/_8$"
BOOK #: 277495

Learn how to transform your bathroom. Over 600 photos and illustrations. 224 pp.; $8^1/_2$"x$10^7/_8$"
BOOK #: 277055

For more information, and to order direct, call 800-631-7795; in New Jersey 201-934-7100.
Please visit our Web site at www.creativehomeowner.com